T0375647

DARWIN'S RESOLUTION:

Evolution or Creation

Ernest L. Brannon

WESTBOW
PRESS®
A DIVISION OF THOMAS NELSON
& ZONDERVAN

Copyright © 2019 Ernest L. Brannon.

All rights reserved. No part of this book may be used or reproduced by any means,
graphic, electronic, or mechanical, including photocopying, recording, taping or
by any information storage retrieval system without the written permission of the
author except in the case of brief quotations embodied in critical articles and reviews.

KJV: Scripture taken from the King James Version of the Bible

WestBow Press books may be ordered through booksellers or by contacting:

WestBow Press
A Division of Thomas Nelson & Zondervan
1663 Liberty Drive
Bloomington, IN 47403
www.westbowpress.com
1 (866) 928-1240

Because of the dynamic nature of the Internet, any web addresses or
links contained in this book may have changed since publication and
may no longer be valid. The views expressed in this work are solely those
of the author and do not necessarily reflect the views of the publisher,
and the publisher hereby disclaims any responsibility for them.

Any people depicted in stock imagery provided by Getty Images are
models, and such images are being used for illustrative purposes only.
Certain stock imagery © Getty Images.

ISBN: 978-1-9736-5325-7 (sc)
ISBN: 978-1-9736-5324-0 (e)

Library of Congress Control Number: 2019901457

Print information available on the last page.

WestBow Press rev. date: 03/26/2019

Darwin's Resolution is a discourse on the reconciliation of the controversy between evolution and Creation in the realm of twenty-first-century science. The discourse presents both sides of the issue to provide a fair assessment for those challenged by life's origin and diversity. The discourse is prepared by Dr. Ernest Brannon, a retired professor of biology and director of the Sciphre Institute. The institute promotes a balanced forum in science, philosophy, and religion on the university campus. The discourse is a contribution of the scientific element of that endeavor.

Acknowledgments

Nancy Payne was most helpful in her hours of editing the manuscript as well as providing cogent suggestions for the discourse. Many thanks.

Dedicated to my treasure.

Contents

Preface

At the beginning of the nineteenth century, the worldview on the diversity of biological life was that God created it that way. That had been the general view previously accepted by many scientists, but that all changed in 1859, with the publication of the book *On the Origin of Species* by Charles Darwin. Ever since Darwin announced his theory on descent with modification, controversy has continued between the proponents of what became known as evolution and those who espoused Creation.

Jerry Coyne, an ardent evolutionist in the Department of Ecology and Evolution at the University of Chicago, convinced that evolution is true, was puzzled by the challenges to the theory of evolution compared to the lack of controversy regarding other theories in the sciences. Of course, Coyne is well aware that such challenges should not be surprising. It isn't the science that is the source of disagreement, and it never has been. Rather it is the premise that life occurred and diversified by chance, or what is referred to as "material cause," rather than by divine decree. That is the real issue behind the controversy. In *Why Evolution Is True*, Coyne made the evolutionist's position quite clear, that teaching Creation in science education alongside of evolution is folly when he said, "Why teach a discredited, religiously based theory, even one widely believed, along side a theory so obviously true. It's like asking that shamanism be taught in medical school alongside Western medicine. Or astrology be presented in psychology class as an alternative theory of human behavior."

That statement underscores the basis of the controversy. Evolutionists who deny the existence of God, and thus fall under the new atheist banner with Coyne, consider Creation as religion, not science. This has been an attempt by the new atheists to commandeer science to argue their case against religion, but that misrepresents the issue. The controversy is about the source of life's diversity. Creation is a term that identifies a philosophy about the existence of life. There is no doubt that Creation's prominence as a theistic model is associated with the Bible and thus has a religious foundation, but Creation is substantive in itself as a philosophy, and in the broader context, apart from religion, should not be dismissed from scientific inquiry any more than the Big Bang theory should be dismissed as the instantaneous beginning of the cosmos. The theory that matter, space, and time were suddenly brought into existence from nothing is the conclusion of many astrophysicists based on interpretation of scientific evidence. So how is that inquiry of the Big Bang using science different from an inquiry using scientific evidence to assess the concept of Creation?

In the same context, evolution is a term identifying a philosophy about the existence of life. Some claim that evolution is also a religion, but in that case based on an atheistic model. The claim was accentuated by the statement of Julian Huxley, the grandson of Darwin's famous colleague Thomas Huxley, who called evolution the "new religion" at the centennial celebration of the publication of *The Origin of Species*. Although staunch evolutionists have a strong faith in evolution analogous to religious fervor, evolution is not a religion. It is a philosophy formulated strictly on natural phenomena, rejecting any supernatural involvement. That is evolution's defining difference from Creation.

Therefore, we have two worldviews about the source of life's diversity. Creation implies a Creator as the intelligent cause, and evolution purports a material cause, dismissing the existence of the supernatural altogether. So how is this issue resolved? The only option is to examine the scientific evidence in a fair manner and through that process determine what the evidence indicates about the source of life and its diversity. Understandably, this means examining what is known about the natural phenomenon of life, including change at the molecular level, but it also means working outside the box of what is considered natural phenomena, dismissing the imposed limitation that only material processes warrant any consideration. Science is the search for truth, and truth cannot be confined within a limited scope. Science broadens our understanding, and it provides the tools in search of the truth on this important question.

The purpose of this treatise is to summarize information on the two worldviews about the diversity of life, to show where there is common ground, and to differentiate between the evidence and speculation, between certainty and assumption. The latter three chapters then address reformation of the two worldviews, examine the scientific credibility of the Genesis account of Creation, and finish with the essence of resolution. References to the Holy Bible are from the King James Version, the World Publishing Company, Cleveland, Ohio, 1945.

CHAPTER 1
Introduction

As an undergraduate at the University of Washington, I took freshman zoology from a seasoned limnologist and a very respected scientist who was also an ardent evolutionist. I remember sitting in the lecture where he trivialized belief in God and advocated the theory of evolution as the only explanation for the life-forms we were studying. The professor presented the issue in the same manner of thinking as do many other evolutionists: that belief in God is opposed to scientific rationale.

Although I was raised in a wonderful home with loving parents, religion was not part of that childhood. My parents considered themselves Christians, but only in the nominal sense. We weren't affiliated with any church. However, a Christian friend of my parents transformed my life by introducing me to the purpose of Christ as savior. Unaffiliated with a church, I had little wherewithal to understand God's word, except to comprehend that a loving God said we must have a spiritual birth to appreciate and experience the eternity available to humankind. I accepted that perspective, so ten years later, as a university freshman, hearing respected professors speak of God as a myth and associating themselves with a totally materialistic perception of life was unsettling. It made me realize that belief in God was alien to many in the academic world of science I was entering. How could these men and women professing great knowledge be wrong? A seed of doubt can easily be sown.

Many have experienced similar situations in science education. Excluding a superior intellect responsible for what is observed in the cosmos is common in the world of academia and most prominent within the biological sciences. That reality is the influence of two related factors. First, the majority of university science educators are adherents to evolutionary philosophy, indoctrinated during their own student educational experiences. Their research and study in science on what is measurable material phenomena is then interpreted consistent with evolutionary thinking, which then appears as though Darwinism is validated.

The second and most pervasive factor is the parody that science has disproven God. Ever since descent with modification was proposed by Darwin[1] as the explanation of life's diversity, evolution has become the framework of the biological sciences and God as Creator marginalized to the point of myth. This was exemplified in the *New York Times* November 2006 publication[2] entitled "God vs. Science," as though science is contrary to the existence of God. The article featured a debate between Richard Dawkins, the Harvard evolutionist arguing against religion, and Frances Collins, the director of the Human Genome Project and recently the director of the National Institutes of Health, who was supporting faith in the supernatural. The fact that the debate was cast in the framework of questioning whether the supernatural is germane with what science reveals underscores the cynicism of society towards belief in the Genesis account of Creation.

Information is filtered through the human thought process, and thus preconceptions in the context of our social and spiritual frameworks influence how such information is interpreted. Students of science who are exposed only to natural philosophy will tend to interpret scientific issues about life in that framework. Although few biologists have had direct experience working on evolutionary theory, it has become the major influence in the thinking about what constitutes the foundation of the biological and physical world.

Social influences are implicit in how we view the nature of the world. Knowledge about the world we live in is due to scientific inquiry, and those scientists who increase our knowledge of life, the world, and the cosmos deserve much credit for their research accomplishments. Much credit must also be given to those scientists who have challenged fraudulent attestations in the scientific literature and textbooks, such as the Piltdown man and Haeckel's embryos, and their scrutiny has served to maintain the credibility of science. The fact of the matter is that natural cause is a logical explanation for natural phenomena, which is reinforced by empirical observations of the mechanisms and processes at work.

But is that the whole story? Creationists in science believe they have a deeper perspective of what needs to be included in the range of subjects under the definition of science, and a broader framework needs to be applied to what is considered relevant in the structure of life. The belief that all phenomena of life, the Earth, and even the cosmos can be explained through natural laws, involving physical, chemical, and molecular relationships, apart from any supernatural intervention, origin, or authorship, is referred to as "naturalism." It is a term that means everything in nature is wholly the result of material processes.

It is important that scientific reasoning avoid rejecting other viewpoints in the pursuit of knowledge and truth. In the scientific venue, when legitimately different views exist on a subject, one is obliged to recognize those views and to consider them in a fair manner. From a strictly pragmatic perspective, the narrow point of view that excludes the Creation option that may contain keys to understanding life's beginning and diversity should be a concern to every scientist. Even with the alleged circumstantial evidence of common descent, a broader understanding of its implications will be missed if the singularity of material cause is the only interpretation allowed in scientific analysis. Worse still, by limiting the search of inquiry, truth may be overlooked, which will have broad implications not only for the scientific community but those committed to theological precepts, as well.

Background of the Controversy

Before Darwin proposed the origin of species, which later became known as the theory of evolution, the origin of life-forms on Earth was generally accepted as having been created more or less in their present appearance and structure. God, the supernatural force, as the Creator in Genesis of the Bible, was espoused by great thinkers like Isaac Newton[3] (1686), in his magnum opus *Principia*, William Paley[4] (1802), in his treatise on *Natural Theology*, and Louis Agassiz[5] (1857) in his *Essay on Classification*, where their deliberations were on the manner of God's Creation, and not whether the biblical account of Creation should be questioned. The suitability of life-forms for their particular environment was attributed to a plan by the Creator as the worldview at that time and fell within the arena of divine providence. Richard Owen[6] (1804), a renowned anatomist and paleontologist, believed all vertebrates were structural variations of the same divine blueprint.

There is little doubt, however, that other scientists of that day did not adhere to any belief in God, but only in an unresolved dynamism behind the appearance of life. The issue was really about the existence of life's diversity in the many forms observed in the world, as well as the forms contributing to the fossil record no longer in living evidence. These scientists sought other explanations about life that did not include any divine oversight or providence. Not least among these was Jean-Baptiste Lamarck,[7] best known for his theory on evolution and inheritance of acquired characteristics that appeared in *Philosophie Zoologique* as the key to the diversity of species. Others who entered the controversy of that period included Alfred Russel Wallace, Robert

Chambers, Geoffroy Saint-Hilaire, and Georges Cuvier, all with different versions of the evolution of life.

Given the premise among many in the scientific community that life had arisen by some form of non-biblical spontaneous generation, the scientific forums on the geological record, paleontology, and biological classification provided an intellectual climate in the mid-1800s that was preconditioned to accept alternatives to Creation. Naturalism, especially with regard to the diversification of life-forms, was the alternative pursued by many in the scientific community, but the defining mechanism was missing.

Charles Darwin[8] entered the altercation at the most opportune time and provided such an appliance in his proposition entitled *On the Origin of Species by Means of Natural Selection, or the maintenance of favored races in the struggle for existence.* When Darwin published his ideas on the origin of species as descendants of simpler forms through the process of natural selection, disconnected from any divine element, anti-theists enthusiastically greeted his thoughts as a revolutionary ideology. They embraced the idea that the diversity of life was the result of Darwin's mechanism of natural selection, a process where accumulation of favorable traits for survival resulted in transformations of the organism, and eventually, with sufficient time, divergence into many different life-forms. Natural selection was thought to have eliminated the need of divine engineering, and among many of the intellectuals of the nineteenth century, that was a welcome alternative to natural theology.

That perspective solidified among scientists over the next century, demonstrated at the centennial celebration of the publication of *The Origin of Species.* One of the most enthusiastic participants in the celebration was Julian Huxley,[9] a prominent advocate of the evolutionary theory during the twentieth century.

He announced, "In the evolutionary pattern of thought there is no longer either need or room for the supernatural. The Earth was not created, it evolved, as did all the animals and plants that inhabit it, including our human selves, mind and soul as well as brain and body."

Those philosopher-scientists had established a beachhead of popular consent in the scientific community, and during the following years, their partisans elevated the concept as a fact of science. Ernst Mayr[10] stated, "Evolution is thus a fact, not a conjecture or assumption." Stephen Jay Gould[11] similarly felt so strongly about the theory that he considered it to be "one of the firmest facts ever validated by science."

Scientists began to take a pragmatic view about that which could be observed in life and how understanding could only be engaged through the complex and interactive processes revealed by the scientific method. Science was defined as the inquiry about the factual state of the natural world through understanding of matter and the validated laws that facilitated diversity in physical form. Religion was relegated to the search for spiritual meaning and ethical values. By little more than proclamation, Creation and any reference to divine intervention were viewed as religion and excluded from life's scientific equation. Naturalism took preeminence as the foundation of science, and the theory of evolution was its exemplar. Evolution, by natural selection of random genetic events, without purpose and undirected, became the dominant worldview of the scientific community.

However, scientific advancements have challenged two of the basic tenets of naturalism: chance and randomness. Cellular research has revealed that the smallest unit of life is a system with complexity and details of synchrony in structure and function that many consider to defy the theory of material cause by chance processes. How can systems that are programmed in such intricate detail, involving the genetic code that translates information in the genome (genetic makeup) into physical assemblies as mechanisms to sustain cellular life, be reduced to chance events that are random, without purpose, and undirected? What was the source of information coded in the DNA of the cell, which is the instruction book on most aspects of bodily growth and function? Creation theory purports there is more to life than evolution. Creationists in the scientific community don't know the details of how Creation was performed, but they recognize the fingerprints of a superior intellect in those things that were made.

We cannot resolve the matter of the supernatural, but we can look at the scientific evidence alleged to support either evolution or Creation to judge the validity of the theories. If the evidence is convincing in both cases, then it would appear that some reconciliation must be made to resolve the disparity.

Ideological Sources

To describe the two worldviews and the scientific evidence used in their support, I refer to the scientific rationale given by scientists considered experts in their fields of study who have presented their points of view with evidence on the respective subjects in the written record. Primary reference material listed below includes ten books by scientists considered authoritative on the subjects of evolution and Creation, and two textbooks by professors in biological science.

The first of the reference materials in the evolutionary arena is the book by Charles Darwin[12] that started the controversy on the origin of life's diversity: *On the Origin of Species by Means of Natural Selection, or the maintenance of favored races in the struggle for existence.* His contribution to the biological sciences has been profound and is the foundation on which subsequent expansion of the evolutionary theory is based. Although not the originator of evolutionary thinking, the concept of natural selection as the mechanism is attributed to him.

The second reference is the writings of the late Ernst Mayr,[13] who I believe was the most gifted and outstanding evolutionist of the twentieth century and a person much admired during my graduate years. His work still represents the most authoritative material on evolution. At the time of Mayr's death at 101 years of age, he was a professor emeritus in the Museum of Comparative Zoology at Harvard University. One of his last books, entitled *What Evolution Is,* is an excellent reference on the evidence used in support of Darwinian evolution and one that is used here to convey the evolutionist's basic position.

Jerry A. Coyne's[14] book entitled *Why Evolution Is True* is the third authoritative representation of present-day thinking of the staunch evolutionists. Coyne is a well-respected faculty member in the Department of Ecology and Evolution at the University of Chicago and presents what is considered the logic and proof of Darwinian evolution.

In the area of theistic evolution, reference is made to two outstanding books. The first is *The Language of God* by Frances S. Collins,[15] a renowned geneticist and leader of the Human Genome Project, which was completed in April of 2003. He went on to be the director of the National Institutes of Health. Although Collins recognizes humans as God's creations, his view of evolution is generally consistent with the evolutionists but goes further to purport harmony between the scientific and spiritual worldviews.

The second is *Finding Darwin's God* by Kenneth R. Miller,[16] an authority on evolution and a defender of both evolution and the power of faith. Miller is a cell biologist and professor of biology at Brown University. He is a staunch defender of Darwin and a critic of the Young Earth Creationists (YEC) and the intelligent design (ID) perspectives. His work can be viewed as a bridge between the two worldviews.

In the area of intelligent design, three substantial works are referenced. The first is the *Signature in the Cell: DNA and the Evidence for Intelligent Design* by Stephan C. Meyer,[17] a prolific writer on ID. The book is a rigorous exposition on information in the cell that challenges naturalism's orthodoxy. Meyer is a senior fellow at the Discovery Institute and director of the Discovery Institute's Center for Science and Culture.

Darwin's Black Box by Michael Behe[18] is the second reference on intelligent design. Behe, also the author of *The Edge of Evolution*, is a professor of molecular biochemistry at Lehigh University. His postulate on irreducible complexity has had a monumental influence on the first-cause debate in the scientific community.

The third book is *Icons of Evolution: Science or Myth?* by Jonathan Wells,[19] which is an essay examining and characterizing the claims of evolutionists. Wells challenges the most frequently cited evidence that evolutionists use in support of Darwinism. He completed doctorates in theology and in molecular and cell biology. Wells is senior fellow at the Discovery Institute.

In the area of the Young Earth Creationism (YEC), the book *What Is Creation Science?* by Gary Parker and Henry Morris[20] presents the basic position of the YEC view on the origin and development of life. Both Parker and Morris taught in the sciences, Parker in biology and evolution, Morris in the physical sciences, at five different universities. Morris was the founder of the Institute for Creation Research (ICR).

The book *Creation Basics & Beyond: An In-Depth Look at Science, Origins, and Evolution* is introduced by Jason Lisle,[21] director of research for ICR. It is a commentary of ten experts in their respective fields on the fundamental big-picture facts on the origins debate from the YEC's perspective. Five of the authors are scientists: two in biology, one in physics, one in astrophysics, and one in geology. Two are science writers, one is a medical doctor, and two theologians.

The two textbooks included in the reference material provide the general information on biological science. The first is *Biological Science* by Scott Freeman,[22] a principle lecturer and researcher at the University of Washington. Freeman provides the fundamentals of biological science in a comprehensive manner, posing questions that highlight information available in the range of subject matter covered.

The second text is on foundational biology, *The Riot and the Dance* by Gordon Wilson,[23] a professor at Saint Andrews College in Moscow, Idaho. Wilson presents the foundation of life with a practical overview of the cell, its organelles, and protein-building mechanisms.

The focus of this review is on the scientific information most relevant over the last half century, and how that information is interpreted by the proponents of evolution and Creation. There is some allusion to the Bible associated with theistic perspectives because of the background in reference to Creation, but the emphasis is on the science. The state of the evidence presented in support of the two worldviews on the diversity of life will be presented as interpreted by the referenced authors, and those references will be listed in sequence at the end of each chapter.

Endnotes

1   Charles Darwin, *The Origin of Species by Means of Natural Selection or the maintenance of favored races in the struggle for existence* (London: J. Murray, 1859), AVENEL 1979 edition.

2   David van Biema, "God vs. Science." *Time* magazine 168, No. 20 (2006).

3   Isaac Newton, *Philosophiae Naturalis Principia Mathematica* (1686).

4   William Paley, *Natural Theology: or, Evidences of the Existence and Attributes of the Deity; Collected from the Appearances of Nature* (Philadelphia: John Morgan, 1802).

5   Louis Agassiz, *Essay on Classification in Contributions to the Natural History of the United States,* Vol. 1 (Boston: Little Brown & Company, 1857).

6   Richard Owen, *Archetypes and Homologies of the Vertebrate Skeleton.* (London: John Van Voorst, Paternoster Row, 1848).

7   J. B. Lamarck, *Philosophie zoologique, ou exposition des considerations relatives a l'histoire naturelle des animaux,* 2 vol. (Paris: Dentu, 1809).

8   Darwin, 1859.

9   Julian Huxley, *The Centennial Celebration of the Publication of The Origin of Species* (1960).

10 Ernst Mayr, *What Evolution Is* (New York: Basic Books, 2001), 264.

11 Steven Jay Gould, "Darwin's More Stately Mansion," in *Science* 284, 1999, 2087.

12 Darwin, 1859.

13 Mayr, 2001.

14 Jerry A. Coyne, *Why Evolution Is True* (Oxford University Press, 2009).

15 Frances S. Collins, *The Language of God* (New York: Free Press, Simon and Schuster, 2006).

16 Kenneth R. Miller, *Finding Darwin's God* (New York: Harper Collins Publishers, 1999).

17 Stephan C. Meyer, *Signature in the Cell: DNA and the Evidence for Intelligent Design* (New York: Harper Collins, 2009).

18   Michael Behe, *Darwin's Black Box* (New York: Free Press, Simon and Schuster, 2006).

19   Jonathan Wells, *Icons of Evolution: Science or Myth? Why Much of What We Teach about Evolution Is Wrong* (Washington DC: Regnery Publishing, Inc., 2000).

20   H. M. Morris and G. E. Parker, *What Is Creation Science?* (Arizona: Master Books Inc., 2001).

21   Jason Lisle, *Creation Basics & Beyond: An In-Depth Look at Science, Origins, and Evolution* (Dallas: Institute for Creation Research, 2013).

22   Scott Freeman, Biological Science (NJ: Prentice-Hall, 2002).

23   Gordon Wilson, *The Riot and the Dance* (Moscow, ID: Canon Press, 2015).

CHAPTER 2
The Worldviews on Life's Diversity

When twenty-first-century evolutionary theory is argued in contrast with Creation, the advocates of evolution generally compare their ideology with what is actually nineteenth-century interpretation of scripture, when in reality it should be contrasted with the twenty-first-century scientific assessment of Creation. Creation is not a static philosophy; it has progressed over time as greater understanding of life has advanced. Evolution theory has also changed since its conception in the mid-1800s. In both cases, it is important to put the two worldviews in their present renderings to appreciate the real differences they represent. So let's look at the definitions as they apply in the current controversy.

What Is Evolution?

In the biological sciences, the theory of evolution has come to mean the process responsible for the diversity of all forms of life. It was initially proposed by Charles Darwin[1] in 1859. Darwin did not use the term *evolution* until later in his publications. Rather, he referred to it as "descent with modification" in his book *On the Origin of Species*. Darwin's theory was proposed as the material cause of life's diversity, with all organisms originating through common descent by the natural selection of random variation. Thereafter, scientists have referred to that process as Darwinism or the theory of evolution.

Ernest L. Brannon

After the occurrence of first-life, the advocates of Darwinism assert that all of life can be explained by natural selection working on the blind chance of variability occurring in the genetic code encrypted in the deoxyribonucleic acid (DNA) of the chromosomes within the cells of individuals. Variation is the result of either chromosomal recombination or mutations that alter the nucleotide sequence making up the strand of DNA. Changes that impact the subsequent generation of sexually reproducing organisms are those that occur in the meiotic cells destined for reproduction. Such changes can result in structural, functional, or energy-producing systems that sustain a particular life-form. Beneficial mutations in the genome of an organism are selected over the original simply by the improved survival they impart to the resulting offspring. Those members of the population that possess the beneficial constructs produce more surviving progeny than the originals and eventually displace the former. It is a natural process in response to environmental conditions favoring those chance genetic alterations that improve the fitness of the organisms, and those changes are credited to culminate in diversity within the lineage of the organism. Evolutionists allege that those changes accumulate and eventually are responsible for isolated segments of the lineage diverging from their parental source. They form new types of organisms that over time have developed into the entire variety of life-forms that exist in the world. This process is referred to as material cause.

Mayr[2] defined evolution simply as "the gradual process by which the living world has been developing following the origin of life." That definition is a simplified rendering of the process, and in some cases, it would describe changes consistent with the creationist's point of view about adaptation of life-forms.

Coyne[3] elaborated further and more concisely:

Life on earth evolved gradually beginning with primitive species—perhaps a self-replicating molecule—that lived more than 3.5 billion years ago; it then branched out over time, throwing off many new and diverse species; and the mechanism for most (but not all) of evolutionary change is natural selection.

There was a process of synthesis of evolutionary theories initiated in the late 1940s by Ernst Mayr, Theodore Dobzhansky, George Simpson, Julian Huxley, Ronald Fisher, J. B. S. Haldane, and Sewall Wright. They brought together some of the competing models from genetics, paleontology, and systematics into one unified theory, referred to as the modern synthesis,[4] neo-Darwinian evolution, or just neo-Darwinism as the biological piece of naturalism. In essence, it purports that all life was derived from a common origin, the process of which occurred gradually over hundreds of millions of years by natural selection of random mutations involving functional benefits. This is referred to as functionalism. The process was a natural phenomenon with no purpose, undirected, and devoid of any supernatural force, with life beginning approximately 3.5 billion years ago and henceforth diversifying—all by chance and natural selection alone. Denial of a supernatural force is the element that sets naturalism apart from Creation, and while that position is consistent with atheistic evolutionists, it isn't the case with all evolutionists.

Many scientists supporting evolution do so as a matter of faith in what they were taught, while others accommodate evolutionary theory with faith in the supernatural. But some of the most ardent evolutionists, such as Mayr and Coyne, have indulged in serious study to present evidence in support of their position. Coyne[4] describes six components involved in the evolutionary process that represents the general theory.

1. The first and most significant are changes that occur in the DNA strand referred to as mutations. Without mutations,

variation in the molecular structure of the DNA strand would not exist. Mutations are the foundation of genetic change. They are alleged to occur by chance.

2. Next is gradualism. The stability of the genome is such that change occurs infrequently in the concept of time. Unless something induces abrupt nucleotide alterations or mutations of the regulatory genes, the genome of an organism will accumulate changes very slowly, if at all.

3. Then there is splitting or budding. The parental lineage splits through allopatric events such as geographic isolation of the original population into two separate segments that are denied interbreeding opportunity. Mayr[5] identifies the more common condition as budding, whereby a derived lineage through speciation separates from the parental lineage by allopatric means (isolation), and the new population diverges from the latter by their separate accumulation of genetic alterations.

4. The fourth feature is common ancestry. This means that if one can go back in the history of a species' lineage, it will eventually lead to the ancestor from which two lineages separated and followed separate paths. The concept of neo-Darwinism is that if one were able to go back in history far enough, one would eventually find the single common ancestor of all living organisms. Grouping the lineages along their most similar DNA relationships would render the phylogenetic evolutionary tree of life. (See figure 1.)

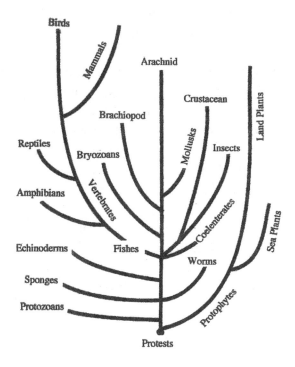

Figure 1. Phylogenetic tree of life.

5. Natural selection is the second-most significant feature of evolution. This is the selection of a mutation by the survival benefit it provides the progeny phenotype, which refers to the observable features of the organism. A mutation generally changes a particular nucleotide, referred to as an allele, along the sequence of the DNA strand. Beneficial alleles are generally passed on through the population simply by the fact that more progeny that possess the benefits of those altered advantageous constructs will survive. But as Coyne[6] described, natural selection is not chance. It is a filtering of the variation, whether to the survival advantage or disadvantage. It is a molding force accumulating genes that make individuals better able to cope.

6. The final feature on Coyne's list is processes other than natural selection that can cause evolutionary change. These fall under the category of genetic drift. In primarily small populations, changes in the gene frequencies can occur by circumstances that allow a segment of a population to survive unrelated to fitness. An example would be the chance survivors of members of a population from a flood. Such circumstances can establish the genetic constructs on which reproduction is configured and thus determine the characteristics of the future population.

These six components describe the general nature of evolution. But to get to the basics involved in the interpretation of the scientific data related to the process, it is important to understand how evolution is viewed among advocates of neo-Darwinism.

Classes of Evolution

Scientists refer to two classes of evolution. Mayr[7] defined the difference:

When we review evolutionary phenomena, we find that they can be assigned rather readily to two classes. One consists of all events and processes that occur at or below the level of species, such as geographic variation and speciation. At this level one deals almost exclusively with population phenomena. This class of phenomena can be referred to as microevolution. The other class refers to the processes that occur above the species level, particularly the origin of new taxa, the invasion of new adaptive zones, and, correlated with it, often the acquisition of evolutionary novelties such as the wings of birds or the terrestrial adaptations of the tetrapods [vertebrates with four legs] or warm bloodedness in birds and mammals. This second class of evolutionary phenomena is referred to as macroevolution.

Separation of evolution into two classes representing relatively small changes confined primarily within species, and the other involving major changes resulting in different types of organisms, indicates there is a logic for that distinction. For that reason, it is worthwhile to give it some attention.

Microevolution

Microevolution is a term that originated among German scientists at the turn of the last century. It meant small changes. In the late 1930s, Dobzhansky,[8] the famous evolutionary geneticist and a prominent contributor to neo-Darwinism, used it in a more fundamental reference to evolution. Microevolutionary phenomena occur within species, and almost all involve observable changes exclusively at the population level. The most common changes in phenotype result from recombination during meiosis (cell division forming gametes) in sexually reproducing organisms. Before the paired chromosomes within the cell separate, segments of each pair can exchange genes via crossing over and reformulate a construct of alleles different from the pattern of either parental chromosome.

Mutations are the other source of variability. Mutations are changes of single alleles or other alterations in an organism's genome. Most often, they are changes in nucleotide sequence on the DNA strand, increasing genotype (the genetic construct) diversity. Deleterious mutations are the most common and are selected against. Neutral mutations are those that appear to have no effect on the phenotype and can be carried in the genome of the individual with no apparent influence until confronted with altered environmental or physiological conditions that may induce an effect. Beneficial mutations have a positive effect on the survival of the individual possessing the altered allele. Although beneficial mutations are very rare, they result in greater reproductive success, and ultimately those with the trait displace the other members of the population.

Microevolution is considered synonymous with adaptation, and there are many examples of that process. Adaptation means the environment is selecting the phenotype that is most in synchrony with present environmental conditions. It is ongoing either as a stabilizing process in relatively stable conditions or as a divergent process, where adaptation is induced by a change in the environment with survival implications. Genetic diversity of a population is made up of its members and, when taken as a group, demonstrates a normal bell-shaped curve on any given variable trait (figure 2). When that trait has survival benefits, synchronization occurs through the selected advantage of those individuals in possession of the appropriate genetic construct that provides the best fitness to cope with environmental conditions being confronted. Those individuals possessing the survival advantage contribute at a higher frequency to the next generation and would be represented by the mode of a bell-shaped survival abundance curve, similar to the one shown here.

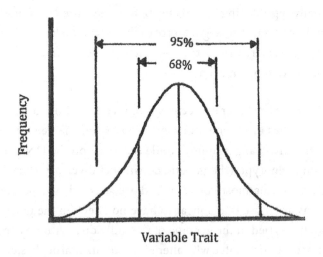

Figure 2. Normal curve

An example of adaptation is maturation timing in Pacific salmon (*Oncorhynchus*) in response to freshwater temperatures.[9] Salmon are anadromous; they begin life in freshwater, migrate to sea to take advantage of the more abundant food resources, and as adults return to their freshwater stream of origin to spawn and die. The female deposits the eggs in a redd (nest) dug in the stream, where they are immediately fertilized, and then she covers them with gravel, where they incubate over the winter months. The embryos and hatchlings (alevins) are sustained by their yolk reserves during the incubation period. In the spring when the yolk is depleted, the fry emerge from the gravel, grow to the fingerling stage in the fresh water, and then migrate downstream to start their marine residence. The timing of those events affects survival. Emergence has to synchronize with the spring bloom in food resources for optimum success of the emerging progeny.

Return and spawn maturation timing of adults is a genetic trait selected by the survival success of their progeny. Because salmon are cold-blooded, the rate of development and growth of the incubating young, and hence the length of the incubation period, is controlled by the stream temperature. This is a very critical relationship where tenths of a degree in mean incubation temperature makes a significant difference in the length of the incubation period. Exposure to very cold temperatures requires as much as nine months, whereas in warm temperatures, incubation will take as little as three months.

Thus, in cold streams, optimum maturation timing of adults occurs in late summer to provide sufficient incubation time at those low temperatures for fry emergence in the spring of the following year. In progressively warmer incubation temperatures that increase rate of development, optimum adult return and maturation timing occurs proportionally later, as late as winter, to synchronize fry emergence with the most favorable spring timing. Each stream will differ in mean incubation temperature, resulting in a range of spawn timing patterns consistent with the temperature pattern of those respective streams (figure 3). The relationship between the timing of maturation and fry emergence is an adaptation that represents the greatest survival success.

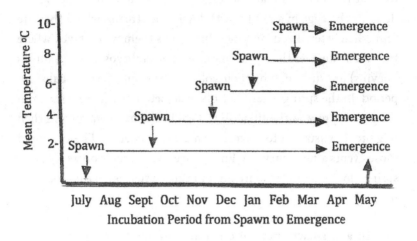

Figure 3. Effect of mean temperature on the length of incubation time for Chinook salmon embryos.

Because of this critical influence of temperature and the different temperature regimes among streams, salmon cannot randomly spawn in any stream to successfully reproduce. They must return not only to the same stream year after year, but more specifically they must home to the same general reach of that stream to facilitate adaptive timing, because temperatures vary over the length of the stream, as well. This is accomplished by juveniles imprinting on the sequence of odors experienced from the point of emergence and along their descent to marine waters, and then subsequently as returning adults to follow that odor pathway home to the same general reach of stream.

As salmon stray and colonize other streams, those adults with maturation timing closest to the new optimum for a given stream will produce more progeny, initiating the beginning of a new salmon run. Natural selection will fine-tune maturation timing of subsequent generations to synchronize optimum fry emergence with their new home stream temperature pattern. This represents microevolution in action and is the mechanism largely responsible for the difference in the time of year Pacific salmon populations return to their home streams from June to December throughout their range.

Transfer of Sacramento River Chinook salmon to New Zealand in the early 1900s resulted in the successful introduction of the species to the Southern Hemisphere.[10] By natural selection, the founders that originated from a fall spawning stock in the Sacramento River expanded in range from early to late spawn timing consistent with the incubation temperatures available in New Zealand streams. The key to success in colonizing new streams with different temperature regimes is the selection of the appropriate maturation timing from the variability among members of the parent population. Those fish with the right timing requirements will form a new temporally separate cline and eventually establish a population distinct from the parent population.

Microevolution is understood as a normal process in the organism's ability to accommodate to environmental challenges and is responsible for the preservation of the species to the extent genetically possible in dynamic environments. The diversity of phenotypes generated within a sexually reproducing population provides the means to adapt to the host of environmental challenges. Although genetic alterations at the microevolutionary level may involve as little as a single allele, more often, several genes engaging many alleles are eventually involved in the process, culminating in diversity.

Macroevolution

Macroevolution, the second class of evolutionary phenomena defined by Mayr, involves changes above the species level that include the origin of new taxa and the acquisition of evolutionary novelties such as fins, wings, eyes, and warm-bloodedness. Changes at that level of magnitude result in alterations in form. Such major changes are not observed taking place, and that is because in a relatively stable environment, changes at the macro level are alleged to occur over long periods of time involving millions of years, and this makes it difficult to relate theory with real-time understanding. Gradualism is considered a feature of macroevolution because it allegedly involves the accumulation of small changes over that time period, and those small changes are microevolutionary in origin. Evolutionists consider microevolutionary alterations of the genome as the first steps in progressing on to macroevolution. Microevolutionary evidence is treated as proof of macroevolution, because evolutionists view the process as a continuous progression of small incremental changes that eventually result in different kinds of plants and animals, essentially new taxa from that of their respective ancestors.

Lacking the ability to observe macroevolution directly, several indirect lines of evidence are in support of the evolutionary theory, and they will be given attention in subsequent chapters. But the existence of fossils is some of the earliest indirect evidence used in support of the theory. There is no question that fossils show major differences in the diversity of ancient life and also demonstrate major differences between ancient and more recent life-forms within the same typological lineage.

In theory, macroevolution should show the history of life slowly changing over time into different versions of plants and animals that progress in diversification to that observed in present life-forms. That is the case as described by Coyne. Mayr[11] agreed but points out that new types often appear abruptly, without evidence of immediate ancestral forms, and generally show long periods of stasis. The fossil evidence indicates that some taxa have remained the same for hundreds of millions of years. But given that macroevolution is said to account for new forms of life and the origin of novelties, how do we rationalize a standstill or stasis of structural forms for such long periods? In theory, the answer has to do with genetic variation and the process of natural selection itself. In order for change to occur to any degree, it requires that the environment provide the opportunity. Without new environmental conditions that select for appropriate variants in gene frequencies, there are no ready mechanisms for altered genes to be promoted in the phenotype, and in most cases, that means evolution may remain at a standstill over very long periods of time.

Geophysicists have recognized that the Earth has gone through major changes before a relatively stable environment ensued, but there were large disrupting events that occurred thereafter, as well. Proceeding to what is referred to as the Cambrian explosion,[12] where different body forms of animal life appeared over a relatively short period of a few million years, it is suggested that substantial alterations in the Earth's environment involving major changes such as an increase in atmospheric oxygen and changes in water chemistry permitted much greater opportunity for aerobic respiration.[13] The sudden appearance of skeletonized multicellular animals may have been in part a response to opportunities induced by those environmental changes.

Rapid change can occur in members of founder populations because they start with a small number of individuals, and they are on the perimeter of the environment that has supported the more stable parental population. New environments represent opportunities for changes in the organism's genome related to survival benefits under those regimes. Major differences in physiography of an area can provide a new adaptive zone, where several alterations in the genotype can be favored and expressed as a distinct evolutionary change, accelerating separation from the parental form.

The three foremost adaptive zones—landmasses, water, and air—historically offered major environmental opportunities for bursts of change to take place. For example, in order for birds to have become successful invaders of the air, natural selection had to favor the variability of the incipient form that limited maximum size, reduced weight per unit of mass, caused an alteration of form, acquired hollow bones, developed wings from forelimbs, grew feathers, and acquired the physiological wherewithal to fly. Also within that zone, thousands of different environmental conditions existed for selection of other traits to occur that would result in a variety of forms and functions. But once those niches were filled, new opportunities must have occurred in order for microevolution to proceed. A stable environment would limit those opportunities and thus slow the rate of change, even to the point of stasis. Such a phenomenon is demonstrated to be widespread in the fossil record among populous species. Niles Eldredge and Steven Jay Gould[14] pointed out that after the successful changes of a species in an adaptive zone, it may remain unchanged for millions of years. For example, the origin of the lungfish, *Lepidosirenidae,* has been placed during the carboniferous period three hundred forty million years ago. Change in lungfish fossils appeared in the first seventy million years, but over the last two hundred fifty million years, there was little further change.

Mayr[15] commented, "Such a drastic difference between the rates of evolutionary change in young and mature higher taxa is virtually a rule." Two major factors contribute to that phenomenon. One factor affecting evolutionary change is population size. Large populations are much less responsive to change because of their greater diversity and gene flow. They are large in number because natural selection has developed a phenotype that is highly successful in their expanded range. Consequently, large population size contributes to stasis.

The other related factor cited by Mayr[16] is that natural populations that have undergone thousands of generations of selection are near the optimal genotype. That condition is called normalizing or stabilizing selection, resulting in a persistent stasis by culling any deviation that would alter the optimal form. The stable genotype is diverse enough to accommodate environmental variation.

Genotypes can also reach a limit in their capacity to change. Mayr,[17] referring to such a genotype that has persisted through time, concluded, "All mutations of which this genotype is capable and that could lead to an improvement of this standard phenotype have already been incorporated in previous generations. Other mutations are apt to lead to a deterioration [of fitness] and these will be eliminated by normalizing selection." So the inability of a well-established, highly fit population to meet new environmental challenges can be the result of not having the necessary variance available at that particular time, or it may also be that the genotype has reached its limit in the capacity to make such changes for the better.

Correlated mutations, which involve two or more mutations to make a functional change, is another difficulty that leads to a slower process for an organism to accommodate to a given circumstance. The probability of two or more mutations occurring in synchrony is the multiple of their individual probabilities. Such circumstances reduce the chance of such change occurring, leading to extended stasis.

Related to the phenomenon of correlated evolution are gene interactions that will impact the function of other traits. The phenotype is not affected just by the correlated mutations facilitating a given change of a trait, but often includes the combined influence of the altered alleles along the DNA strand on other functions or traits that are under the influence of the same alleles. If a change in a gene affects more than one trait by an interaction disrupting multiple functions, it greatly expands the potential for negative influences. The consequence of such circumstances increases the possibility that the mutation will be eliminated by natural selection, and that will also result in extended stasis.

However, when major alterations of the environment occur, inhabiting organisms will experience a corresponding change in the selection pressure on their phenotypes. If the environmental alteration is abrupt, the selective pressure may favor major phenotypic alterations in a short period of time, geologically speaking, less than five million years, for example. Under those circumstances, the opportunity for fossils of intermediate forms to accrue will be limited. This can appear as a saltation (abrupt change) in the phenotype, leaving what would be interpreted as a major gap or discontinuity in the structural forms within the taxonomic lineage.

The problem is that saltation does not conform to the gradualism consistent with neo-Darwinian theory. Gould and Eldredge[18] considered the absence of gradual changes and intermediate forms as a characteristic that is almost universally observed in the fossil record, and they called the comparatively rapid change followed by a long period of stasis "punctuated equilibrium." Punctuated equilibrium is a departure within the camp of Darwinian evolutionists, where gradual change as the rule does not describe what has been observed. The pattern, in contrast, has been rapid changes bound by long periods of stasis as the general nature of the fossil evidence. However, Mayr[19] considered punctuated equilibrium as just another form of macroevolution, and while it represents what has been observed in the fossil record, he did not consider punctuated equilibrium a radical departure from neo-Darwinism.

Therefore, in retrospect, the fossil evidence is not entirely consistent with the concept that has been promulgated by evolutionary theory. However, in spite of that contrary evidence most evolutionists have accepted without question that macroevolution occurs gradually over great lengths of time as a continuum of incremental microevolutionary alterations. The fact remains that two levels of evolutionary change as defined by Mayr are recognized as separate classes, and that is an important distinction to be discussed in later chapters.

But there is another criterion that is also an important distinction in the determination of evolutionary change, and that is its irreversibility, or Dollo's law, described by Theodore Dobzhansky and others. Dobzhansky[20] said in effect that biological evolution meant change in an organism that progressed to the point where reversion to its ancestral form was no longer possible. Technically, Dollo's law means that the level of change ascribed to neo-Darwinism, specifically that level of change recognized in modern synthesis theory at the macro level, is really the only change that can legitimately be classified as evolution. As demonstrated in adaptation of organisms, microevolution is within the range of reversibility and technically would not qualify as evolution under the irreversibility definition, even though Dobzhansky recognized the process as the pathway to macro-change. Irreversibility is an important distinction with significant implications about how scientific evidence is interpreted. It means that once an evolutionary pathway has been established, such as the transition of the walking forelimbs of a tetrapod to wings, returning to the previous condition of its ancestor is no longer an option.

To summarize, there are two classes of evolutionary phenomena. Microevolution refers to changes leading to diversity within a general type of organism, or the level of variation induced within a distinct kind of plant or animal. It is functional as adaptation, can be observed, and is reversible. There is no controversy with that level of change; creationists and evolutionists are in accord on microevolution. Macroevolution is another matter. It involves the formation of different kinds of life-forms and novel anatomical structures that occurred over ages past, and in the technical sense, it is ultimately the level of change that is irreversible. Macroevolution is the change associated with the generation of new taxa in the Linnaeus classification system that is recognized above the species level. It is a concept of much controversy within the scientific community and remains primarily an inferred phenomenon, because it is alleged to occur by the accumulation of micro-changes at a rate too slow to observe.

The interchange in use of the term *evolution* referring to both macroevolution and microevolution is confusing in the literature and also confusing to the public. Most instances of cited evidence of evolution are observations and experimentation that are microevolutionary in nature. But the meaning of the term *evolution* within the scientific community carries the connotation that changes are the transformation of a taxon into a new major taxonomic form of life, or the acquisition of an entirely new structure, and a term synonymous with macroevolution. Therefore, in the context of this treatise, evolution will infer changes at the macroevolutionary level.

Creation

In the biological sciences, the concept of Creation means that life was brought into existence by a supernatural force. It had its origin in ancient times as a religious concept accepted by Jews, Christians, and Muslims, who believe that life was formed, manufactured to unfold, or planned by God as the Creator. Up to the mid-nineteenth century, the life-forms on Earth were generally thought to have been created more or less in their present appearance and structure by God, perhaps as spontaneous events. Early Christian society did not give much attention to how God created those different life-forms or how life itself came into existence, except to believe that it was in response to the command of God. Scripture does not say how Creation was accomplished, only that there was a time element involved. It is disingenuous for the critics to characterize creationists as being content with such a parochial point of view, because society in general has not been preoccupied with details of how life started, except to recognize that it is complex and involves a phenomenal process inconsistent with the view that it was a happenstance event.

The present and more comprehensive view of Creation is reminiscent of the concept expressed by Richard Owen,[21] the nineteenth-century typologist who believed that life-forms were preordained by natural laws that resulted in different types, referred to as the primal order. Different kinds of life-forms were not the result of adaptive selection but occurred as the outcome of causal constraints of natural biological properties as specific structures, referred to as structuralism. So there were the two opposing theories on the origin of life-forms among scientists in the mid-nineteenth century that characterized the difference between evolution and Creation that have continued to the present day: functionalism and structuralism. Philosophically, functionalism says that life-forms are entirely the result of cumulative incremental microevolutionary changes in response to environmental conditions. In contrast, structuralism stipulates that organisms are adaptive expressions constrained within given physical structures originating as separate types. While microevolution will facilitate adaptive changes within typological lineages or archetypes, such changes are confined within the limitations inherent in the lineage.

With the advancement of science and the magnitude of diversity within species apparent through the study of systematics, genetics, and molecular biology, the view of Creation has expanded as science has gained greater knowledge about the universe and life within it. The expanded postmodern Creation paradigm is referred to as "contemporary Creation" or "Creation theory," representing an integration of the different Creation points of view referenced in this treatise. Contemporary creationism recognizes that natural processes observed in the world conform to natural laws but are not attributed to happenstance. Natural processes and natural laws are considered the works of an intelligent agent, the Creator, and thus represent a deeper reality responsible for natural cause than chance. Design is considered the manifestation of the plan of an intelligent cause in which life-forms are endowed with mechanisms in structure and function for a purpose through the alliances of the affiliated cell constructs.

Creation theory recognizes microevolutionary processes in the context of adaptation, the mechanism to accommodate change when phenotypes are confronted with environmental alterations. The phenotypic form is the responsive component that meets those changing demands through natural selection. Most Creation scientists believe that microevolutionary processes are considered critical elements in the preservation of different life-forms, as well as inducing diversity. They recognize the role of mutations in building diversity as the fundamental component of change in the sustenance of life-forms. Creationists agree with the evolutionist that natural selection is the process that establishes such changes in the genome of the individual and that reproductive success leads to such changes that can spread through the population, but those processes are constrained within the archetype.

The Creation paradigm is presented as a process initiated by intelligence, the omnipotence behind the mechanisms that endowed life to exist and subsequently to unfold in the diversity of the living organisms witnessed over the element of time. There are differences in the creationists' community of scientists regarding the details and timing of the Creation events. There are also differences in how the role of chance is perceived. But all creationists agree that life and its diversity were the work of the Creator. The difference among creationists is in the matter of process. What was meant by the words "God created"? What were the mechanisms that the Creator embedded in the Creation events that were responsible for life and its diversity?

That is why the concept of macroevolution is a major issue. Contemporary creationists limit the idea of microevolution when it comes to the formation of major taxa that make up the diversity of the living world. Are the major divisions in the diversity of life the result of progressive changes accumulating to the point of different kinds unfolding through some form of evolution instigated by the Creator, or do phyla or classes under the Linnaeus classification system represent discrete entities as kinds that were created separately in the beginning? Creationists differ among themselves on these issues.

Classes of Creation

The meaning of Creation given in the definition above is the general view among scientists who adhere to the concept, segregated into at least three categories of how Creation proceeded, with variations existing even within those categories. Most similar to nineteenth-century natural theology is the Young Earth Creationist (YEC) view[22] that the Biblical six days were twenty-four hours in length, and Creation was accomplished over the six-day period. When Creation occurred is not fixed among the YEC adherents, but in general, they believe in a young Earth scenario: less than ten thousand years ago. Gary Parker and the late Henry Morris were notable Creation scientists in the YEC movement, and most recently, that view was defended by members of the Institute for Creation Research (ICR), represented by Jason Lisle, the institute's director of research. Members of this persuasion base their belief on what they consider the literal interpretation of the Genesis account of Creation, and believe they are faithful to the word of God, the Bible, which takes precedence over all other considerations.

The second group is the intelligent design (ID) theorists.[23] They base their position on science and avoid arguing from a religious position. ID theorists assert that the universe, the physical laws, and certain aspects of nature are best explained by the actions of an intelligent agent. Members of the Discovery Institute are the most prominent ID theorists at the present time, including Steven Meyer, Jay Richards, Michael Behe, and Jonathan Wells. ID theorists deal principally with the science and do not identify the intelligent agent; they assert that the incredible complexity of the cell and the information system that determines its structure and function are best explained by intelligent cause. They believe life is beyond chance and natural selection and, in that regard, might be considered similar to Richard Owen's primal order, or laws of form, rather than adaptive origin. Although ID adherents tend to avoid the religious aspect of the controversy, their recognition of an involvement of an intelligent agent in the proposition of life justifies their being placed in the creationist camp insofar as this work is concerned, although they would not identify with creationism and can agree with some aspects of evolution.

The third class placed in the Creation camp is the theistic evolutionists, perhaps best represented by Frances Collins[24] and Kenneth Miller.[25] Theistic evolutionists accept most of neo-Darwinism as the mechanism responsible for life's diversity. They accept common descent from an original simple life-form and natural selection of positive mutations that induced genetic variability to ultimately diversify life-forms into all of the varieties that have existed though the history of life to the present. However, they advocate that science and religion are compatible and believe a supernatural element is affiliated with life. They believe in God but ascribe to evolution's pathway in nature. As stated by Miller[26] in addressing what constituted God's methods:

> No one should pretend to know the answers to such questions, but neither should anyone assume the great range of evolution's outcomes somehow runs contrary to the demands of faith. It may demonstrate instead the Creator's determination to fashion a world in which His creatures' individual choices and actions would be free to affect the future. And it is only in such a world that conscious beings would face true moral choices, and know the certainty of genuine peace made possible by such a Creator.

That difference places them outside the evolutionists' camp and is why they are included among creationists in this work, although they dispute both the YEC and ID positions on Creation.

Looking at the Evidence

In the scientific examination of the two worldviews on the diversity of life, much of the controversy rests on the different interpretations of the evidence. Concrete facts are not disputed, but rather, it is how those facts are interpreted and assumptions made at the onset that determine how those facts are applied. So what about the evidence? What is the science in support of the two worldviews? Both Mayr and Coyne state that evolution is a fact without qualification. Certainly, there is no question about the unassailable evidence for microevolution, but they are not referring to that level of change. They are referring to the level of change that qualifies as macroevolution. But the process for determining what is fact and what is implied in evolutionary theory is not as straightforward as in other scientific arenas. Mayr[27] has made that point very clear. He stated, "Evolution is a historical process that cannot be proven by the same arguments and methods by which purely physical or functional phenomena can be documented. Evolution as a whole, and the explanation of particular evolutionary events, must be inferred from observations."

The level of change referred to as adaptation of an organism is considered the process that leads to macroevolution through the accumulation of such micro-adaptive events. It is based on inference from observations of fossils on down to the DNA complex involving the universal genetic code and the effect of mutations altering allele sequences. The evolutionist says that while those systems appear to have been designed, that is only illusory.[28] They appear as designed and orderly because of the great length of time involved in refining fitness in synchrony with the environment through natural selection, asserting material cause is undirected, without purpose, and the result of random mutations.

The contemporary creationist's response is that the inferential hypothesis about fossils and changes in the DNA complex is very much influenced by the observer's frame of reference. The evolutionist limits interpretative descriptions within the box of naturalism. Alternative possibilities are excluded, which many scientists feel is ironic, given that science champions the open mind and the search for truth. Limiting analysis fixes the manner in which discoveries in science must be interpreted. Eliminating design from the options biases the discussion. Neo-Darwinian ideology is adamant about mutations being random, undirected, and without purpose. But in some cases, mutations have been reported to be nonrandom and appear under the influence of cellular mechanisms that depend on the environment[29] and that in some way are similar to the cell's ability to activate transcription, depending on circumstance. Nonrandom mutations represent a disparity in the interpretation of evolutionary theory, and there are implications about design in the evidence that should not be ignored. Rigid exclusionary interpretation of the evidence can lead to false conclusions, and in the sciences, that would have far-reaching implications. Resolution can only be achieved by giving a fair hearing to the different points of view.

An item that needs clarification between evolution and Creation theories is the difference in the magnitude of change that is possible within typological lineages.[30] As discussed above, evolutionists view macroevolution as the accumulation of microevolutionary changes that occur above the species level, all the way up to kingdom. An example is the change that is observed to have occurred in the family of the horse, *Equidae*. Starting fifty-five million years ago, a small form called *Eohippus* progressed in size and form to culminate with the modern horse.[31] Evolutionists consider those progressive changes as macroevolution. In contrast, contemporary creationists view the progressive changes in the horse family to represent adaptive changes that occurred within the typological lineage of *Equidae* and thus do not qualify as macroevolution under Creation theory. How macroevolution is defined has a major impact on how evidence is interpreted, which will be discussed further in subsequent chapters.

In the following chapters, information is presented on the science relevant in ten different categories used to support the two worldviews. In each category, there will be a short commentary, after which the perspective of the evolutionists will be given in support of their position, followed by the perspective of the creationists, and ending with a conclusion on the merits of the issue. We start at the beginning, regarding the cosmos, time, and matter as the foundation that permitted life to occur.

Endnotes

1   Darwin, *The Origin of Species.*

2   Mayr, *What Evolution Is,* 286.

3   Coyne, *Why Evolution Is True,* 3.

4   Coyne, *Why Evolution Is True,* 3–14.

5   Mayr, *What Evolution Is,* 191.

6   Coyne, *Why Evolution Is True,* 129.

7   Mayr, *What Evolution Is,* 188.

8   T. G. Dobzhansky, *Genetics and the Origin of Species* (New York: Columbia University Press, 1937).

9   E. Brannon, M. Powell, T. Quinn, and A. Talbot, "Population Structure of Columbia River Basin Chinook Salmon and Steelhead Trout and Application to Existing Populations." Reviews in *Fisheries Science* (12, 2–3, 2004): 99–232.

10 T. Quinn, M. Kinnison, M. Unwin, "Evolution of Chinook Salmon (Oncorhynchus tshawytscha) Populations in New Zealand: Pattern, Rate, and Process," *Genetica* 112–13 (2001): 493–513.

11 Mayr, *What Evolution Is,* 189.

12 Graham Budd, "At the Origin of Animals: The Revolutionary Cambrian Fossil Record," *Current Genomics.* **14** 6 (2013): 344–54.

13 S. Freeman, *Biological Science* (2002), 492.

14 Niles Eldredge and S. J. Gould, "Punctuated Equilibria: An Alternative to Phyletic Gradualism." In T. J. M. Schopf, ed., *Models in Paleobiology* (San Francisco: Cooper & Co., 1972), 82–115.

15 Mayr, *What Evolution Is,* 196.

16 Mayr, *What Evolution Is,* 135.

17 Mayr, *What Evolution Is,* 135.

18 S. J. Gould, and N. Eldredge, "Punctuated Equilibria: The Tempo and Mode of Evolution Reconsidered," *Paleobiology* **3** 2 (1977): 115–51.

19 Mayr, *What Evolution Is,* 270.

20 T. G. Dobzhansky, *Genetics of the Evolutionary Process* (New York: Columbia University Press, 1970).

21 Richard Owen, *On the Anatomy of Vertebrates*, vol. 3 (London: Longmans, Green and Co., 1866).

22 J. Lisle and J. Johnson, *Creation Basics & Beyond* (2013), 29.

23 P. E. Johnson, *Darwin on Trial* (Washington DC: Regnery Gateway, 1991).

24 F. S. Collins, *The Language of God*.

25 K. R. Miller, *Finding Darwin's God*.

26 Miller, *Finding Darwin's God*, 275.

27 Mayr, *What Evolution Is*, 13.

28 R. Dawkins, *The Blind Watchmaker* (New York: Norton, 1986).

29 S. Waldherr, T. Eissing, and F. Allgower, "Analysis of Feedback Mechanisms in Cell-Biological Systems," *Proceedings of the 17th World Congress* (Seoul, Korea: The International Federation of Automatic Control, 2008).

30 J. P. Brock, *Evolution of Adaptive Systems* (Academic Press, 2000).

31 Mayr, *What Evolution Is*, 18.

CHAPTER 3
the Beginning

Before astronomer Edwin Hubble[1] proposed that stars beyond our galaxy were speeding away from us, scientists considered the universe to exist as a point in infinity: no beginning and no end. However, using Einstein's theory of relativity, a Russian mathematician, Alexander Friedman,[2] and a Belgian astronomer, George Lemaitre,[3] developed models on his theory from which they concluded that the universe was expanding. Thus, if you went backward in time, you would reach a point where nothing existed before. Astronomers feel that point represented the beginning of the universe.

Where there was nothing before, suddenly the physical universe flashed forth at great speed and continued to expand in magnitude, having come from a speck that itself came from nothing. Nothing is defined as the lack of matter, energy, and all space-time dimensions. The beginning took form as energy packaged in protons, neutrons, and electrons, and they in turn formed all of what is observed in space.

The concept of a beginning having started from nothing to form all that is observed in the universe, including time itself, is difficult to comprehend. Fred Hoyle, an English astronomer who refused to recognize that the beginning of the universe would suddenly come into existence in a nanosecond, mockingly called it the Big Bang and, as an alternative, developed the stationary universe model.[4] But the evidence supported the concept of a beginning, and the Big Bang name has persisted to the present.

The Big Bang was not a chaotic event, as would be descriptive of an explosion, but rather an event that has been described as an orderly speed of expansion. The process produced hydrogen and helium, and stars and energy centers, that in turn were involved in the production of other elements, with carbon as the critical element that allows the optimal bonding to nitrogen, oxygen, and other elements required for life to exist. As astrophysicists and astronomers study the universe, they find specific relationships that represent an extreme in what could be called fine-tuning. It was an orderly beginning.

In *The Creator and the Cosmos*, the astronomer Hugh Ross[5] identifies several unique characteristics of the cosmos and Earth that were compatible with the existence of life. The following twenty traits were selected from among those that Ross listed as having significant influence in permitting life to exist:

1. The universe has the right gravitational force constant, the proportionality constant in the force of attraction between two bodies. Gravity also challenges our understanding. Astrophysicists show that gravity increases with the mass of the celestial body, but the gravitational force is quite precise. If the gravitational force were greater, stars would be too hot, and they would burn too quickly. If the gravitational force were less, the stars would remain cooler, nuclear fusion would not occur, and no heavy elements would be produced. Therefore, the gravitational force constant had to be within a specific range to permit the right conditions to unfold in the universe for life to exist.

2. The universe had to have the right expansion rate and had to occur within certain limits, with little range in variability. If it were faster, matter would have streaked away too rapidly, and the galaxies with their stars and planets would not have formed. Conversely, if the expansion rate were slower, the universe would have collapsed upon itself shortly after the

Big Bang. The expansion rate occurred at the right velocity, with gravitational and electromagnetic forces that permitted the consolidation of matter into galaxy clusters of stars and planets with different expansion rates. This permitted the right conditions on Earth for the existence of life.

3. The universe had to have the right nuclear force—that strength of attraction and repulsion that exists in the particles of energy that define the elements. The protons with their positive charge, the electrons with their negative charge, and the neutral neutrons are all balanced in the atoms they form. If they were not balanced, with the negative charge offsetting the positive charge, the present atomic structure, which is the foundation on which the cosmos and all life exists, would not have formed. The difference in the size and weight of protons and electrons, and the balance between their positive and negative charges, are still much of a mystery.

4. The creation of matter, starting with hydrogen and then helium, with small amounts of beryllium, boron, deuterium, and lithium in the Big Bang, was followed later by all the other elements in the universe produced in the nuclear furnaces at the core of the stars. Energy is consolidated as protons, neutrons, and electrons, forming chemical elements that are substances with distinct chemical properties and are the components of matter as the substrate of the Earth. Five of those elements (carbon, hydrogen, nitrogen, oxygen, and phosphorous) are among the most important elements in life-forms. The configurations of the energy bundles dictate how the atoms join to form their molecular structures. They are stable, do not interchange back and forth, and are predictable in their behavior. The five elements are at the right ratio to support life. If there were a marked imbalance from the present ratio of these elements, there would be disruptions in the building blocks or resources necessary to support life.

5. The age of the universe is also within the right range that permitted life to exist. When the Big Bang occurred, the processes associated with the aging of the universe did not permit life to exist, except for a period within the overall aging timeline. Using NASA's Wilkinson Microwave Anisotropy Probe, the universe is shown to be approximately 13.7 billion years old, but there is only a window of opportunity where conditions could be suitable for life. Earlier in time, the conditions in the universe would have been hostile to life. If the universe were older, astrophysicists indicate that no solar-type stars would exist in a stable burning phase in the right location of the galaxy, the relationships among the celestial bodies would not have been established, and our solar system would have terminated.

6. Distance between stars must be within certain limits for rocky planets to form and planetary orbits to be stable enough for life. If the mean distance between stars were greater, the density of heavy elements would be too low for rocky planets to form, and if the distance were less, the planetary orbits would be destabilized.

7. Our galaxy is unique in that it is located in a loose group of galaxies on the far edge of the Virgo supercluster of galaxies. Most galaxies are in denser clusters that interfere with one another and create conditions that are unstable for the existence of life. The Milky Way is in the right position in the universe to allow the celestial conditions to be stable enough to permit the existence of life. A galaxy must be spiral, like the Milky Way, to provide stability in the orbits of the planets and stars. Only 5 percent of the estimated hundred billion galaxies are spirals. The rest are elliptical or irregular, and their instability limits the possibility of life.

8. The Milky Way galaxy is also located in the right position in the universe with respect to other galaxies, with the right number of neighbors, and in the right time window for life on

Earth. No mergers with neighboring galaxies have occurred, and none are imminent. A safe galactic environment exists for our present age, and such conditions have allowed the right environment in our solar system for life on Earth, the only planet where such a condition appears to exist.

9. The orbit of our sun, and hence the accompanying planetary bodies, must have exceptional stability to maintain the conditions suitable for life. If the average distance between galaxies were less, the sun's orbit would be too erratic for a stable Earth environment. If the sun's orbit were erratic, the instability of our sun's solar system would not allow the conditions suitable for life. The number of such solar-type star systems is rare and underscores the unique situation that we must attribute to exceptional circumstances.

10. The location of our sun is between the two spiral arms in our galaxy, and that has permitted it to remain in a safe path around the center of the Milky Way. Further displacement from its present position would make it vulnerable to instability and erratic orbits. The location between two spiral arms accentuates the limited range of conditions that must occur in our galaxy to provide the environment for life on Earth.

11. The sun must be a star within a specific mass in order for life to exist. If it were more massive, it would burn too rapidly and erratically for life. If it were less massive, flaring would be more violent and frequent. The planet would have to be closer to receive sufficient heat from a star of smaller mass, and that lengthens the rotation speed to months, such as is evident in Mercury and Venus. The number and complexity of circumstances necessary for Earth's environment to be suitable for life makes happenstance unbelievable.

12. Another feature that makes Earth suitable for life is Jupiter. Its mass and distance from Earth are right for Earth's protection. If it were farther from Earth, or of less mass, it would not

have diverted asteroids and comets from hitting the Earth. If Jupiter were closer or of greater mass, it would cause Earth to have an unstable orbit. Consequently, Jupiter is an important partner of Earth in our solar system and another component in the equation favoring life on Earth.

13. If supernova eruptions were closer, radiation would exterminate life on Earth, and if they were farther away, the density of heavy elements would be too low for the formation of rocky planets. These limitations underscore the narrow range of parameters placing our solar system where it is in the universe.

14. The colliding body that hit the primordial Earth and ripped away the material that coalesced to form the moon reduced the dense atmosphere around the Earth and allowed sufficient sunlight to penetrate to the Earth's surface. Two significant conditions were introduced by that Earth-changing collision. One was the change in atmospheric conditions from a density that probably would have limited life's diversity to one that encouraged nearly unlimited penetration of light. The second was that it created a moon that is relatively large, which in turn provided for greater tidal circulation and marine refreshing.

15. Earth is also a rare planet in the universe in that its orbit is nearly circular, whereas most are more elliptical. This can be considered as a unique circumstance allowing the existence of life as we know it. The near circular orbit reduces the temperature extremes that would otherwise occur with the seasons. Life would have been uncertain under the influence of an elliptical orbit as the planet passed closer and then farther in its path around the sun.

16. The Earth's rotation speed is just right, and if it were different by more than a few percent, there would be serious problems for life. Slower rotation would cause the present temperature extremes to become more excessive over the rotation period. If the rotation speed were faster, it would cause wind velocities

to increase to speeds exceeding our worst hurricanes. Jupiter, for example, rotates every ten hours, and wind velocities on that planet reach 1,000 mph. Rotation speed is just one of the characteristics of Earth that we take for granted, but it represents another narrow limit that permits life as we know it.

17. Of great importance is the presence of water occurring in gaseous, liquid, and solid states, which appears unique in the universe. Water would not exist if it weren't for the correct atmospheric pressure, temperature, rotation speed, and chemical composition of our planet. The atmospheric pressure is right for the water cycle and diversity of life. Higher pressure would reduce the evaporation phase, and lower pressure would cause too much evaporation. Either condition would alter life support and change environmental patterns suitable for life.

18. The Earth's distance from the sun affects the stability of the water cycle. If it were closer, it would be too warm, creating a greater vaporization phase, and farther away, it would be too cool, solidifying water as ice.

19. Water is also unique because of its polarity, in that oxygen (O) with a partial negative charge (-) bonds to two hydrogen atoms (H) with a partial positive charge (+), forming a bend along the single plane of the three-dimensional structure. This polarity allows the water molecule to attract other charged molecules that remain in solution as ions that can act both as a base and an acid, giving it a greater capacity to contain dissolved substances than any other liquid. If the polarity of water were greater or less, it would not possess its present solvent properties, and the heat of fusion and vaporization pressure would not permit life. It is a characteristic that not only permits life to exist but is also a major component in the composition and support of life.

20. Water can absorb a large amount of energy, and thus it doesn't readily change in temperature, but temperature affects its form. It evaporates into the atmosphere as a gas and renews its purity. It recycles as rain to replenish the land. As a liquid, its density increases with decreasing temperature, until it reaches 4°C, and thereafter becomes less dense, resulting in a less dense solid crystalline structure at 0°C. That feature makes a major difference to the environment of the Earth. Lakes and oceans recycle and exchange with their surface water, and ice floats rather than accumulating in deep-freeze beneath the surface. With its neutral pH, water is a hospitable environment that makes life possible.

These twenty characteristics of our universe, the Earth, and matter point out the unique circumstances that came together in the cosmos to enable life to exist. The expanse of space (exceeding 13.7 billion light-years in size), the forces forming the universe in its present arrangement, the life of stars and supernovae, the phenomenon of black holes, the possibility of dark matter, the creation of energy in the beginning, the micro elements and ratios that provided the Earth with a unique substrate from which the physical aspect of life is supported, and all coming from nothing, are concepts that are challenging to grasp.

The probability of all those variables coming together in just the right combinations for life makes happenstance occurrence implausible. But it happened within very narrow limits in atmospheric composition, atmospheric pressure, gravity, radiation, and temperature that define the environmental conditions in which life can exist. How do we explain the cause of these phenomena?

Evolutionist Perspective

The fact that the attributes of the cosmos and Earth appear to feature life is not disputed by most scientists, but there are differences about the reason for such conditions. The general theory is that life was able to occur because those conditions just happened to characterize this particular planet, and such conditions allowed a form of life to occur that was defined by those environmental parameters. Different forms of life are thought to exist elsewhere in the billions of galaxies of our universe, and in those cases, life will be defined by the parameters that exist in those situations.

There are the multiverse theories that speculate the existence of an infinite number of random universes, as promoted by Carl Sagan several years ago in his televised series on the cosmos.[6] Given such an assembly of infinite universes, there would have to be one that has all the features necessary to support life, and we just happen to be in that particular universe.

Other cosmological theories have been proposed in contrast to the Big Bang model. One that was given serious attention is the steady-state model.[7] The hypothesis is an infinite universe with no beginning and no end. As the universe continues to expand, the steady-state model posits that the voids resulting from expansion will be filled by the spontaneous self-creation of new matter, maintaining the same cosmic density. The ongoing creation of matter was given as an act of nature over infinite time, and with infinite time comes the infinite number of galaxies, one of which would have all the right conditions for life, and it just happens that we are experiencing that galaxy.

Another hypothesis is the cyclic or bouncing universe,[8] where over infinite time, there is an oscillating model of expanding and shrinking phenomena. An expanding universe that has sufficient mass could be brought to a halt by its gravity. Gravity then reverses the process, shrinking the extensive volume back to where space ceases to exist. Then another explosive reaction begins another cycle of expansion and regression. This describes the process that allows an infinite number of universes, but in sequence where at some point, all the right conditions assemble to result in a cosmic environment that would permit life-promoting conditions to exist. And by happenstance, we are experiencing the particular point of expansion in the cycle.

There are other models as alternatives to the Big Bang theory, but the forces that could explain the existence of the universe and how it was formed remain unknown. Yes, one can conclude that life is unique, but consistent with evolutionary theory, it is concluded that life occurred by chance as the result of what was able to fit in with the admittedly unique conditions present on Earth, making it only appear that Earth was prepared for life when it was simply the other way around. Life was an advantageous event that fit into the conditions that were present. The universe has billions of galaxies, and there are most likely many other Earth-like environments in which some forms of life may also exist, simply by the nature of the celestial environment that can induce it as a function of circumstance.

Creationist Perspective

The steady-state hypothesis would predict the appearance of galaxies of various ages—youthful, intermediate, and very old—but they all appear to be very close to the same age, so the evidence is contrary to that of the steady-state model. The cosmic background radiation confirmed the Big Bang and invalidated the steady-state argument.[9] The problem with the multiple universe theory is the inability to test it, so it has no scientific validity and must be set aside. The cyclic universe models suffer from the same problem as the multiverse hypothesis. There are no ways to test those theories, so they have to be dismissed.

Many cosmologists believe that it was impossible for a universe suitable for life to come about by chance. Technically, the chance of it occurring would be the product of multiplying the probability of each of the independent chance events ($A \times B \times C \times D$, etc.) that were necessary for an environment to exist in which life would be possible. The total number of independent events required is unknown, but if the very conservative probability of each of just the twenty listed above were one in a thousand, then the probability of all twenty events would represent a chance smaller than the level considered impossible to occur.

And that is the issue. Those cosmologists believe that the complex organization of the universe is attributed to the anthropic principle,[10] defined by Merriam-Webster's Collegiate Dictionary as "the universe must have properties that make inevitable the existence of intelligent life." Those astrophysicists recognize that life would not exist apart from the narrow limits demonstrated in the order of the universe, and such order is the result of some unknown force, referred to as the mind of the cosmos.[11] While in their view, the mind of the cosmos is not the God of the Bible, it at least points out that as more knowledge is acquired through the sciences, more scientists recognize the level of organization required for the provision of life is so phenomenal that chance is not an option.

An alternative to chance has to be proposed, because the order and complexity of the cosmos progressing to the ultimate forms we see in life today are cast within narrow tolerances in the origin and structure of matter. A chance event of such an improbable occurrence compared to the manifestation of an omnipotent plan leaves chance in an infinitely weaker position of ever having occurred.

Consequently, the phenomena that produced the life-giving characteristics of the cosmos must remain an implausible mystery. Just the short list presented above supports the position that purpose was responsible for the assembly of such provisions, and the events that progressed were predestined as a comprehensive and complete plan unfolding from the moment of the Big Bang. Creationists call that intelligent cause, as declared in Psalm 19:1: "The heavens declare the glory of God; and the firmament showeth his handiwork."

Conclusion

Scientific evidence indicates that the universe had a beginning when the cosmos sprang forth in the form of energy packaged in protons, neutrons, and electrons, and they in turn formed all of what is observed in space, having come from a speck that itself came from nothing. It is referred to as the Big Bang, but it occurred in an orderly manner with fine-tuning of all the right features that permitted life to exist on the planet Earth. While there is insufficient scientific knowledge at this time to understand how the Big Bang was brought about, the degree of fine-tuning that occurred testifies that something more than chance was responsible. The neo-evolutionists believe that it was a unique astrophysical phenomenon that science will eventually be able to ascertain. The creationist feels it corroborates the Genesis account of the beginning. While one does not negate the other, the evidence of the organization and fine-tuning of the universe consistent with the anthropic principle appears to favor implementation by an intelligent cause.

Endnotes

1   "Hubble's Law and Expanding Universe," *Proc Natl Acad Sci U S A* 112 11 (2015): 3173–75.

2   A. Friedman (trans.), "On the Curvature of Space," in *General Relativity and Gravitation* 31 12 (1999): 1991-2000.

3   G. Lemaître, "A Homogeneous Universe of Constant Mass," *Royal Astronomical Society* 91 (1931), 483–90.

4   F. Hoyle, "A New Model for the Expanding Universe," *MNRAS* 108, 372 (1948).

5   H. Ross, *Creator and the Cosmos: Reasons to Believe* (Nav Press, 2001), 263.

6   C. Sagan, *Cosmos* (New York: Random House, 1980).

7   C. O'Raifeartaigh, B. McCann, W. Nahm, and S. Mitton, "Einstein's Steady-State Theory: An Abandoned Model of the Cosmos," *Eur. Phys. J. H* 39 (2014) 353–67.

8   H. J. Blome and W. Priester, "Big Bounce in the Very Early Universe," *Astron. Astrophys.* 250 (1991), 43–49.

9   A. A. Penzias and R. W. Wilson, "A Measurement of Excess Antenna Temperature at 4080 Mc/s," *Astrophysical Journal* 142 (1965), 419–21.

10 J. D. Barrow and F. J. Tipler, *The Anthropic Cosmological Principle* (Oxford University Press, 1983).

11 T. Nagel, *Mind and Cosmos* (Oxford University Press, 2012).

CHAPTER 4
Against All Odds

Neo-Darwinists are generally not involved with beginning of life, referred to as abiogenesis, but it is considered relevant in the assessment of the evidence because the concepts are not exclusive. What was the origin of phenotype? The origin of the cell, its ability to translate information into structure and function, to replicate, and to utilize energy are faced with the same challenges in theory as the origin of diversity. What is it that allowed life to start in what some believe was an environment hostile to life? The large mass of inorganic matter that came together to form the Earth contained carbon, supplemented by interplanetary dust and comets that subsequently, with oxygen, hydrogen, and nitrogen, were synthesized to form organic compounds. But how those structures were translated into life, incorporating the information that organized and controlled subsequent function and replication, is an unknown.

The elemental components making up the chemistry of life are distinctive. Hydrogen, the first element created by the Big Bang, has a single proton and one orbiting electron, and with carbon, it's the essential component in all organic molecules. Carbon is the most versatile of atoms because of the four unpaired electrons in its outer shell. Oxygen, like carbon, has several critical roles in organic compounds. It has the major role in respiration by going to the cell sites as an electron acceptor and picking up carbon, neutralizing the four unpaired electrons and carrying the carbon for exhaustion as CO_2.

Nitrogen, along with the other elements, is a major player in amino acids, nucleotides, and lipids, and thus essential in protein, nucleic acid, and membrane structure. Although carbon, oxygen, and nitrogen are similar in some ways, they have markedly different functions in the composition of matter and in their roles in living organisms. The structural configuration of protons, neutrons, and electrons gives molecules complexity, which is the basis for their reactivity, and hence the functions they have in living organisms. The mystery is in the particles that constitute their atomic structure. Atoms are made up of the same minute particles of energy. The atomic mass unit (amu) of protons and neutrons are the same in all of the elements (1.6605×10^{-24} g), with electrons at much less mass: only $1/2000^{th}$ of a proton.[1]

Ultimately, these essential molecules for life had to be gathered and isolated within a permeable membrane barrier. Certain combinations of those molecules were stimulated to differentiate into various specific assemblages, incorporate other molecules as energy that was used to sustain the system, and become what we call a cell, the smallest form that can exist as independent life, able to replicate by its own instructions. The ability of an entity to acquire certain molecules for use in chemical reactions and to replicate is the secret of life. Chemical replication is presented as the first step in life's process, along with the substrate from which life started.

The important point is that inorganic elements are not random configurations of energy and atomic structure. They have a distinctly ordered composition and join in the formation of specific compounds. The compounds are not involved in a mass of other dysfunctional molecular combinations of the elements. These are ordered arrangements that fit the concept of design. Deoxyribonucleic acid (DNA) has a distinct configuration that is replicated precisely, as are specific proteins, carbohydrates, and lipids. The manner in which they are structured determines their function and the roles they have in the conception of life. The two worldviews differ in significant ways on how life was conceived, so let's examine those differences.

Evolutionist Perspective

Naturalism calls the process involved in the assembly of biomolecules that led to the first primitive cell chemical evolution. It occurred in the formation of specific compounds from different molecules as simply a feature of their atomic structure, resulting in a mass of reactants. Some of those reactants were potentially functional in fortuitous combinations that formed bio-viable compounds as the result of chance. Chemical evolution theory asserts that relatively high concentrations of the right chemical ingredients, rich in carbon, had accumulated in the warm aqueous environment covering much of the Earth,[2] and these randomly combined into progressively more complex compounds that subsequently polymerized into prebiotic forms.

Originally, it was thought that the atmosphere of the early Earth was in a reduced state, where electrons were gained and available to be given up. It was commonly held that a reducing atmosphere originated from interstellar gases largely composed of methane (CH_4), hydrogen (H_2), ammonia (NH_3), and water vapor. When those components were exposed to high energy levels, they underwent chemical reactions that produced the chemical complexes as the next stage in chemical evolution. Lightning was considered an energy source that might have stimulated such interactions, but kinetic energy, either in the form of electricity, light, or heat, would have been necessary in the right environment to initiate those chemical complexes.

In 1953, an attempt was made to test such a scenario in what has been referred to as the Miller/Urey[3] experiment. Stanley Miller was a graduate student under Harold Urey, a professor at the University of Chicago who supported the hypothesis, and Miller assembled a closed apparatus with a reducing atmosphere in which he inserted heat and an electric spark to simulate lightning. The apparatus and experimental setup that Miller developed can be observed in any college biological textbook on the beginning of life. The result of his work was the formation of some simple amino acids, formaldehyde (H_2CO), hydrogen cyanide (HCN), and several other organic compounds, some of which were common in living organisms. Those results were reported in material published by the National Academy of Sciences[4] as evidence that the building blocks of life were produced in the Earth's original atmosphere, thought to be a reducing atmosphere lacking oxygen.

The reducing atmosphere has since been challenged.[5] Given the extensive volcano activity that geologists believe characterized the new Earth's cooling environment, it is assumed that gaseous elements and compounds ejected from the volcanoes dominated the atmosphere with N_2, H_2, H_2O, and CO_2. Oxidized carbon holds electrons much tighter than reduced carbon, and no chemical evolution takes place. However, when those chemicals are bombarded by high-energy photons of sunlight, some methane, acetaldehyde (H_4C_2O), formaldehyde, and hydrogen cyanide are formed. Although gaseous carbon was spewed into the atmosphere, the exposure to sunlight would have induced the occurrence of reduction reactions that would have allowed opportunities for some amount of those critical compounds to form and chemical evolution to advance.

Another theory on the initial state of chemical evolution is that hydrothermal vents deep in the ocean floor could provide the right conditions.[6] Superheated water from these vents has been found to contain carbon molecules, and under pressure and temperature conditions near those vents, both kinetic energy and reduced carbon are available. Consequently, origin-of-life theorists suggest that such a situation induced chemical reactions that formed the necessary intermediates of chemical evolution. Water, with its unique solvent properties as a liquid with slight negative and positive charges, and an insulator against temperature extremes and atmospheric perturbation, allowed these compounds to combine through spontaneous reactions.

Either way, origin-of-life theorists assert that chemical evolution was stimulated by heat (deep hydrothermal vents), sunlight, or electrical pulses (lightning) that resulted in reduced carbon compounds. Amino acids and other carbon compounds were then generated through the transfer of kinetic energy into chemical energy, forming carbon bonds that resulted in complex carbohydrates, proteins, and nucleotides. The ocean, or isolated shallow bays, became a rich prebiotic soup of mega-concentrations of these compounds, and over time, some of these molecular compounds polymerized to form constructs of complex prebiotic macromolecules that were able to self-replicate and become the first forms of primitive life.

Although complete chemical complexes have not been formed in laboratory attempts, the fact remains that some amino acids and other organic compounds have been formed under laboratory trials, and while those conditions may not have been representative of the Earth's early atmosphere, it is relevant that some organic compounds associated with living organisms were formed under simulated conditions. That is important in the evolutionist's argument for life having originated by an undirected natural or material cause. Origin-of-life scientists suggest that in some such manner, proteins, carbohydrates, and nucleotides, which are required for life, were formed in the prebiotic soup in the form of ribonucleic acid (RNA) when exposed to kinetic energy,[7, 8] even if that type of environment was limited to only certain areas conducive for such formations.

Origin-of-life scientists have considered the candidates capable of initiating the chemical evolution of macromolecules responsible for first life were DNA, RNA, and proteins, because of the function they display in cellular processes (covered in more detail later).

Since proteins are extremely variable and complex, and don't replicate themselves except as infectious amyloids,[9] they were less likely candidates as the primary component in life's beginning. The double-stranded DNA molecule has not been observed as a catalyst of chemical reactions in an organism except as deoxyribozymes,[10] which are not always catalytic, and thus many scientists consider it to be less likely as the prime candidate for first life. However, the versatility of RNA as both a template for replication and as a catalyst make it a likely candidate, and that started concentrated research in that arena that became known as the RNA world.[11, 12]

Because it has the ability to replicate, over time, RNA would have become a dominant molecular form in the prebiotic soup. Its positive feature as a catalyst would have induced reactions that eventually were refined by chemical evolution and selection from among random combinations into functional proteins, nucleotides, and sugars. In some of the laboratory manipulations of chemicals and energy, such as the application of spark-discharge between electrodes in a water-vapor atmosphere containing carbon compounds, lipids were represented among the molecules produced. The premise is that the spontaneous formation of the bilayers when phospholipids are in water resulted in a structure of little spheres or liposomes capturing water inside.[13, 14] This provided the containment that was necessary as a primitive membrane to isolate the ribonucleotide strand in the presence of the right composition of other components. Contained within the primitive membrane and in the presence of an energy source, that characteristic increased their abundance over all other compounds, enabling prebiotic progress towards a living cell. The key to that progress was replication and the presence of an energy source.

Requirements for Primitive Life

Origin-of-life scientists also recognize the challenges with the concept. The formation of the right chemicals and their presence within a lipid envelope may satisfy the material needs, but the processes of division and replication of the incipient cell are critical events that also must occur by some mechanism. Ribonucleotides may be able to replicate themselves, but much more than ribonucleotides must replicate in cellular duplication, and replication must be in synchrony with and apportioned within the dividing lipid envelope. In theory, the processes that were successful in producing a living parent cell occurred by chance among multiple trillions of trillions of other primitive molecular processes that existed in the hypothetical nutrient broth of the early ocean bodies but were irrelevant to life. It was by chance that the right chemical assemblies came together that could replicate and by that feature went on to dominate the rich broth as primitive cells.

The requirements for primitive life identified by origin-of-life scientists include at least eighteen conditions before life could have a beginning through natural processes.[15] Those conditions are (1) a prebiotic soup characterizing certain bodies of water. (2) The presence of carbon compounds, along with (3) molecular ribose, (4) nitrogen bases, and (5) phosphate. (6) The presence of proteins, as well as (7) the assembly of RNA, with (8) specific catalyzing enzymes for protein production. (9) The presence of catalyzing enzymes for RNA replication, and (10) a very high abundance of RNA. (11) The existence of a primitive but functioning membrane that enclosed organic molecules, with (12) the ability of the membrane to selectively diffuse some molecules and retain others. (13) The tendency of the membrane to divide along some level of synchrony with RNA, and (14) the occurrence of a mechanism that would segregate ribonucleotide replicates within the presumptive sister cells. (15) The presence of an energy source, along with (16) an energy transfer system to sustain the process. (17) The presence of the right catalyzing enzymes for energy production, and (18) the presence of a relatively stable environment.

Origin-of-life theorists consider that all eighteen requirements were satisfied by chance occurrence. It is not suggested that the molecular components and cell membranes of the primitive assemblies that would have first formed the replicating molecule were like those of the present day. Understandably, much more complexity and structure evolved in the cellular functions we are now able to observe. Similarly, membranes would have evolved extensively over that which constituted enclosures of the incipient cell, but the theorists in the origin of life believe that cell organelles and lipids behave in such a manner to put their faith with some confidence in chemical evolution theory as a rational explanation for the beginning of life. Origin-of-life scientists believe such a beginning, which developed into what is called the prokaryote cell, with cytoplasm containing chromosomes and basic forms of organelles within a membrane, will ultimately be shown to have occurred by the natural laws of chemistry and physics under unique but rare conditions. Essentially, the assembly of the chemical elements and compounds forming primordial structures will be shown as the consequence of certain conditions that are representative of what existed in the early Earth's environment.

The conditions that formed the first cell and stimulated its duplication are as yet unknown. With the absence of explicit evidence regarding the nature and composition of the early Earth environment, opportunity to duplicate those conditions will depend on laboratory research and scientific inference. Present-day conditions are not representative of the early Earth. Bacteria consume all unprotected organic matter, and once they evolved in the past, they would have conceivably eliminated nonfunctional prebiotic compounds accumulating from chemical reactions, as well as eliminating any chance of primordial cell forms from developing henceforth. The search of life's origin via natural laws of chemistry and physics will continue, and at some point in the future, it is expected that research will disclose how first life assembled.

Creationist Perspective

Creation differs from chemical evolution, but the evidence used in support of naturalism's viewpoint is also consistent with the contemporary creationist's account in many respects. Science has shown that the material composition of life is made up of the basic components of matter found in Earth's composition. That in essence describes the dust of the ground, the chemical composition of matter on Earth. So both views consider that life was formed from the elements of the Earth.

As with evolution, Creation theory also recognizes the role of water, proteins, carbohydrates, lipids, nucleic acids, and an energy component, each of which is unique in their composition and function. Life unfolds in the orderly sequence of those compounds being synthesized in a manner comparable to a temporal blueprint. The process follows a coded program in DNA so that each developing component progresses in time and place in an orderly manner.

No one denies that nucleotide sequences are the blueprint for building proteins, the essential elements of life. There is an orderly program that builds ribosomes, the endoplasmic reticulum, the mitochondria, and the other organelles of the cell. Those organelles are in turn destined for specific duties of manufacturing, fine-tuning, and delivery of the cell products to the various sites for their use. They are programmed to recover, disassemble, and segregate the waste generated for recycling or disposal. Every scientist recognizes that unzipping of a specific section of the DNA double helix strand by RNA polymerase, and assembling of the designated protein, are all programmed in a precise manner. Similarly, the function of the cell organelles, facilitated by energy transfer enabling the cell to sustain itself, is an orderly system. Glycolysis and the Krebs cycle represent very complex patterns of electron sharing and energy potential, and they follow progressive interactive relationships based on elemental and molecular structure, the enzymes that catalyze the reactions, and the feedback that regulates the system and eliminates CO_2 in respiration. There is no discord here. The creationist agrees with the evolutionist that the development of the cell and all its functions are not an accretion of random processes resulting in an overwhelming conglomeration of functionalist compounds, but a programmed system with specific functional end points.

So where does the Creation story depart from that of chemical evolution? The difference is in the first cause. Rather than all of this occurring by chance, Creation theory stipulates that the origin, complexity, and function of the cell are evidence of design by an intelligent agent. Chemical evolutionists recognize the extensive complexity inherent in the cell organelles and their functions as programmed systems but relegate their origin to chance, undirected, and without purpose. To the creationist, such logic is flawed. It is a stretch to think that a living system that demonstrates programmed sustained functions in all aspects of its existence would in like manner not have originated by a systematic plan. There are no examples of even much simpler machines, manufacturing mechanisms, or data processing systems that occur by chance. All such systems are conceived, designed, and implemented by intelligence. Creation of life is considered the origin of what many scientists refer to as the anthropic principle,[16] the cosmos centered on the existence of humans. Therefore, contemporary creationists attribute the programmed systems involving the extensive complexity inherent in the cell organelles and their functions as evidence of design and, therefore, indicative of intelligence.

But the evolutionist will ask, what about the evidence that has shown organic compounds that ultimately make up living organisms can be formed naturally under the right conditions? For example, the Miller/Urey experiment and subsequent laboratory trials that verified that organic compounds, including some amino acids, could be formed in an environment with the presence of kinetic energy. That is true. However, the point isn't that bio-viable compounds can be formed naturally under certain conditions, but that evolutionists assume those natural phenomena are happenstance events. They fail to appreciate those organic assemblages as evidence of an encoded system endowed to contribute to a life-forming application. Creation theory suggests that intelligent cause would have provided the appropriate mechanisms for the creation of life to be assembled from the dust of the ground by design, not chance. If the mechanisms were by chance, there would be pervasive accumulations of remnant functionless compounds as testimony of such coincidental events. Even the hypothesized ubiquitous sea of nutrient-rich broth is challenged. If it had existed, there would have been extensive nitrogen-rich mineral deposits in Precambrian sedimentary rock, but there is no evidence that such deposits exist.

Moreover, the limited Miller/Urey results were forthcoming from a strongly reducing environment, dominated by hydrogen, methane, ammonia, and water vapor, in the absence of oxygen.[17],[18] Scientists now believe that such an environment never existed on the primitive Earth.[19] Since water was present on the ancient Earth, oxygen would have been generated by photo-dissociation of water vapor exposed to ultraviolet rays from sunlight. That would have resulted in free oxygen and hydrogen. Hydrogen would have escaped into space, and the oxygen left behind would have oxidized methane and ammonia. Even sunlight striking CO2 is thought to be an oxygen source under some conditions.

What about the RNA world? RNA has been suggested as the biomolecule responsible for the beginning of life, because it can replicate and catalyze chemical reactions. However, RNA also poses problems. RNA formation has not been demonstrated naturally outside of living cells,[20] so the conditions that would have produced RNA in the environment of the early Earth are unknown. RNA is unstable.[21] There is no mechanism outside the living cell that produces RNA's nucleotide bases thymine, uracil, and cytosine,[22, 23] so their origin is at best uncertain or impossible to form under early Earth scenarios. The origin of ribose, the sugar component in RNA, is also said to be a mystery outside the living cell.[24]

The problem increases because the conditions suitable for ribose formation are contrary to the conditions suitable for base formation. The bases are unstable at high temperatures, and all of them are reactive with other compounds, which would compromise their availability to form an RNA macromolecule without interference.[25] RNA performs limited enzyme functions, doesn't show nucleotide sequencing sophistication to fill all the roles in protein building, does not generate genetic information, and requires an exact duplicate of itself as a template in order to replicate.[26] This makes RNA unlikely as the biomolecule responsible for initiating the synthesis of the primitive cell. Therefore, in order for life to originate from the mechanisms proposed by origin-of-life scientists, it would have required intelligent intent through programmed assembly.

Chance and Probability

It is apparent that the concept of chance assembly of first life has very serious problems, and those problems are accentuated by two other factors. First, one has to put the time frame for life's beginning in perspective. As mentioned above, based on radiometric dating, the Earth is approximately 4.6 billion years old[27, 28] (although the methodology that determined that figure has been challenged[29]). Cooling down and becoming a substrate on which life could subsist comprised nearly the first billion years after the Earth was formed.[30] The earliest fossils are estimated to have existed 3.5 billion years ago.[31] Therefore, under the theory of chemical evolution, life had to occur over a time frame of 100 to 300 million years. That represents an amazingly short length of time in geological terms for chance to have produced what we reviewed above as the basic requirements for life, including all the complex organic mechanisms and machinery associated with the first living organisms. Determining how that might have occurred is the problem that origin-of-life theorists must confront. The concept is based on theories that came from interpretations of laboratory research and educated inference, but in essence, they assume these processes were initiated, transpired, and were brought together simply by chance.

The second problem when contemplating chance is again probability, covered extensively by Steven Meyer.[32] What is the probability of an event occurring? Recall that origin-of-life theorists list eighteen requirements or events that had to happen before a living cell could exist. The probability of all those events occurring is the multiple of their individual probabilities, which is a level of diminishingly low expectation as one advances. Understandably, there will always be the uncertainty about the odds associated with each independent event, but the probability of all these events occurring is so low that such uncertainty makes no substantive difference. For instance, there are twenty amino acids that are involved in protein building, among a very large pool of non-protein amino acids. But if just limiting the example to the twenty that are involved, that means in a pool of unlimited numbers of the twenty amino acids, the probability of a given amino acid starting the sequence of a protein is 1/20, which is true for the second in the sequence, the third, and so on. So the chance of a given amino acid sequence in a relatively short protein chain of 150 amino acids is 1/20 multiplied 150 times. Therefore, as Meyer[33] points out, if the protein was only 150 amino acid sequences long, the probability that a given sequence would assemble in the prebiotic soup would be minuscule.

Evolutionists point out that in many cases, more than one amino acid can serve successfully in a particular sequence without affecting the function of the enzyme, thus increasing the odds of a particular functional enzyme forming. Such a hypothetical example would be an enzyme that can function with either glycine or leucine in the eighth sequence position, and with alanine or tryptophan in the sixtieth position. That makes four different combinations that can occur without changing the function of the enzyme, or four combinations that represent the same given functional sequence.

Research on the odds of the formation of an enzyme's functional amino acid sequence versus a specific amino acid construct of the same length has in fact taken place. In 2004, Douglas Axe[34] reported on his work using a tested method to determine the ratio of a functional sequence of a 150-amino acid section of the enzyme that performs a specific function in bacteria, against all possible amino acid sequences of that length. His estimate of a ratio of 1 in 10^{77} that a functional sequence in that enzyme would occur by chance confirms the minuscule probability of that occurring.

However, Ian Musgrave[35] indicates that such low probabilities are mistaken. Some molecular constructs self-assemble, bypassing the probability problem. Moreover, a probability of 1 in 10^{77} doesn't mean that 10^{77} trials have to be taken before the right sequence comes up, but rather it can occur at any point in such a random assembly, even the first, fifth, or tenth trial in the 10^{77} probability, greatly reducing the time that such an assembly would potentially occur. Further, prebiotic compounds comprised an ocean full of potential protein constructs numbering unimaginably, in the multiple trillions of opportunities and combinations all occurring at once and repeatedly, effectively reducing the time element of abiogenesis.

Although Musgrave's analysis may be feasible, it doesn't make the improbability within reach. There are many related problems with the chance assembly of proteins in the prebiotic soup. Amino acid sequences in proteins are linked together in chains with peptide bonds, but non-peptide bonds form in equal frequency in laboratory mixtures of free amino acids. In the prebiotic soup, one can assume, therefore, that amino acid linkages with non-peptide bonds would form frequently enough to disrupt proteins from forming. The probability of a peptide bond forming under those conditions would be 1/2, and in a protein chain of 150 amino acids, the probability would thus be $1/2^{149}$, or 1 in 10^{45} chances of 150 peptide bonds forming without non-peptide interference.[36]

Another problem is the equal frequency of the left-handed amino acids with their right-handed mirror images.[37] Proteins are made up of only the left-handed isomeric forms. In a prebiotic soup with equal frequencies of each, the chance of a 150-amino-acid protein forming would also be $1/2^{150}$, or 1 in 10^{45} possibilities.

Consequently, in a prebiotic soup of left- and right-handed amino acid isomers, the chance of forming all peptide bonds in a 150-amino acid enzyme with a specific function would be the multiple of their probabilities, or $10^{45} + 10^{45} + 10^{77}$, coming to approximately 1 chance in 10^{167} that the enzyme would synthesize. Those odds are much lower than the level of probability considered below which an event will likely never occur. Since most proteins are made up of chains much longer than 150 amino acids, that improbability will increase with the increasing size of the amino acid chain. That extremely improbable event is made even more improbable by the presence of the many other compounds in close proximity in the prebiotic soup that would markedly interfere with the chance of a functional amino acid chain forming.

And this is the chance of only one specific enzyme. There are thousands of specific enzymes in protein building, in RNA replication, and in catalyzing functions for energy production that must be formed to facilitate the first primitive cell. The probability of that occurring is < 1 in 10^{167} times the number of enzymes involved. That leaves the assembly of all the structural proteins, enzymes, and nucleic acids of the first primitive prokaryote organism having been formed by chance within the confines of a primitive membrane with such an extremely minuscule probability that it is considered absolutely impossible. That was the only conclusion of both Sir Fred Hoyle in 1983 and Douglas Axe in 2004, with estimates of less than 1 chance in $10^{4,000}$ as the odds of producing the proteins necessary for the origin of a one-celled organism.[38]

Apart from the unfathomed problems of the extreme low probabilities in chemical evolution, the RNA world, and the time element for these processes to occur, there are still other issues that must be considered. In the same manner that amino acids have mirror images (chirality) with left- and right-handed structure in equal frequency, sugars also have left- and right-handed structures, but in the case of living cells, only the right-handed sugars are involved. This adds to the problem of chance assimilation of these compounds without interference in building functional constructs. The reciprocal of the very low probability of functional compounds forming by chance in prebiotic soup is the near-certainty of nonfunctional compounds accumulating and overwhelming the landscape, but they appear to be absent in geological formations that formed in the prebiotic early Earth.

Perhaps the most difficult problem of all confronting origin-of-life evolutionists is to resolve the source of information indigenous to the structure and function of the first cell. That issue has not been addressed. The fortuitous assembly of matter and the utilization of energy to sustain the cell thereafter is a conceptual challenge, but it also required the development of information that preserved the prescription of structure, function, and replication. If chemical evolution was a chance process, how was that information implemented and encoded in a polymer language? And how did the coded transcription/translation system evolve to extract those coded elements to duplicate structure and function? Contemporary creationists submit that random chance of life represents an infinitesimally minute probability, but given that it did happen, then it is logical that a functional element was responsible, which would imply a programmed assembly by intelligent cause.

Conclusion

Chemical evolutionists are committed to the search for mechanisms that will demonstrate how natural processes could have produced a living cell, including the information that prescribes the DNA blueprint. Such predisposition goes down to energy particles of the basic atomic structure forming compounds in a unique way, with detail and specificity ultimately identified as the endowment of life. Origin-of-life theorists suppose that the process occurred by natural laws and the unique nature of isolated biomolecules that formed in the presence of energy induced prebiotic progress towards a self-replicating cell.

The process of life's beginning related to natural laws and information is not just the venue of chemical evolution theorists. Creationists agree there was a complex process involved in the assembly of matter into a living entity. While the details of life's assembly are unknown, the evolutionists believe the process was a fortuitous construct, but creationists believe the process was possible only by the implementation of intelligent cause. The fact of the matter is that proposing such a process by chance creates a probability crisis. Contemporary creationists recognize the existence of natural laws and information in the synthesis of life, but the processes are viewed by the creationist as the fingerprints of God, and thus their concept of how those processes unfolded is different from that of the chemical evolutionist only with regard to their origin: design rather than chance. The probability crisis is resolved by intelligence that foreordained the circumstances for life to be assembled from the dust of the ground. The fact that all cellular processes follow programmed structural and functional developments makes design a feasible conclusion.

Endnotes

1 Freeman, *Biological Science*, 23.
2 Freeman, *Biological Science*, 41–54.
3 Freeman, *Biological Science*, 42.
4 J. Wells, *Icons of Evolution*, 26.
5 R. Shapiro, *Origins: A Skeptic's Guide to the Creation of Life on Earth* (Summit Books, 1986).
6 Freeman, *Biological Science*, 43.
7 Behe, *Darwin's Black Box*, 171.
8 Freeman, *Biological Science*, 55–57.
9 Saroj K. Rout, M. P. Friedmann, R. Riek, and J. Greenwald, "A Prebiotic Template- Directed Peptide Synthesis Based on Amyloids," *Nature Communications* 9(2018): 234.
10 S. K. Silverman, "Deoxyribozymes: DNA Catalysts for Bioorganic Chemistry," *Organic and Biomolecular Chemistry* 19 (2004).
11 S. C. Meyer, *Signature of the Cell*, 296.
12 Behe, *Darwin's Black Box*, 171.
13 Freeman, *Biological Science*, 73.
14 Wilson, *Riot and the Dance*, 38.
15 J. Jortner, "Conditions for the Emergence of Life on the Early Earth: Summary and Reflections," *The Royal Society* (2006).
16 B. J. Carr and M. J. Rees, "The Anthropic Principle and the Structure of the Physical World," *Nature* (1979), 278.
17 Freeman, *Biological Science*, 42.
18 J. Tomkins, *Creation Basics and Beyond*, 187.
19 Wells, *Icons of Evolution*, 18–22.
20 G. F. Joyce, "RNA Evolution and the Origins of Lif," *Nature* 338 (1989), 217-224.
21 Meyer, *Signature of the Cell*, 301.

22 R. Shapiro, "Prebiotic Cytosine Synthesis: A Critical Analysis and Implications for the Origin of Life," *Proc. Natl. Acad. Sci.* (1999), 96.

23 Tomkins, *Creation Basics and Beyond*, 189.

24 Meyer, *Signature of the Cell*, 303.

25 G. F. Joyce, "The Antiquity of RNA Based Evolution," *Nature* (2002), 418.

26 Meyer, *Signature of the Cell*, 304–19.

27 G. Brent Dalrymple, "The Age of the Earth in the Twentieth Century: A Problem (Mostly) Solved," Special Publications, Geological Society of London, 190, 1 (2001).

28 N. Mazhenov and S. Shalkarbekov, "Non-Radiometric Dating of the Age of the Earth: Implications from Fossil Coral Evidence," *Int J Adv Innovat Thoughts Ideas* 3 (2015): 160

29 Hebert, *Creation Basics and Beyond*, 233.

30 J. G. Ogg, G. Ogg, and F. M. Gradstein, "A Concise Geologic Time Scale," *Elsevier* (2016), 20.

31 Mayr, *What Evolution Is*, 215–28.

32 Meyer, *Signature of the Cell*, 204–14.

33 Meyer, *Signature of the Cell*, 212.

34 34. D. Axe, "Estimating the Prevalence of Protein Sequences Adopting Functional Enzyme Folds," *Journal of Molecular Biology* (2004), 341.

35 I. Musgrave, "Lies, Damned Lies, Statistics and Probability of Abiogenesis Calculations (1998), www.talkorigins.org/pdf/abioprobcalc.pdf.

36 Meyer, *Signature of the Cell*, 206.

37 Paula Y. Bruice. "Organic Chemistry"(4th Edition) *Pearson Education Books* (2004).

38 Meyer, *Signature of the Cell*, 213.

CHAPTER 5

Molecular Structure
of the Cell

The basic component in the phenomenon of life is seen in the form of a cell, consisting of a membrane around cytoplasm that contains all the structures that sustain the operation of that living unit. There are three general domains that constitute the biosphere of unicellular microorganisms. Bacteria are one, and they are ubiquitous, living in the soil, in water, and in other organisms. They are essential in digestive systems, decomposition, and recycling of nutrients. Archaea, the second domain, are like bacteria but very different in biochemical characteristics; they are genetically distinct from bacteria. They are found in extreme acidic and alkaline environments. Both bacteria and archaea are prokaryotes, consisting of a simple internal structure with no nucleus or membrane-bound organelles. Eukarya are the third domain. They have a nucleus within the cytoplasm and many membrane-bound organelle structures. All animals fall within the eukaryote domain.

The eukaryote cell is described by molecular biochemists Michael Behe (Lehigh University) and Scott Minnick (University of Idaho)[1, 2] as a system of small machines that manufacture cell products, each type having specific functions. That is very different from Darwin's understanding of the cell, which was consistent with the early nineteenth-century explanation that protoplasm was only a semifluid living substance, with little or no structure. Protoplasm is a term that now includes the mixture of all the molecular material of the cell, including the nucleus, nucleic acids, the organelles, proteins, lipids, and polysaccharides. Over the last few decades, knowledge of the cell has exploded, and while this account is only a cursory synopsis, an overview of the cell and its functions is necessary to arbitrate the worldview perspectives on biological life. The following section is a brief description of the eukaryote cell, according to the present understanding of cell structure and function.

Cell Structure and Function

The eukaryote cell is a molecular system that represents the multifaceted composition of cellular structure (figure 1). Inside the membrane surrounding the cytoplasm containing all the organelles is the nucleus, filled with the chromatin matrix near the center of the cell.[3, 4] The nucleus, enclosed in a double membrane called the nuclear envelope, surrounds the chromatin material, which takes form as chromosomes. These units contain polymer instruction codes that control the developmental process of the organism, its cellular differentiation, protein structural components, regulating enzymes, and cellular function.

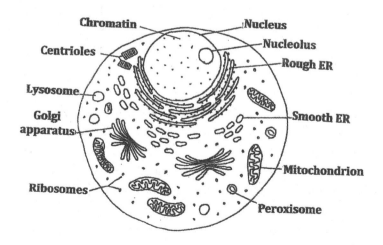

Figure 1. Eukaryote cell structure with nucleus and organelles

The polymer instructions are distributed among the several chromosomes, the number of which vary with different life-forms, but are specific within each. For example, humans have twenty-three pairs of homologous chromosomes, while fruit flies have four. Each chromosome is a long strand of linked molecular configurations called nucleotides, made of molecules of phosphate, a 5-carbon sugar, and one of four different nitrogen bases. The linked nucleotides form what is known as deoxyribonucleic acid (DNA), the polymer language in the cell that is associated with nearly all inherited characteristics of the organism.

The nucleotide segments along the DNA molecule are the codes for the different proteins and organismal characteristics. These segments of DNA are referred to as genes, either singularly or in combinations. The genetic structure of an organism is thus determined to a large extent by the composition of the DNA molecules making up the chromosomes, and that structural composition represents the genome or genotype of the individual. The genetic constitution of the genotype is what determines the physical and behavioral traits of the organism, and those observable traits make up the individual's phenotype. An alteration of a nucleotide on the DNA strand that changes a given sequence in the code, deletions of a segment of the strand, or its duplication, are referred to as mutations. In general, a mutation can be expected in every hundred thousand duplications of a chromosome. Most mutations are deleterious, resulting in the dysfunction of the resulting protein. Some are neutral, having no effect, but can be carried on in the genome of the surviving individual. A few of the mutations are beneficial and result in improved performance of the phenotype. Advantageous mutations in the form of new genetic constructs can expand through the population by the selective benefit it provides to survival of the progeny and thus the reproductive prowess of the organism in producing more offspring.

The basic composition of all life-forms is made up of water, fats, carbohydrates, minerals, and proteins. Excluding water, proteins make up about 48 percent of the mass. They are composed of polypeptide strings of amino acids. Each set of three nucleotides along the DNA strand form the code or codon for a specific amino acid. There are twenty different amino acids that are the building blocks of all proteins in living organisms, and it is the particular set of codons along the DNA strand that designate the composition, structure, and function of the proteins. All combinations of the four nucleotides are involved over the length of the chromosome, and the number of sets of codons in the structure of proteins ranges in the tens of thousands.

The critical step of protein building occurs in the ribosomes (figure 1). Ribosomes are assembled in the nucleolus of the nucleus and then transferred into the cytoplasm. Ribosomes translate the polymer codons for amino acids into proteins. The series of codons are transcribed from the respective segment of the DNA strand by an enzyme that forms a single strand of messenger ribonucleic acid (mNRA), which carries the transcribed polymer code from the nucleus to the ribosome in the cytoplasm. The polymer strand is then decoded by transfer RNA (tRNA) through a process that translates the polymer series of codons on the mRNA molecule into a linked polypeptide series of amino acids constituting the respective protein.

Proteins formed in the ribosomes are carried into the rough and smooth endoplasmic reticulum (ER) for processing.[5, 6] ERs (figure 1) are organelles in the cytoplasm that occur as a series of flattened compartments and tubal structures, where proteins are prepared for secretion, and where fatty acids, phospholipids, and glycoproteins are synthesized. Depending on their destination, some proteins are altered by enzymes adding carbohydrates to the side chains. In the process, the proteins are concentrated in membrane-bound vesicles for transportation to another organelle, the Golgi apparatus (figure 1) contained in the cytoplasm, which is a series of flattened sac-like structures (cisternae) where further modifications are made to the carbohydrate side chains. The Golgi apparatus functions as a vesicle-processing and distribution center for the proteins secreted from the organelle, with address labels or markers for hundreds of predetermined destinations in or outside of the cell.

Protein building requires energy, and the mitochondria organelles shown in figure 1 are the energy centers of the eukaryotic cell.[7] These organelles contain the enzymes that catalyze the reactions of aerobic respiration, oxidizing carbohydrates and fatty acids to produce adenosine triphosphate (ATP). This molecule stores and transfers energy and is hydrolyzed to produce free energy for work. Glycolysis occurs in the cytoplasm of the cell, changing glucose into pyruvate through a chain of ten distinct sequential chemical reactions. The pyruvate is carried to the mitochondria, where it goes through what is called the Krebs cycle,[8, 9] passing on reduction products to the electron transport chain in the inner membrane of the mitochondria. ATP production involves a sequential reaction series involving eight carboxylic acids, enzymes, and chemical cofactors, producing the energy that enables all organismic functions and thus all life processes. Glycolysis and the Krebs cycle are carefully regulated by feedback mechanisms that manage the energy supply for maintenance and accelerated demands.

Cell structure is not just organelles floating in the membrane-bound cytoplasm. The centrosome, made up of two centrioles (figure 1), is the major microtubule-organizing center. The centrosome involves a mass of proteins that organize microtubule structures of the cell's cytoskeleton, providing stability to the shape of the cell.[10] Microtubules are also formed as highways on which the membrane-bound protein vesicles are transported to their destinations within the cell and to the cell membrane for secretion from the cell. They are also involved in cell division, transporting chromatids of the dividing chromosomes along microtubules to each centriole at the cell poles as the cell divides.

Then there are the lysosomes and peroxisomes (figure 1), organelles that facilitate recovery of cell materials that are no longer functional after use. The lysosomes[11] are organelles that recycle proteins and worn-out organelles. Used proteins are transported to lysosomes for reprocessing, where their amino acids are extracted for reuse in other molecules. Peroxisomes[12] are organelles that degrade fatty acids and amino acids that are discarded and reduce hydrogen peroxide resulting from the degrading process into water and O_2. These organelles act as waste-processing centers that recycle waste in reusable forms for cellular functions.

All of these structures of the cell are made up of proteins. While only twenty amino acids are involved in protein building, there are thousands of different proteins constructed from those peptides involved in every aspect of body structure and activity. Proteins make up muscle, collagen, connective tissue, skin, body organs, hair, and other tissues. Most of the proteins are enzymes that catalyze chemical reactions such as respiration and oxidize carbohydrates and fatty acids into energy as ATP for cellular use. Others perform intracellular maintenance; some are for organelle construction and others for RNA processing. Proteins also function as antibodies that protect against invading diseases. Proteins are involved in bone structure, formed by specialized cells (osteoblasts) that secrete a material containing calcium compounds for strength and hardness of bone material. Hematopoiesis, the production of red blood cells, occurs from bone-marrow protein.

The function of each protein is determined by the composition of amino acids linked along the strand, and the three-dimensional (tertiary) or four-dimensional (quaternary) folding complex structure of the amino acid assembly. The complexity of proteins is demonstrated in figure 2, which shows the maze of amino acid threads, coils, sheaths, spirals, and helices in physical form portrayed as a step above the molecular configuration. These structures represent stable arrangements by the position and linkages of the amino acids and peptide bonds. Thousands of different protein assemblages exist, each with specific functions based on their tertiary and quaternary folding configuration determined by the millions of constituent molecular constructs.

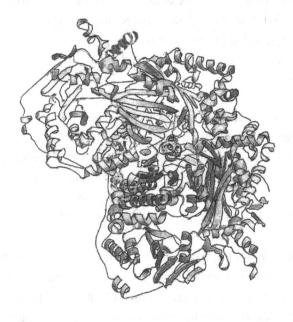

**Figure 2. A facsimile model demonstrating
the complex structure of a protein**

The next section presents an overview of cellular processes and programmed functions that are critical in understanding the phenomenal complexity of the system. Although the terminology may be unfamiliar in many cases, to alleviate the problem, technicalities are minimized, and figures have been included to assist in understanding cellular processes. If the reader is well acquainted with the material or isn't interested in further detail, this section can be passed over, going directly to the evolutionist's perspective.

Cellular Detail and Processes

Cellular processes and functions are determined in large measure by the sequence of nucleotides on the DNA strand. The structure is a linked series of nucleotides, each consisting of a phosphate group, a deoxyribose sugar (a 5-carbon molecule), and one of four molecular units called nitrogen bases:[13] adenine (A), guanine (G), cytosine (C), and thymine (T) (figure 3). The bases are shown only to demonstrate their chemical structure and henceforth will be designated with their respective capital letters along with P for the phosphate group and S for the 5-carbon sugar. These specifics are important only in providing a broad understanding of the mechanisms functioning within the cell.

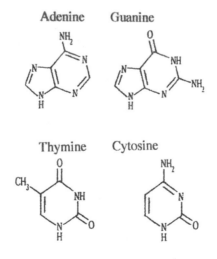

**Figure 3. The chemical structure of the
four nucleotide nitrogen bases**

The long strands of nucleotides that make up the chromosomes are formed by the phosphate group (P) linked to the 5-carbon sugar (S) of one nucleotide, which is linked to the phosphate group (P) and the 5-carbon sugar (S) of the next nucleotide, and so on (figure 4). The phosphate-sugar molecular series is referred to as the backbone of the strand. Nitrogen bases are attached as molecular side chains to the 5-carbon sugar groups. The makeup of the respective strand exists as a series of any combination of the four nucleotides.[14] The strands vary in length and can include thousands of nucleotide combinations.

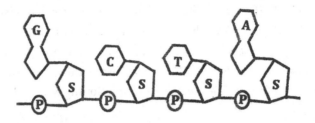

Figure 4. A single nucleotide strand with base side chains

The nucleotides making up a chromosome occur as two cross-linked strands, referred to as a coiled double helix. Its appearance is analogous to a twisted ladder, with the nucleotide bases that are attached to the sugars of one strand linked by weak hydrogen bonds to the bases attached to the sugars of the partner strand. These bonded base pairs form the rungs between the two phosphate-sugar backbone strands or poles of the analogous ladder (figure 5). The bases forming the rungs are paired in specific combinations, with the A base on one strand of the double helix always paired across with the T base on the other strand, and the G base of one strand always paired with the C base of the other, forming reciprocal partner strands. This makes the partner strand of the double helix in what is referred to as an antiparallel construct.[15] The base pairs are positioned in antiparallel alignments and are given linked stability by the weak hydrogen bonds between the partner strands. This molecular strand of the double helix is the construct of DNA.

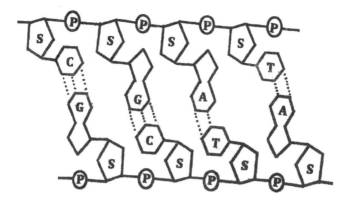

**Figure 5. The structure of DNA double helix,
with hydrogen bonds between base pairs**

The double helix strand of any combination of the four nucleotides is the DNA genetic code in the cell, which is associated with all inherited characteristics of the organism. Each strand is about six to nine feet long. To accommodate that length of DNA, the strands are coiled further by winding twice around numerous spool structures[16] (nucleosomes), each made up of eight histone proteins, which form the spool base around which the double helix winds before proceeding to the next spool (figure 6). The spooled DNA/protein bundles are held in particular shapes by specialized proteins forming larger coils of a compact DNA-protein complex that makes up the composition of the chromosome.

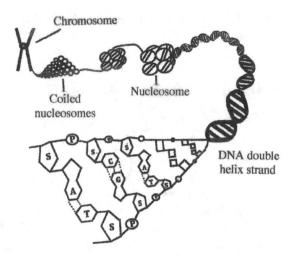

**Figure 6. DNA double helix coiled around
nucleosomes forming the chromosome**

The codons representing a particular protein on the DNA strand
have start and stop locations that identify that part of the strand to
be copied. A specific enzyme in the nucleus of the cell monitors the
strand for that series of codons and binds to the DNA double helix,
inducing the respective segment to unfold from its coil.[17] With the
help of a promoter enzyme, it chemically binds to the right location
on the single DNA strand and transcribes each nucleotide in sequence
beginning at the start marker, forming a separate single molecular
strand. That strand is the RNA molecule, where the 5-carbon sugar
is ribose in place of deoxyribose, and a slightly different base, uracil
(U), is substituted for thymine (T) and is henceforth always paired
across with adenine (A) in antiparallel construct of the RNA strand.
The ciphering process for the antiparallel code selection is unclear.

Transcription proceeds until reaching the stop marker on the DNA
strand for that particular protein, which results in the formation of
an RNA antiparallel strand consistent with the code sequence of
that section of DNA (figure 7). Because the transcribed section of

DNA must have only the pure code sequence to be translated into the protein, any noncoding intervening segments of the transcribed RNA strand are removed by a molecular machine called a spliceosome. The machine excises the intervening segments from the strand and splices together the adjoining coded segments to provide a pure coded strand for translation. The resulting RNA strand is called messenger RNA (mRNA) for the respective protein.[18]

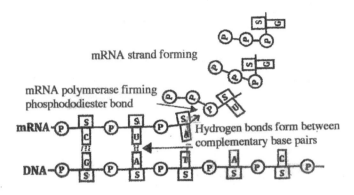

mRNA strand forming

mRNA polymrerase firming phosphododiester bond

mRNA

Hydrogen bonds form between complementary base pairs

DNA

DNA strand as template

Figure 7. Transcription of DNA to mRNA strand by a special RNA polymerase enzyme

That is only the first part of the protein-building story, so stay with me for the next part. The mRNA strand then leaves the nucleus through a special door in the nuclear membrane and transports the linear code to one of many ribosomes among the numerous organelles, or little machines, shown earlier in figure 1. Ribosomes are made up of two RNAs and thirty proteins, assembled in the nucleolus of the nucleus and then transferred into the cytoplasm. Ribosomes translate the polymer code carried by the mRNA into proteins. A particular mRNA goes to the surface of a ribosome, and the strand is decoded by tRNA through a process that translates the polymer series of codons on the mRNA molecule into a linked series of amino acids (figure 8). Each mRNA three-nucleotide unit codon is matched with the three-nucleotide anticodon representing the particular amino acid by the appropriate tRNA complex inside the ribosome and links it to the series of corresponding amino acids forming the polypeptide strand of the particular protein.[19]

Once the amino acid joins the polypeptide strand, the tRNA unit then disengages, and the next tRNA slips in with the right anticodon match with the next codon of the mRNA strand as it moves along the ribosome. How the enzyme determines the match is uncertain. The process of matching and disengaging continues until the series of codons that constitute the respective protein polypeptide is completed.[20] The translation phase of the complex protein building involves activators, tRNAs, proteins, and many synchronized steps, each of which has a specific function.

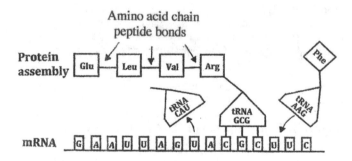

Figure 8. Translation of codons of the mRNA strand into amino acids by tRNA on the surface of ribosomes

The next phase of protein building is to identify the front end of the molecule with special markers or labels and then transport the protein from the ribosome along the microtubules to other specific destination organelles, where they are altered for specific duties.[21] These marker tags on front of the different proteins are entrance keys into the various destination organelles that induce the organelle or cell-wall pore to exclusively open. Then the markers drop off after guiding the protein to its specific destination. Some proteins leave the ribosome in an inactive state until needed for specific functions.

The centrosome microtubule-organizing center forms the tracks on which the membrane-bound protein-packed vesicles are transported for use by the vesicle transport system. Vesicle transport along microtubule tracks is a fascinating process. A molecule called kinesin is a motor protein that converts chemical energy into mechanical energy to do work.[22] The molecule is two intertwined polypeptides forming the stalk, with a double tail region and two heads. The tails connect to the vesicle (cargo), and the two heads at the other end of the intertwined stock bind to the microtubule and ATP (figure 9). It is thought that when each head binds to ATP, it induces a change in the shape of the protein, causing it to move. As the process alternates between the two heads, the kinesin walks down the microtubule to its destination, just as a biped moves along a sidewalk. It has been shown that cells have a number of different kinesin proteins that are specialized for different types of vesicles. These kinesin motor proteins, which move cargo throughout the cell, are also involved in the structure of both the cilia and flagella of cells.

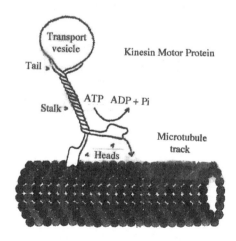

**Figure 9. Portrayal of a kinesin protein with tails bound
to cargo and two heads walking on a microtubule**

It is well known that growth of the organism occurs by cell replication, referred to as mitosis,[23] resulting in the exact duplication of the cell. The human cell contains a set of twenty-three chromosomes that came from the female parent and twenty-three chromosomes from the male parent. These chromosomes are referred to as homologous pairs, essentially twenty-three pairs for a total number of forty-six chromosomes. The forty-six chromosomes are referred to as a diploid (2N) set. Division starts by the homologous chromosomes of the original cell forming exact copies of themselves, with the centromere maintaining a connection between the original and the copy as sister chromatids. When cell division is initiated, the replicate strands of the chromosomes separate to each side of the dividing cell. Upon completion of the division, each cell will have exact reciprocal copies of the parent strands as a diploid set (figure 10). The new cells in turn subsequently divide and follow the same process in producing multiples of the original cell during growth of the organism.

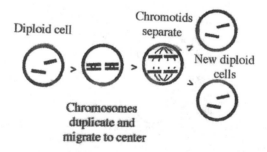

**Figure 10. Mitosis or cell division in
nonreproductive somatic cells**

There is a remarkable feature of the system when the DNA strands duplicate during cell replication. The double strands that make up the double helix of the DNA separate, and each separate strand becomes a template for the synthesis of the new antiparallel strand. A special enzyme moves along the template strand and constructs the new partner strand by placing the incoming nucleotides in matching (antiparallel) sequence, consistent with the nucleotide sequence of the template.[24] In the process, there is an occasional error or mismatch in the sequence. However, the new partner strand is proofread by a DNA enzyme, and when an error occurs, the enzyme will correct mismatches in nucleotide sequence by replacing the discrepancy with the appropriate matching nucleotide. This proofreading process is responsible for the major reduction of potential mutations in DNA replication. The organelles also duplicate and divide with the respective daughter cells during cell division through processes less well understood.

In eukaryotic organisms, cell division for the production of gametes follows a different and exceptional pattern that imbues diversity. The original diploid set of homologous chromosomes duplicates as in mitosis, but during the process, sections of the paternal and maternal chromatids cross over in recombination, with the result that the homologous sets are represented by a mixture of each parental chromosome.[25] The newly reassembled homologous duplicated sets segregate, with one set of each homologous chromosome migrating to a daughter cell in the first cell division, giving each daughter cell a diploid set that represents reciprocal mixtures of the original parental chromosomes. But in meiosis, those cells divide again without duplication, producing four daughter cells with one haploid (1N) set of chromosomes each (figure 11). These haploid cells are the gametes, and because they went through recombination, they contain a unique mixture of parental chromosomal segments. When the gamete of the female is joined by the gamete of the male in fertilization, the resulting cell or zygote (fertilized ovum receiving homologous chromosomes from each parent) is then in diploid form, representing a new set of homologous chromosomes for continued mitotic development as a heterogeneous offspring, unlike either parent. Reproductive cells are the only ones that will carry mutations to the next generation.

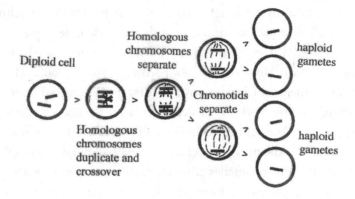

**Figure 11. Meiosis or cell division in
reproductive cells forming gametes**

Mutations that occur during cell divisions forming the gametes (meiosis), or during recombination of the genes in the set of chromosomes of the gametes, are the changes passed on in sexually reproducing organisms. So if the probability of a mutation is 1/100,000, and the chance of it being neutral or beneficial is a probability no greater than 1/10,000, that would mean only one mutation in a billion will result in a positive change in progeny.

Such a low rate potential isn't a problem in numerous rapidly reproducing bacteria, where quadrillions reproduce every hour. That rate of bacteria reproduction would mean potentially beneficial mutations are present continuously in large numbers. But that is not the case in animals. Their low rate potential is the result of long generation times, especially in some that can take years to reproduce. That reality has a major impact on how rapidly change can occur within most animal populations and is a factor in extending the time before a substantial change can be observed in some species.

Geneticists have shown that epigenetic[26] (non-genetic) sources of information also influence gene expression. Complex biological systems appear to require more than what is determined by DNA. For example, the cytoskeleton of the cell discussed earlier is essential in cell stability and in the delivery of cell products to specific locations. The cytoskeleton is made up of proteins, but the pattern of the structure is determined by the centrosomes, including the internal tracks (microtubules) for transport of the essential molecules to exact destinations in the cell. Centrosomes are made up of two centrioles that are passed on in cell division and duplicated in the daughter cell, but centrioles have no DNA.[27]

Similarly, sugars on the cell surface have a role in intercellular communication and have a great capacity for information, but DNA does not determine their location. Protein patterns in the cell membranes are transmitted directly from parent to the daughter membrane during cell division rather than by gene expression. Epigenetic information is thought to be involved in development of body plans and cellular complexity but is not subject directly to the effects of mutations of nucleotide sequences.

At a given point, cells differentiate into specialized features of the body plan. Although all cells originate by division from the original cell and thus all carry identical genes, as the embryo begins to develop along its respective body plan, the cells start differentiating for specific functions that are controlled in part by regulatory genes. The cells that were duplicating the parent cell change and take on the new form consistent with the respective body part, differentiating further into specialized configurations within that body part such as the retina, nephrons, follicles, organs, appendages, skeleton, and so on. As the body plan unfolds, the challenge is knowing how those changes are ciphered. Major components are the homeotic genes high in the controlling hierarchy of cell behavior. They control the kind of organs that are formed, determine the anterior-posterior axis, and regulate gene expression. Some of what geneticists have referred to as "junk" DNA, making up most of the chromosome's length, were originally thought to be no longer viable[28] but have been shown to have a role in regulating cell differentiation and other functions.[29]

While this is a cursory review of the structure of life at the molecular and organelle levels, it vividly demonstrates that the transformations that the cells go through are indeed complex and beyond marvelous. It is a mystery in many respects how all of the different organs—the liver, heart, lungs, kidneys, eyes, digestive system, and other functions— come from the one original cell programmed to differentiate along separate developmental pathways to fulfill the blueprint of that plan. Early in this differentiation process, a cell can be transferred to another body part, where it assumes its new role by conforming to the requirements of the receiving organ or appendage. If left longer before transfer, it will no longer conform to the new site when transferred and will continue as if in its original location.

The DNA strands of those multiplying cells are the same, but at a critical point when growth changes into differentiation, the protein products in the cell change accordingly. The information decodes changes to conform to the requirements of different components of the body plan. Apart from the digital genetic code on the DNA strands, it appears that regional aspects of the DNA strands have an influence on how information is formatted to meet body-plan requirements. Genome loops, interacting clusters, and linear proximity of the DNA strands exert influences on genetic instructions. All information is in the cell but undergoes mechanisms that are not readily apparent in the protein-generating pieces of DNA. The process is more complex with genes that involve many different sites on the DNA strand for the development of a particular trait, and the complexity of advanced life-forms testifies to the many combinations and interactions that are involved in the inherent constructs that form the organism.

Evolutionist Perspective

There is no doubt about the structure of life. Molecular biology reveals a complexity and an organized sequence of events at the molecular level that appear designed to achieve function for purpose. That too was what early nineteenth-century naturalists had concluded about animal life observed in nature. But that was only an illusion exposed by Darwin when he published his treatise on the origin of species. While life appears designed, Dawkins[30] asserts that it is because of the length of time that living organisms have been subject to the processes of genetic variation and natural selection that allowed the adaptive integration of the organism with its habitat. What was true for animal life adapting to the changing environment through small advantageous changes accumulating over time is true for the molecular mechanisms responsible for those observable refined changes. Life arose through what is called chemical evolution, and it progressed henceforth by similar mechanisms at the molecular level. Dynamic changes have accumulated in small increments over great lengths of time, and that is the key to developing the molecular complexity of the cell through evolutionary processes by natural cause.

The synchrony between the biological world and its environment occurs because of the changes that transpired through the happenstance of ongoing variation in nucleotide arrangements and natural selection. Variations responsible for the changes observed in organisms are transformations in the molecular framework of the cell that proved to be advantageous alterations. Darwin was unaware of the cellular mechanisms, but his observations and rationale in developing evolutionary theory associated with animal and plant life at the organismic level involve the same principles at the molecular level: chance variation followed by natural selection and the accumulation of those small changes over great lengths of time.

Ernest L. Brannon

There is much in molecular biology that demonstrates the validation of evolutionary theory. The most impressive evidence of evolutionary relationship of all life-forms are the universal nature of cellular constructs, the DNA code, translation of the code, and protein building and function. These features common in most life-forms demonstrate a mutual affiliation consistent with the concept of common descent. Evidence in support of ancestral origin is the presence of compatible genes found in life-forms as divergent as flies and humans.[31]

Phylogenic relationships of life-forms using molecular data have been relatively consistent with the evidence that originally established those relationships based on morphological analysis. These data could be called molecular anatomy, because they offer the same type of information forthcoming from morphological data, except at a much finer level. Molecular data provide estimated molecular time frames of relationships that weren't possible with morphological data. Animals that show morphological similarities also show similarities at the molecular level, which supports the proposition of common descent. Although DNA sequences are taken primarily from living organisms rather than from fossils, the degree of their similarity is the basis on which relationships are developed, and those relationships provide the information used to develop molecular trees of life. The trees vary depending on the DNA sequence but provide another parameter used with morphological and physiological data that confirm phylogenetic relationships.[32]

Corroborating evidence on common relationships is the research that has shown dysfunctional regions or inactive genes on the chromosomes that represent a series of loci no longer coding for proteins. When genes become inactive or dysfunctional, they are referred to as pseudogenes; these inactive genes have been classified as junk in the jargon of molecular biologists. Junk is composed of a variety of nonfunctional DNA in the form of degraded genes, duplicated sections of the DNA strand, and ancient repetitive elements (AREs),[33] as pointed out by

Frances Collins of the human genome fame, mentioned previously as an authority on the genetic code. Pseudogenes can provide some of the potentially strongest data on evolution. For example, when one compares occasional genes between humans and chimpanzees, a dysfunctional piece of DNA can be found in humans that involves the same loci as the dysfunctional piece of DNA in chimpanzees.[34] These data are interpreted as evidence of the common descent of these life-forms when separated from their common ancestor.

Common descent is most conclusive among mammals because of the level of research on these life-forms. Comparing the mouse and human genomes, which have been worked out rather precisely, Collins states that the order of protein coding genes along the chromosomes is remarkably similar in these life-forms. For instance, virtually all of the genes on the human chromosome 17 are found on mouse chromosome 11. He also referred to the evidence of "jumping genes" that are in the same locations on the chromosomes of humans and mice, as well as throughout the mammalian genre. He says:

> Even more compelling evidence for a common ancestor comes from the study of what are known as ancient repetitive elements (AREs). These arise from "jumping genes," which are capable of copying and inserting themselves in various other locations in the genome, usually without any functional consequences. Mammalian genomes are littered with such AREs, with roughly over 45 percent of the human genome made up of such genetic [material]. When one aligns sections of the human and mouse genomes, anchored by the appearance of gene counterparts that occur in the same order, one can usually also identify AREs in approximately the same location in these two genomes ... in a position that is most consistent with their having arrived in the genome of a common mammalian ancestor.

Ernest L. Brannon

Evolutionary theory specifies that diversity of life-forms is the result of accumulative microevolutionary changes that can result in even very complex structures. The eye is an example. It is an organ of complexity in cell types and function, all evolving at the molecular level by small progressive changes of some advantage to the organism. Darwin[35] was aware of the difficulty in advancing the concept that natural selection was able to produce the mammalian eye. However, he reasoned that if gradual changes from a simple optic nerve coated with pigment to the perfect and complex vision organ was shown to presently exist in different forms of life, then it wasn't a problem in concluding how it could be formed by natural selection. In essence, the progressive steps in advancing complexity of the eye that occurred correspondent with the advancement in the complexity of life-forms provides the evidence of how the eye evolved from a small fortuitous light-sensitive spot to the complex camera-type eye through a series of small steps over great lengths of time.

Coyne[36] reiterated the argument in more detail:

A possible sequence of such changes begins with simple eyespots made of light sensitive pigment, as seen in flatworms. The skin then folds in forming a cup that protects the eyespot and allows it to better localize the light source. Limpets have eyes like this. In the chambered nautilus, we see a further narrowing of the cup's opening to produce an improved image, and in ragworms the cup is capped by a protective transparent cover to protect the opening. In abalones, part of the fluid in the eye has coagulated to form a lens, which helps focus light, and in many species such as mammals, nearby muscles have been co-opted to move the lens and vary its focus. The evolution of the retina, an optic nerve, and so on, follows by natural selection. Each step of this hypothetical transitional "series" confers increased adaptation on its possessor, because it enables the eye to gather more light or form better images, both of which aid survival and reproduction. And each step of this process is feasible because it is seen in the eye of a different living species. At the end of the sequence we have the camera eye, whose adaptive evolution seems impossibly complex. But the complexity of the final eye can be broken down into a series of small, adaptive steps.

So while the complexity in programmed structure and function of the cell and its organelles appear to have been designed, natural selection of altered molecular constructs have only made it appear as if the systems were designed. These molecular phenomena are the result of the refining influence of natural selection through the accumulation of micro-changes over long periods of time. Programming is the result of trait reoccurrence induced by the fortuitous nucleotide combination of the particular gene or set of genes responsible, and that will be maintained in the DNA code until replaced by another more advantageous mutation.

Creationist Perspective

The molecular biology of the cell is a phenomenal example of a system that has a predetermined design in its structure and function. To the creationist, it is entirely implausible that a system of coded information transcribed and translated from a polymer language into a living entity made up of organized, interactive, complex elements with an integrated purpose could occur by chance. Scientists see design and purpose in the molecular structure of the cell, and that is because there *is* design and purpose. No other interpretation makes sense of even the simplified description of the cell presented in this discourse.

The DNA code, existing in the form of a double helix with the strands wound around the histone bundles, the sequence of unfolding the DNA strand by a special enzyme for transcription of the code, proofreading, and its transfer as mRNA from the nucleus to the ribosomes for translation, are amazing features that follow a programmed process. The series of events in translation of the mRNA code in the ribosomes by tRNA, the manner in which the different tRNA units are readied, the enzymes that are associated with each predetermined step of transfer, and proofreading initiated for corrective action, are all extraordinary indeed. In addition, the cytoskeleton, its organization by the centrosomes, and the kinesin walking proteins that carry the manufactured cargo along the microtubules to specific sites in the cell are features indicating a prescribed organization. These events fit into a master design of a functioning system of different cell types in the composition of the organs and tissues making up an organism's body plan, all coming from a single cell that replicated and diversified in construct and function for the greater purpose of life. Billions of molecular units are involved that require specific relationships in the functions of the cell that can only be ascertained as evidence of omniscient intelligence.

Given that the cell demonstrates the complexity of a master design, it is most logical that an intelligent cause would have been responsible for its origin. And if that is the case, then how is the interpretation of the evidence used in support of neo-Darwinism rationalized? Evolutionists attribute the presence of life's diversity to natural phenomena referred to as material cause. In other words, life evolves by small accumulative changes that result from the happenstance of randomly occurring mutations or chance alterations of the nucleotides as mistakes in the DNA construct. But in the Creation saga, what is identified as material cause is, in reality, the result of circumstance, where physical laws or biological prodigies are the manifestation of universal principles established by the Creator at the beginning of time. Natural phenomena should be considered as the tools of the Creator, and much of what is observed as the result of material cause had an intelligent origin, even the application of chance itself.

Certainly, at the species level, genetic variability and natural selection are mechanisms that allow an organism to integrate with an ever-changing environment, and that requires adaptation via molecular adjustments. Adaptation is a marvelous biological accommodation of environmental variability. Whether or not adaptive change progresses on to the magnitude of change that would result in transition of archetypes is an unresolved question, but that too would have been the prerogative of the Creator. The point is that one doesn't know the mind of God, nor his methods, but the evidence indicates the existence of a master plan in the structure and function of the cell, and such intelligible information would have been initiated at the highest level prior to the cell's beginning.

The information is ciphered as digital code that has been revealed by meticulous investigations of molecular biologists, and that code is common in all organisms. With the exception of some viruses, DNA, RNA, and the protein-building process are universal in all life-forms. Some sequences of DNA protein coding regions are the same among all organisms, from bacteria to humans. Humans and chimpanzees share 100 percent of DNA sequences that code for proteins.[37] Such similarity is used as an indication of lines of relationship, but while the similarity of genes between humans and chimpanzees has been interpreted to mean a common lineage, such a conclusion is based on an interpretation consistent with the model that is being applied. The evolutionary concept of common descent is the Darwinian model. The more analytical alternative is that similarities imply a nearly universal design evident in all life-forms, just as DNA is the genetic code in all of the animal kingdom, established as life's provision at conception. Universal design in which all of life was given the same basic molecular machinery in the creation of diverse phenotypical form is an omnipotent characteristic of divine authorship. Relationships demonstrated in morphological and molecular features in support of universal design are not always compatible with the concept of common origin. Humans and mice share 99 percent of DNA sequences that code for proteins,[38] but in this case, molecular similarity doesn't represent a close relationship.

Pseudogenes are another area where the thinking has been changing about common origin. Pseudogenes were considered nonfunctional and have been called "junk." Humans carry about two thousand pseudogenes in their genome of thirty thousand genes.[39] While the location of a particular pseudogene at the same location between viable DNA sequences in both humans and chimpanzees has been thought nonfunctional in coding for proteins and assumed to have originated from a common source, there is reason to reconsider that assumption. There is no evidence that pseudogenes are nonfunctional in some other aspect of expression. Humans and chimpanzees have a high degree of morphological similarity, so the presence of allele units in similar locations would be expected. Moreover, there is evidence that pseudogenes are involved in protein production, and there are numerous examples of pseudogenes involved in gene regulation and expression.[40] The AREs or jumping genes have also been shown to provide regulatory functions of gene expression,[41] so the concept of noncoding DNA that constitutes the majority of the DNA strands is being modified from the original assertion that they were junk.

The point is that research showing functional properties of noncoding classes of DNA challenges the evolutionary assumption that noncoding protein DNA is the remnant of genes that became inactive in the common ancestor and were passed on to its subsequent descendants as evidence of evolutionary relationship. Function trumps assumption. The presence of common noncoding DNA sequences stems from their role in regulating gene activity, and they are positioned in relationship to that function. They are widespread and reflect the common design of these incredible structures that provide such universal application.[42]

There are many unknowns about the information coded in the DNA of the cell, and the influence that information exerts upon the molecular mechanisms is not entirely understood. Science has yet to determine what force organizes the molecular mechanics of the cell to follow such a predetermined distribution and function. When the elements making up the ribosomes are separated but in close proximity, they will self-assemble. How is that realized? Cell division is also a mystery in many ways. What induced the cell to divide and the organelles to self-replicate in synchrony? During transcription of the two unfolded segments of the DNA strands, both segments code for separate proteins. Each segment is antiparallel to the other, so while the two protein products are different, they are complementary, because the code on one segment obligates the antiparallel code of the other. How were the antiparallel code combinations synchronized?

The questions could go on, but it is apparent that all of this involves stored information that appears functionally predestined. How such a complex system of information originated is yet a mystery, and the code is far more comprehensive than computer digital codes programmed by intelligent agents, so it is logical that such an advanced polymer language would have originated from a more advanced intelligence.

Ever since Darwin, the eye has been an issue in rationalizing evolution theory at the morphological level of an organism. The eye is a unique organ because it can utilize the phenomenal aspect of light. Images are discernable by light's reflection off the surface of objects. Darwin[43] commented about the evolution of the eye being difficult to conceive because it is a complex marvel, capturing reflected light, which involves a totally unique structure in our understanding of sensory systems. He reasoned that if gradual changes from a simple optic nerve coated with pigment to the perfect and complex vision organ was shown to exist in different forms of life, then it wasn't a problem in seeing how it could have progressed by natural selection. However, Michael Behe,[44] as a molecular biochemist, says that when scientists remark that the eye can be explained simply by evolution proceeding from some single-celled animals that have a light-sensitive spot with a little pigment behind it, or in multiple-celled animals that have a pigment-backed light-sensitive cell in a little cup that gives it better direction-finding ability, they are grossly ignorant of what is required at the molecular level for such so-called "simple" mechanisms of even primitive eyes to form by happenstance. And of course, how simple is a simple light-sensitive cell at the molecular level?

To the evolutionist, the sequence from simple eyespots made of light-sensitive pigment to the protective cup, to the transparent cover, to the lens, to the focusing muscles, optic nerve, and retina, represents a series of hypothetical steps through natural selection because such a sequence is consistent with the accepted Darwinian model that would allow no other explanation. However, the alleged evolution from the simple to the complex eye isn't based on progress demonstrated in a series of fossils advancing over time but rather is a contrived sequence based on the formation of eyes seen in different living species consistent with their needs. The conjecture is contrary to the evidence. The trilobites came on the scene in the early Cambrian period over five hundred million years ago with advanced compound eyes showing optic double lenses with a refracting interface to focus.[45] There is no evidence of small adaptive steps evolving into this complex eye. They simply appeared with the trilobites in the absence of any precursory forms as the most advanced eyes conceived, and those advanced eyes were present when those animals first appeared.

Contemporary Creation posits that the complexity of the cell and the polymer language engaged go beyond what could be accountable by the neo-Darwinian model. Investigations in the molecular biology of the cell have advanced our understanding of the presence of very complex interactive systems, their physical constituents, and their functional relationships. These aspects point to a common material design attributed to an omnipotent metaphysical force as the origin of the biochemical matrix of life.

So what mechanisms were employed in the creative process? Did the Creator's master plan include molecular processes that unfolded over time, as suggested by theistic evolutionists, or were the life-forms structured in a shorter time frame as discrete units, consistent with what is apparent in the fossil evidence of the Cambrian explosion? Both options can be viewed as substantive alternatives for the assembly of different life-forms, but it is apparent there was a provision that allowed for life to form in nearly an unlimited diversity involving mechanisms yet to be ascertained.

Conclusion

The detail of the digital code of the DNA double helix is an astounding feature controlling most of an organism's development, differentiation, and growth. The facts demonstrate that the sequence of nucleotides on the double helix of antiparallel DNA strands in the cell nucleus are coded information using only four letters or digits for nearly all the functions of life. Segments of the double helix as digital codes separated by an enzyme along with start and stop markers are transcribed in the construction of an RNA messenger, transported to the ribosomes outside the nucleus, and translated into the construction of different proteins with specific functions for the processes of living. The cell is able to replicate and differentiate into different structures, and those structures are not the random assembly of pieces, but dynamic entities of complex systems that follow predetermined pathways. These are evidence of programmed phenomena.

The resolution of how that came about requires a look at the evidence. Evolutionists recognize that the processes that occur in a predictable manner in the cell are largely programmed in the genetic code. Contemporary creationists agree and recognize that fine-tuning and the overwhelming complexity of the cellular mechanisms and functions at the molecular level are evidence of programmed processes. That is the reality. The issue is whether or not such programming could originate by any other means than by an intelligent cause. In non-biological phenomena throughout the world, programming is conceived by intelligence. Although only the fundamentals of cell structure were presented in chapter 5, the demonstrated complexity in structure and function are sufficient to effectively argue that intelligence was also involved in the conception of cellular life. Just the linear succession of protein formation by DNA transcription, RNA proofreading, spliceosome refitting, translation of codes assembling amino acids into proteins, and transfer of proteins by kinesin walking proteins to designated sites is convincingly attributed to intelligent cause.

Endnotes

1 Behe, *Darwin's Black Box*, 4–5.
2 S. A. Minnich and S. C. Meyer, "Genetic Analysis of Coordinate Flagellar and Type III Regulatory Circuits in Pathogenic Bacteria," *WIT Transactions on Ecology and the Environment* (2004), 73.
3 Wilson, *Riot and the Dance*, 55.
4 Freeman, *Biological Science*, 93.
5 Wilson, *Riot and the Dance*, 69.
6 Freeman, *Biological Science*, 97.
7 Wilson, *Riot and the Dance*, 72.
8 Wilson, *Riot and the Dance*, 108–109.
9 Freeman, *Biological Science*, 118–28.
10 Wilson, *Riot and the Dance*,76–79.
11 Wilson, *Riot and the Dance*, 71–72.
12 Freeman, *Biological Science*, 93.
13 Wilson, *Riot and the Dance*, 116.
14 Wilson, *Riot and the Dance*, 117–18.
15 Freeman, *Biological Science*, 61–62.
16 Wilson, *Riot and the Dance*, 118–19.
17 Wilson, *Riot and the Dance*, 122–23.
18 Wilson, *Riot and the Dance*, 123.
19 Wilson, *Riot and the Dance*, 124.
20 Wilson, *Riot and the Dance*, 127.
21 Freeman, *Biological Science*, 97–101.
22 Freeman, *Biological Science*, 107.
23 Wilson, *Riot and the Dance*, 143–51.
24 Freeman, *Biological Science*, 238–40.
25 Wilson, *Riot and the Dance*, 153–60.
26 F. Perri and others, "Epigenetic Control of Gene Expression: Potential Implications for Cancer Treatment," *Crit Rev Oncol Hematol* (2017), 111.

27 W. Marshall and J. L. Rosenbaum, "Are There Nucleic Acids in the Centrosome?" *Current topics in developmental biology* (2000), 49.

28 Collins, *The Language of God*, 111, 117.

29 J. Wells, *The Myth of Junk DNA* (Seattle: Discovery Institute Press, 2011).

30 R. Dawkins, *The Blind Watchmaker* (New York: Norton, 1986).

31 Collins, *The Language of God*, 127.

32 M. V. Filatov and others, "A Comparison between Coral Colonies of the Genus Madracis and Simulated Forms," *Proc. R. Soc. B* 277, 1700 (2010).

33 Collins, *The Language of God*, 135.

34 Collins, *The Language of God*, 138.

35 Darwin, *The Origin of Species*, 217.

36 Coyne, *Why Evolution Is True*, 153.

37 Collins, *The Language of God*, 127.

38 Collins, *The Language of God*, 127.

39 Coyne, *Why Evolution Is True*, 72.

40 R. C. Pink and others, "Pseudogenes: Pseudo-Functional or Key Regulators in Health and Disease?" *RNA Society* 17, 5 (2011).

41 L. Pray, "Transposons: The Jumping Genes," *Nature Education* 1, 1 (2008):204.

42 R. K. Slotkin and R. Martienssen, "Transposable elements and the epigenetic regulation of the genome," *Nature Reviews Genetics* 8(2007).

43 Darwin, *The Origin of Species*, 217.

44 Behe, *Darwin's Black Box*, 22.

45 R. A. Fortey and B. D. E. Chatterton, "A Devonian Trilobite with an Eyeshade," *Science* 301(2003):1689.

CHAPTER 6
Descent with Modification

Charles Darwin didn't have the advantage of what science has disclosed about the cell and the mechanisms of inheritance, but as a naturalist, Darwin was a keen observer and made much from his observations of plant and animal life. His worldwide voyage on the HMS *Beagle* provided a rich background on the variety of life-forms, their variation within types, and the nature of the environment in which they were successful. That experience accounted for much of the material in his thoughtful contemplation about life over the succeeding years. Darwin also indulged in research in the laboratory of his garden, specimen archives, museum galleries, and dove cots. Selective breeding of pigeons was evidence that Darwin used in developing his theory of descent with modification through natural selection. He associated with a group of pigeon fanciers who bred them artificially, selecting variable traits that would be reproduced and maintained in subsequent generations, creating bloodlines or breeds of domestic pigeons, all having originated from the rock dove or pigeon, *Columba livia* (figure 1).

Figure 1. Rock pigeon

The extensive amount of variation that was present in pigeons and drawn out through selective breeding programs influenced Darwin's thinking about natural selection as the source of all the varieties he observed in wild flowers and animals. He concluded that in the wild, the morphological variation that naturally occurs among individuals of a population would be subject to natural selection favoring the variant most successful reproductively under the environmental circumstances. Reproductively beneficial changes would subsequently spread throughout the population over successive generations, changing the population accordingly. This was recognized as adaptation, but Darwin carried it further.

Darwin's concept[1] was that small-scale changes in the morphology of individual organisms were random, and those that were beneficial alterations would eventually accumulate. Since those changes were random, if a segment of a species became isolated, that segment would accumulate novel changes that would make them slightly different from the parent population. With time and further accumulation of small changes, the isolated segment would represent a divergent species. He considered that these small changes accumulating over great lengths of geological time would result in macro-changes, or modifications, leading to different kinds of plants and animals, and eventually would represent the extensive diversity of all life-forms, all having come from that original common ancestor.

Evolutionist Perspective

The modern synthesis or neo-Darwinian evolutionary theory is the expansion and hardening of Darwin's original concept. The perspective still maintains that once life originated from the first living cell, all life thereafter evolved by natural selection of the genetic variation from mutations in those primitive cells. The changes accumulated to result in all the differences observed in historical and present life-forms. The variations from mutations were random, undirected, and without purpose, except that natural selection gave them purpose in a nondeterministic manner.[2]

First organized cellular life is thought to have begun 3.5 billion years ago as the precursor of the prokaryotes, primitive one-celled organisms. Working through such a scenario, the first primitive cell advanced through natural selection of novel mutations and continued to acquire complexity in genetic structure. DNA somehow replaced RNA as the repository of structural and functional information, and RNA then took on its primary role of transcription from DNA to protein synthesis in the ribosomes, forming the specialized catalyzing enzymes for the great variety of functions, including the energy machines of glycolysis[3] and the Krebs cycle.[4] Changes in the genetic structure were caused through alterations of nucleic acid composition by substitution, duplication, or deletion of nucleotides, as well as disruptions in sequential transcription of the nucleotides in the genetic code by mRNA.

Natural selection in the development of the first cellular life-forms (prokaryotes) is understood to have taken great lengths of time, remaining in a primitive state for a billion years. These prokaryotes then diversified along two lines identified as bacteria and archaea, distinguished by differences in the molecular components of their cell membranes and cell walls as they separated along their divergent trajectories.[5, 6] Since there is no evidence of reproduction other than cell division in these life-forms, the cell attributes had to occur by each cell singularly accumulating all mutagenic changes that expanded the genome as the repository of information on acquired cell structure and function. Unlike sexual reproduction or meiosis, where advantageous mutations can be leveraged by passing them on to progeny and eventually spreading throughout the population by greater reproductive success, single-cell organisms that reproduce simply by cell division share advantageous mutations by lateral transfer from one to the other of the same species (or between species).

A bacterium can attach itself to another bacterium and in the process transfer pieces of DNA or copies of DNA directly into the receiving cell.[7]

Eukarya, characterized by a cell nucleus, are thought to have separated from archaea between 2.2 and 1.7 billion years ago. Mayr[8] suggested Eukarya was the result of an integration (chimaea) of archaebacteria and eubacteria, and showed some characteristics of both groups. That resulted in three domains of the proposed tree of life, recognized as bacteria, archaea, and eukarya (figure 2). The origin of the nucleus in eukaryotes is still a mystery, but it is associated with the advancement in life's complexity. Evolutionists suggest that single-cell life existed for nearly three billion years in forms without any change, apart from acquiring the nucleus, until multicellular organisms appeared around 550 million years ago, and then only from within the Eukarya domain.[9]

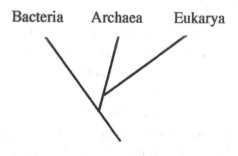

Bacteria   Archaea   Eukarya

Figure 2. Showing three domains

Advancement in complexity required the acquisition of new genes. The most common cited scenario in building new genes is the duplication of sections of DNA sequences along the double helix of the chromosome.[10] The duplicate sequences would then be free to mutate with no immediate consequences, because transcription by the RNA polymerase occurred with the original sequence and would bypass the duplicate or altered sequence that took on the position in the DNA strand as an intron. Therefore, the bypassed section would not be subject to natural selection and could accumulate alternative mutations until by some mechanism, they were pulled into service as a new gene. The process of new genes would have taken place as small steps in the advancement of the evolutionary process.

That process of small steps, described by Dobzhansky as microevolution, is considered the first step of the macroevolutionary process. Mayr[11] states, "It is important to emphasize that all macroevolutionary processes take place in populations and in the genotypes of individuals and are thus simultaneously microevolutionary processes." Therefore, neo-Darwinists consider microevolution as the mechanism responsible for major changes by the continuing process of altering the genotype in response to environmental challenges or simply improvements of function, and those small changes can accumulate to eventually result in macro-change.

Microevolution is something that is possible to observe, and it can involve as little as a change of a single allele among the great number housed on DNA strands of the chromosomes. Macroevolution, by contrast, is implied by the presence of major changes in the fossil ancestors of living organisms. Such changes involve many sites in the organism's bank of genetic loci. Most mutations are deleterious, but some are neutral, and a few are beneficial. Deleterious mutations are lost with the death of the organism or hidden as recessive alleles. Neutral mutations can be carried in the genome and contribute to genetic variation, and the beneficial mutations theoretically result in the displacement of the original form with the more effective phenotype possessing the advantageous genetic construct. It is the accumulation of these advantageous mutations, or the otherwise neutral or recessive alleles under the right circumstances over great lengths of time, that in isolation are the mechanisms that result in the formation of new kinds of organisms.

Therefore, neo-Darwinian orthodoxy purports that through the process of gradually accumulating small mutagenic changes by natural selection spread over geological time, macroevolutionary changes will occur in the formation of new taxa and the acquisition of novel features. The small changes are functional at the organismic level, or adaptive in nature, and improve the fitness of the descendants in their habitats. Neo-Darwinism is thus built upon the exclusivity of microevolutionary principles, culminating in macro-morphological differences from the ancestral form, leading to phyletic segregation.

Primary Evidence

In her book *Darwin's Origin of Species*, Janet Browne,[12] a professor of history in science at Harvard, asserts that the Galapagos finches and the peppered moth are the most influential field studies of evolution. Given that neo-Darwinian orthodoxy conveys macroevolution as a very gradual process of accumulating microevolutionary changes over millions of years, natural selection at the micro level is considered important evidence for evolution as the essence of macroevolutionary theory.

Jonathan Weiner's prize-winning book, *The Beak of the Finch*,[13] is a very interesting and well-written iteration of the process of natural selection among the finch species of the Galapagos Islands. The Galapagos finches rose to significance from Darwin's voyage on the *Beagle* when he visited the islands and sent a number of bird specimens for analysis to the English ornithologist John Gould, who identified them all as finches. Thereafter, they became known as Darwin's finches, attributed largely to David Lack[14] in his book *Darwin Finches*, although Darwin didn't recognize their significance or even their extent of diversity at the time of his collection. The number of finch species in the Galapagos has been debated, but they were originally separated into thirteen species among the islands.

The information source of Weiner's book was the work of Peter and Rosemary Grant, who spent decades of their lives returning to the Galapagos Islands to study the finches. The research was detailed and exhaustive, with perhaps the best account ever given of the varied life history and response of any animal to the selective pressures imposed by different but stochastic environments. The Grants' research was directed at the several species of finches segregated and for the most part isolated by the islands they inhabited. Once isolated, specific adaptations were facilitated by selection of those traits that gave the different finch species advantages to access different food sources available on the islands.

The Grants studied most closely the finches characterized by distinctly different beak morphology;[15] the sharp-beaked ground finch, the large and small cactus finch, and the large, medium, and small ground finch (figure 3.). The variability in size of the latter three tend to overlap, but with three separate modes. This is also true of their beak sizes. In essence, the Grants showed that the beak morphology of the Galapagos finch species was closely aligned with the seed sizes and food sources they specialized on. They also showed that with changing food availability caused by environmental perturbation, the mode in beak sizes changed, and the species abundance also changed. During the later years of the Grants' work, there was also a greater tendency toward fusion among some of the species through the selective advantage of the hybrids, with a pendulum-like swing in the divergence and introgression of features. For these reasons, ornithologists and evolutionists have acclaimed the Grants' study as a classic example of evolution, which Weiner reinforced.

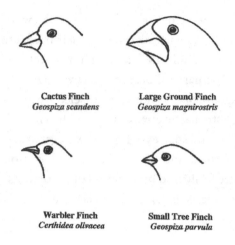

Cactus Finch
Geospiza scandens

Large Ground Finch
Geospiza magnirostris

Warbler Finch
Certhidea olivacea

Small Tree Finch
Geospiza parvula

Figure 3. Facsimile of beak diversity among Galapagos finches.

The second of the most influential field studies of evolution cited by Browne was the peppered moth, *Biston betularia*, that became famous in British research by Bernard Kettlewell.[16] The peppered moth shows a strong dichotomy in color, with light gray wings and body, and black spots, giving it a peppered appearance. In contrast, the other morph is the melanic form with a totally blackened body and wings (figure 4). In some of the regions around the industrial areas of England, the melanic form was the dominant phenotype, whereas in the rural countryside, the gray peppered form predominated.

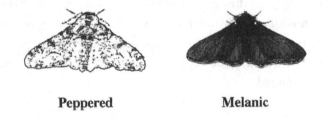

Peppered   **Melanic**

Figure 4. Peppered moth

It was thought that the differences in the percentages of the different phenotypes were the result of natural selection, with the gray form favored in areas where industrial pollution was absent, and the melanic form in areas where industrial pollution coated the woodlands and blackened the trees. Under polluted conditions, the gray phenotype resting on the trees would became obvious to predatory birds, while the black morph would be camouflaged and blend in against the soot-coated bark. The opposite would be true away from industrial pollution, where the color of the grayish phenotypes would blend in with the natural gray lichens on the trees, and the black forms would become more conspicuous. In each case, the hypothesis was that by natural selection, the noticeable form of the moth was eaten by predatory birds, and the more inconspicuous form was overlooked.

Kettlewell tested the hypothesis in the field by releasing marked moths of both phenotypes in the different habitats, subsequently making a census of the survivors by trapping them the following night. In the countryside, the traps recovered a higher percentage of gray moths, and in the polluted area, a higher percentage of the melanic form was recaptured. The conclusion was that predation by birds able to catch the moths contrasting in color with the background on which they rested was the selective force resulting in the numerical differences in the incidence of the phenotypes. The peppered moth became a prime example of natural selection, with the thinking that the hypothesis was confirmed. Kettlewell published an article on his results in *Scientific American* titled "Darwin's Missing Evidence."[17] The phenomenon of the melanic appearance in the industrial polluted areas was referred to as "industrial melanism."

The Kettlewell experiments came under criticism by several scientists over the years, based on the methods he used. Kettlewell released the moths during daylight hours onto tree trunks, but *B. betularia* are night fliers, rest higher in the trees, and seldom are associated with tree trunks. Michael Majerus[18] referred to the problems in his book, *Melanism: Evolution in Action*, but concluded that Kettlewell's explanation was not wrong, it was only incomplete, and felt that further work was needed to show whether birds were the only factor responsible for the differential patterns in abundance of the moths. Coyne[19] was more retrospect, and in his review of Majerus's book, he concluded that the fact that peppered moths do not naturally rest on tree trunks alone invalidates Kettlewell's release and recapture experiments. However, Kenneth Miller with Joseph Levine in their textbook *Biology*[20] still referred to Kettlewell's peppered moth studies as a classic demonstration of natural selection in action. Miller qualified his position on his web page, stating,

> What we do know is that the rise and fall of dark-colored moths, a phenomenon known as 'industrial melanism,' remains a striking and persuasive example of natural selection in action. What we have to be cautious about is attributing 100% of the work of natural selection in this case to the camouflage of the moths and their direct visibility to birds.

Although there is disagreement about Kettlewell's studies and conclusions, the documentation of the different forms of *B. betularia* and the increase of the melanic phenotype in areas where industrial pollution occurred, and their subsequent decrease with the recovery of the gray lichen-covered trees following the reduction of pollution, has shown that natural selection associated with environmental effects is largely responsible. Majerus repeated Kettlewell's work in a six-year study involving releases of 4,864 moths, continued by others[21] after his death. It was confirmed that camouflage and visibility to predatory birds was the overriding explanation for differences in the abundance of the typical and melanic forms of the peppered moth, although there are other cases where the melanic form is not associated with soot-polluted landscapes, indicating that other factors must also have an influence. Kettlewell's vindication demonstrated that differences in predation based on an organism's camouflage, or lack thereof, affects its abundance and thus demonstrates in a most direct way, even under artificial conditions, the influence of natural selection.

Notable in the cited evidence in evolutionary literature are the various bacteria and viruses that have developed resistance to drugs and pesticides in a relatively short time by mutations that replace or substitute susceptible loci. In his chapter on the *Engine of Evolution*, Coyne[22] referred to bacterial resistance to penicillin as a prime example of selection in the process of evolution. He concluded,

> In 1941, the drug could wipe out every strain of staph in the world. Now, seventy years later, more than 95 percent of staph strains are resistant to penicillin. What happened was that mutations occurred in individual bacteria that gave them the ability to destroy the drug, and of course these mutations spread worldwide. In response, the drug industry came up with a new antibiotic, methicillin, but even that is now becoming useless due to newer mutations. In both cases scientists have identified the precise changes in the bacteria DNA that conferred drug resistance.

The immunity that was acquired by bacteria allowed them to survive and reproduce to build resistant strains, rendering penicillin and methicillin ineffective. This was a change in an organism that shows natural selection produced an adaptive response as a pathway around a stressful condition. Coyne equates this to the first step in the long process leading to neo-Darwinian evolution.

Creationist Perspective

Creationists recognize that change takes place in organisms, just as it does in an ever-changing natural environment. Change occurring in an organism is a very basic phenomenon, understood by Creation theorists as a mechanism allowing descendants to conform to environmental alterations, recognized as adaptation. In earlier years, the observations that all forms of life appeared well-suited to the conditions confronted in their environments was explained by natural theology, a condition where the Creator provided the complementary life-form and function that corresponded with the particular characteristics of the natural environment. With the advancement of science over the last century, Creation theorists inspired by Darwinian thinking have expanded their view of natural theology in how the Creator provided for those needs. The contemporary creationist's position is that organisms have the ability to accommodate dynamic environments by natural selection of the immediate descendants with genetic constructs that meet such needs. In most cases, it involves selecting from the range of variability exposed in the gene pool, some of which is expressed by recombination in meiosis, and in other cases occurring by mutations that facilitate the adaptive response.

Adaptation, or adaptive radiation, can be looked upon as organismal life insurance, a preservation mechanism of a population exposed to changing environments, and the mechanism that allows its expansion over a range of geographic diversity, much as Darwin proposed. It represents genetic changes that provide for the synchrony observed between the organism and its environment as the mechanism previously attributed to special creation in natural theology. As Darwin specified, this results in altered characteristics of the organism better suited for the particular environment experienced, and regarding Creation theory, it represents a much more omniscient accommodation of life-form needs than unique but fixed special creations. Adaptation is a mechanism to sustain or improve the fitness of a plant or animal in synchrony with the local environment, but the organism remains in the same relative life-form as before. There is no disagreement among creationists on the process of adaptation and no disagreement for that matter between creationists and evolutionists on that point.

Contemporary creationists differ with evolutionists, however, with regard to purpose. The evolutionist views adaptation resulting from chance mutations as random mistakes in nucleotide constructs that just happen to rarely provide some level of selective advantage to that particular phenotype, given the environmental circumstances being confronted. The contemporary creative view is that mutations are part of the dynamic mechanism that is designed to provide variability for the preservation of life-forms confronting environmental diversity. So the difference again is chance versus design. The unique nature of adaptation is its self-regulating ability as a component of that mechanism but constrained within the limits inherent in the archetype. Versatility through such a mechanism is interpreted as the evidence of an omniscient provider. This is not unlike nineteenth-century theology, except that the Creator's provision is the adaptive mechanism that generates the appropriate phenotypic change as an ongoing phenomenon.

The difference within the creationist community of scientists on variation is the degree to which it can take place. As mentioned in chapter 1, there are those, including the Young Earth Creationists (YECs),[23] who do not believe that change progresses to the point of macroevolution, such as the transition into different kinds of organisms or different archetypes. They contend that macroevolution wasn't demonstrated by Darwin, nor has it been demonstrated empirically since then. They allege that evolutionists have taken adaptive change at the microevolutionary level and expanded it into macroevolutionary theory consistent with the framework of the Darwinian original model. YEC contend that there is no evidence that such major changes actually take place. The operating evidence is only in the area of change within typological lines.

Some intelligent design theorists and theistic evolutionists do not reject the concept of life-forms evolving into more advanced forms that would qualify as macroevolution. However, even within these groups, there are differences in perceptions about what constitutes macro-change. Jonathan Wells is cautious about accepting the claims supporting macroevolution, as demonstrated in his book, *Icons of Evolution,* where he is concerned about the distortion of the evidence to support macroevolutionary theory. In contrast, Michael Behe[24] doesn't appear to have a problem with the age of the universe, nor with the concept of descent from a common ancestor, but disputes that chance can account for complex systems that he attributes to intelligent design. And the more extreme view is advocated by Kenneth Miller,[25] who interprets the evidence along the lines of the neo-Darwinian model, where over great lengths of time, the accumulation of microevolutionary changes by chance variability and natural selection are responsible for forming all taxonomic lineages from a universal common ancestor.

It is fair to conclude that contemporary creationists agree that the evidence compiled on evolution is primarily microevolutionary in nature, which is most apparent as adaptive radiation. They view variability as a basic element in the design of self-sustaining life, but the extent to which such variability can progress is largely based on inference that engenders a level of uncertainty.

Adaptive Variability

As reviewed exhaustively in the preceding chapters, evolutionists consider the microevolutionary mechanism as the defining element in neo-Darwinian theory. This accord was demonstrated in Janet Browne's assertion that the Galapagos finches and the peppered moth are the most influential field studies of evolution. But does that position misrepresent what the studies actually show? Let's look at the evidence.

Recall Dollo's law about the biological distinction that change becomes evolution only when that change is irreversible. That is an important criterion in the discussion of what constitutes evolution. While the Galapagos finches and the peppered moth are evidence of phenotypic change in response to natural selection, they do not provide evidence of the level of change that most people associate with the term *evolution,* involving the origin of different kinds of organisms in the history of life. In decades of study on the Galapagos finches, the Grants demonstrated only adaptive variability among the species of finches. With the strong selective pressure of a limited food supply, a level of introgression of the medium ground finch with the small ground finch and cactus finch occurred, where the hybrids had the advantage. The Grants' research showed differences among Galapagos finches that were reversible, and thus by the criterion of Dollo's law on evolution's irreversibility, their observations would quality only as adaptive change.

Much was made of the Grants' analysis of the marked trends in the evolution of the finches in the short period of only decades, but little is said that after several million years on the islands, the finches are still finches. The Grants' work actually more effectively supports the concept that kinds are constrained within their primary archetype and exercise diversity in structural form around the inherent limits of their genome. The Galapagos finch research has demonstrated only adaptive radiation. The evidence generated by Harvard scientists[26] indicates that beak morphology is driven virtually by two genes, one controlling beak depth and width, responsible for the heavy seed-eating ground finch beaks, and the other controlling beak length, responsible for the slender long beaks of the cactus finches. Genome sequencing[27] has revealed extensive evidence for gene flow throughout the Galapagos finch radiation and brings into question how many species are actually represented.

Classical evolutionary theory on major transformation of kinds was Weiner's assessment of Grants' research on the finches. Weiner[28] referred to the adaptive changes among the finches (in spite of merging of types) as the power of Darwin's process, implying that it was evidence of process leading to greater evolution. The incongruity between the evidence and Weiner's interpretation is characteristic of the ideology that prevails in much of the scientific literature. Empirical evidence of variability and natural selection at the microevolutionary level is used as proof in support of evolutionary theory leading to macroevolution. While the generation of varieties through natural selection among the Galapagos finches is well documented by the Grants, it is apparent that the observed changes don't rise to the level of change that would correspond with macroevolution, as implied by Weiner.

What about the peppered moth? Were the two different phenotypes of the species *B. betularia*—the spotted morph with different patterns on a gray background, called the typical, and the all-black morph, referred to as the melanic form—influential evidence of evolution, as asserted by Janet Browne? The answer to that question is no. Following the publication of *Darwin's Missing Evidence* and the follow-up studies by Michael Majerus, it has been confirmed that Kettlewell's conclusions were for the most part correct. The camouflaged melanic mutant was a morphological advantage when birds predated on the typical form made visible against soot-laden trees, and the opposite was true where soot pollution wasn't present. It appears that natural selection by predatory birds contributed to the abundance of the different phenotypes of the peppered moth, but there is no evidence that it represented something akin to macroevolution. The two forms are of the same species. The melanic form appears to have originated by a mutation of a single allele that altered color pattern sometime early in the nineteenth century. Even if we can agree that the proportions of the phenotypic distributions were related to natural selection, as Kettlewell concluded, it would only be evidence of an adaptive difference representing change at the microevolutionary level. It represents an allelic alteration that gives the population the ability to sustain itself in response to environmental circumstances, although the color incidence would also be influenced by the dominance of the melanism allele.

Now let's put this in perspective. The Galapagos finches and the peppered moth obviously have experienced change, and the finches had an obvious adaptive benefit regarding feeding strategy, but some of those changes have regressed. In the two to four million years that the finches are thought to have occupied the habitat of the Galapagos Islands, the various species appear not to have completely separated reproductively, suggesting they are at least varieties or incipient species that favor different beak morphologies through selection, and those morphologies become stable only as long as the food resources are stable. The differences observed among the finches are significant, but they have occurred within their typological lineage.

The peppered moth is a little more equivocal in terms of adaptation. Although of recent origin, the presence of the different phenotypes in the absence of industrial impacts raises the possibility that more than bird predation is involved in forming the two color morphs. Perhaps dominance of the melanic form is a confounding factor. However, while the term *evolution* implies transcendence of different types of life-forms in the debate on Creation and evolution, in neither case was there evidence that could be interpreted as support for that level of evolution.

So, in both of Janet Browne's influential field studies of evolution,[29] there is no evidence of actual evolution beyond adaptation. At best, only adaptive radiation was shown in finches, and no change in peppered moths except a dimorphism in the proportion of the two phenotypes advantaged by avoidance of predation, depending on the environmental circumstance. Although evolutionists portray microevolutionary evidence as though it represents the process leading to the typological evolution, nothing was demonstrated in the finches or the moths that would support evolution forming different kinds of organisms. These changes only qualify as modification within type.

The same is true of the acquired resistance of bacteria to drugs. Coyne[30] refers to drug resistance in bacteria as an example of natural selection and, by inference, the process that leads to macroevolution. However, drug resistance is only a demonstration of bacteria's ability to adapt. Acquired immunity of bacteria is frequently cited by those in support of neo-Darwinism, but that level of change is not the evolution implied by the neo-Darwinian model. It is not evidence of the transformation of different kinds of life-forms. Bacteria exposed to toxic agents demonstrate that there is sufficient potential in their genetic variability to perpetuate an immune strain. This confirms that through adaptation, organisms are able to adjust to situations in incredible ways to sustain themselves in challenging circumstances. The great variety within typological lineages is very impressive, but it is confined within limits of the general phenotype. The role of natural selection in the process of selecting variation among traits is consistent with Darwin's observations but functional only as adaptation and in a manner with purpose.

Creation theory recognizes that organisms are endowed with the ability to accommodate dynamic environments by natural selection of the immediate descendants, through genetic variability that meets the challenge. It is similar to the proposition of natural theology, with a more impressive difference. Rather than organisms being created in synchrony with their environment, Creation includes an ongoing selection process that continually refines the organism in concert with its environment. Such a mechanism is much more accommodating for life-forms to sustain themselves than fixation of species and speaks of a much more encompassing design provision by intelligent cause than previously recognized even by creationists.

Conclusion

Although creationists and evolutionists agree that adaptation (microevolution) is an ongoing phenomenon that synchronizes the phenotype with environmental dynamics, there is a major difference between the evolutionists and creationists on the subject of cause. Neo-Darwinism is built upon the exclusivity of microevolutionary principles of random mutations and natural selection, culminating in macro-morphological differences that lead to phyletic segregation from a common origin.

The contemporary creationist views life as the result of design by a higher intelligence. The system as we know it from the evidence has purpose, and that purpose is even evident in the adaptation of an organism through which the altered phenotype accommodates to environmental changes. Evidence of descent with modification is confined to adaptive variability and is microevolutionary in nature. Changes at that level are not the evolution implied by the scientific meaning of the term, nor is it the evolution as defined by Dollo's law. While macroevolution via cumulative micro-changes is the focus of evolutionary theory, the evidence doesn't rise above inference.

Endnotes

1 Darwin, *The Origin of Species*, 159–69.
2 Coyne, *Why Evolution Is True*, 121–32.
3 Wilson, *Riot and the Dance*, 105–107.
4 Wilson, *Riot and the Dance*, 108–109.
5 Wilson, *Riot and the Dance*, 204–205.
6 Freeman, *Biological Science*, 7–9.
7 Mayr, *What Evolution Is*, 44.
8 Mayr, *What Evolution Is*, 45.
9 Coyne, *Why Evolution Is True*, 28–29.
10 C. Chandrasekaran and E. Betrán, "Origins of new genes and pseudogenes," *Nature Education* 1, 1 (2008):181.
11 Mayr, *What Evolution Is*, 190.
12 J. Browne, *Darwin's Origin of Species* (Atlantic Monthly Press, 2007).
13 J. Weiner, *The Beak of the Finch: A Story of Evolution in Our Time* (Vintage, 1994).
14 D. Lack, *Darwin's Finches* (Cambridge University Press, 1947).
15 Peter R. Grant and B. R. Grant, *40 Years of Evolution: Darwin's Finches on Daphne Major Island* (Princeton University Press, 2014).
16 H. B. D. Kettlewell, "A Survey of the Frequencies of Biston betularia (L.) (Lep.) and Its Melanic Forms in Great Britain," *Heredity* 12, 1 (1958).
17 H. B. D. Kettlewell, "Darwin's Missing Evidence," *Scientific American* (1959), 200.
18 M. Majerus M. 1998. Melanism: Evolution in Action. Oxford University Press, UK.
19 J. A. Coyne, "Not Black and White: A Review of Michael Majerus's Melanism, Evolution in Action," *Nature* 396 (1998).
20 K. R. Miller and J. Levine, *Biology: The Living Science* (Upper Saddle River, NJ: Prentice Hall, 1998).

21 L. M. Cook, B. S. Grant, I. J. Saccheri, and J. Mallet, "Selective Bird Predation on the Peppered Moth: The Last Experiment of Michael Majerus," *Biology Letters* 8, 4 (2012).

22 Coyne, *Why Evolution Is True*, 142.

23 N. Jeanson, *Creation Basics & Beyond*, 130.

24 Behe, *Darwin's Black Box*, 5.

25 Miller, *Finding Darwin's God*, 291.

26 A. Abzhanov and others, "The Calmodulin Pathway and Evolution of Elongated Beak Morphology in Darwin's Finches," *Nature* 442 (2006).

27 S. Lamichhaney and others, "Evolution of Darwin's finches and Their Beaks Revealed by Genome Sequencing," *Nature* 518 (2015).

28 Weiner, *The Beak of the Finch*.

29 Browne, *Darwin's Origin of Species*.

30 Coyne, *Why Evolution Is True*, 141–43.

CHAPTER 7
Complex Multipart Systems

The science of molecular biology has uncovered a level of cellular sophistication and detail that was inconceivable by Darwinists a century ago. In the molecular arena, there has been expanded knowledge about the workings of the cell that brings a new phase in evolutionary thinking.[1] The concept of trial and error inherent in Darwinian ideology is being revisited in terms of its sufficiency to adequately explain change within multipart cellular components. This has brought a renaissance in thought about design in cell biology as the antithesis of chance, which has come about largely by efforts of the members of the Discovery Institute in Seattle, Washington. Although neo-Darwinists consider complex multipart systems as the primary evidence of more advanced change proceeding on to macroevolution, the problem is that the chance of functional mutations decreases with increased complexity, raising again the question of probability.

Evolutionist Perspective

Evolution at the molecular level is where much of the current work is concentrated, and with the advancements in molecular biology, some controversy has arisen, even among evolutionists, about the Darwinian model. According to Kenneth Miller,[2] perhaps the biggest challenge to neo-Darwinism is not new but again represents the old argument of design that he felt was put to rest by Darwin. Design theorists, such as Michael Behe,[3] argue that some characteristics of cellular mechanisms demonstrate "irreducible complexity," where a particular function is made up of several integrated interactions of components that could not have been a system established over time through progressive stages of evolution. They claim that the system has to occur as a coordinated complete unit with all parts intact. If one of those components is missing, it becomes nonfunctional, and useless features would be eliminated by natural selection. So the allegation is that a multistage system with a specific function could not evolve by accumulating separate nonfunctional steps over time.

Miller rejects that explanation and claims that irreducible complexity is simply the repackaged design argument that was abandoned in the nineteenth century. Organisms appear to be designed for the environments they inhabit, because natural selection over great lengths of time refines the organism for the environment it inhabits. He says:

> What Michael Behe has done is very much in this tradition. He literally has dusted off the argument from design, spiffed it up with the terminology of modern biochemistry, and then applied it to the proteins and macromolecular machines that run the living cell. Once we've figured this out, we ask the key question: Is there anything really so different about proteins and cells that makes the argument from design work better at their level than it does at the level of the organism?

What about the challenge facing microbes when a multipart system is removed from their genetic construct? Can the microbe evolve a pathway around that problem? Jerry Coyne cited a study at the University of Rochester by Barry Hall,[4] where a gene that produced the enzyme galactosidase was experimentally deleted from *Escherichia coli*. The enzyme had previously made it possible for bacteria to break down lactose into components that were used as food. The control region of that gene would turn on the production of the enzyme when lactose was present and turn it off when the lactose was absent. In the presence of the enzyme, the system also could switch on the cell membrane protein, lac permease, that enhanced the entry of lactose into the cell. In the laboratory study, the bacteria with the deleted gene were then placed in a situation where lactose was the only source of food. At first, the bacteria were unable to grow, but then a mutation of another gene took over the role of the missing gene, and some growth was made possible. Another mutation then occurred that increased the amount of the new enzyme, so more lactose could be used. Still further, a third mutation at another location occurred that improved the uptake of lactose and allowed the bacteria to effectively use a food source that had been denied by the deletion of the gene that produced the original enzyme. Not only was a new enzyme produced, but the control region of that gene also mutated, which ensured that the gene was expressed when lactose was present.

Coyne referenced this example to demonstrate evolution of a new complex biochemical pathway that enabled *E. coli* to overcome the challenge by modifying preexisting genes. He pointed out that the experiment showed two other important lessons: "First, natural selection can promote the evolution of complex, interconnected biochemical systems in which all the parts are codependent, despite the claims of creationists that this is impossible. Second, as we've seen repeatedly, selection does not create new traits out of thin air: it produces 'new' adaptations by modifying preexisting features."

Miller[5] used the same *E. coli* study to emphasize evolution's ability to develop a multipart system in opposition to the concept of irreducible complexity that Behe cited as proof of intelligent design, because anything less than the presence of the complete coordinated set of proteins would render the system functionless. Miller's response was:

> Think for a moment—if we were to happen upon the interlocking biochemical complexity of the re-evolved lactose system, wouldn't we be impressed with the intelligence of its design? Lactose triggers a regulatory sequence that switches on the synthesis of

an enzyme that then metabolizes lactose itself. The products of that successful lactose metabolism then activate the gene for the lac permease, which ensures a steady supply of lactose entering the cell. Irreducible complexity. What good would the permease be without the galactosidase? What use would either of them be without regulatory genes to switch them on? And what good would lactose-responding regulatory genes be without lactose-specific enzymes? No good, of course. By the very same logic applied by Michael Behe to other systems, therefore, we could conclude that the system had been designed. Except we know that it was not designed. We know it evolved because we watched it happen right in the laboratory! No doubt about it—the evolution of biochemical systems, even complex multipart ones, is explicit in terms of evolution. Behe is wrong.

Miller[6] goes on to contemplate, "How does evolution produce a biochemical pathway that looks as though it was designed? The answer to that is right here, and it's the same answer that we have seen in other systems as well—by modifying existing structures and proteins to produce new organs, new functions, and especially new biochemistry." This was the point that Coyne made previously, that mutations are changes in existing traits, and thus in order for evolution to build new features or a new organism, it must adapt previous features of its ancestor.

The evolutionist's resolution of the problem is that such complex systems are the combination of separate parts, each of which were honed for different functions progressively over time, and thus in that capacity, they represented precursors that were later co-opted for the new function. The steps for complex multipart systems are the same as that for a new gene. The mechanism involves the gene duplication or duplication of sections of DNA, which are mutations that occur as mistakes during cell division. Once duplicated, that section of DNA would be bypassed and free to accumulate alternative mutations in the genetic code for a protein along a separate path from the original. The protein is then recruited for a different function, where it performs as a product of the new gene in conjunction with other novel proteins in a complex multipart system. Proteins that have acquired altered functions have been documented as a common occurrence.

There are other examples that show evolution leading to complex multipart systems are ongoing. Blood clotting in vertebrates, reviewed by Kenneth Miller,[7] is a case in point. When a cut or tissue trauma occurs, the soluble protein fibrinogen in the bloodstream is activated by an enzyme, thrombin, which removes the activation inhibitors that cover fibrinogen and changes it into a very sticky form that binds together, creating the blood clot. That process is made up of more than twenty different proteins and a sequence of sixteen steps, each involving interactions between a different pair of proteins that culminate in forming the blood clot. The absence of any step would result in the inability to prevent bleeding and thus make the system useless. This is viewed by design theorists as irreducible complexity, where the entire sequence of separate parts must occur together as a system to be functional, and thus inconsistent with neo-Darwinian theory of a progressively evolving mechanism over time. But Russell Doolittle,[8] at the University of California, the foremost expert spanning four decades of research on blood clotting in vertebrates, has worked out a plausible sequence of adaptive processes that were involved in the evolution of the blood-clotting system. The system proposed is a step-by-step advancement accompanying the evolution of life-forms that culminates with the human system. All of the precursors of that system had other non-clotting functions prior to being recruited and adapted for the new combined function as a clotting mechanism through the evolutionary process. The precursors or new factors were the products of gene duplications recruited into other pathways once mutations substituted appropriate amino acids for the new function.

The point that both Coyne and Miller make is that mutations and natural selection are sufficient to form very complex biochemical systems involving the coordinated production of two or more newly evolved genes for a particular cellular function. Such a process has been declared impossible by design theorists because of the extreme improbability that such a synthesis can occur by chance alone. But Coyne and Miller's examples are presented as a demonstration that mutation and natural selection are sufficient to provide the solution to such a challenge.

Then there are situations where a new species develops in a short time frame. As Gould[9] stated, most successful species are highly stable in form and behavior over long periods of geological time. Evolutionary biologists point out that the long time frame for such alterations of a given kind of plant or animal are linked to stable environments where organisms have already synchronized with their habitat, and mutations are not likely to be of any advantage, resulting in genetic homeostasis. In order to have more rapid changes in the morphology or physiology of an organism, it requires substantial environmental modification, which sets a new trajectory for adaptive accommodation. The Galapagos finches, the peppered moth, drug-resistant bacteria, and the synthesis of a complex multipart system are examples where homeostasis was no longer adequate to meet significant environmental challenges, and new trajectories were launched through mutations and selection that improved fitness under those conditions. Some of those changes led to speciation. Coyne[10] points out that in the case of bacteria, where the changes involved result in different ecological descendants, those life-forms are considered distinct species.

An important laboratory study in that regard has been the ongoing twenty-five-year laboratory culture of the bacteria, E. coli, at Michigan State University by Richard Lenski.[11] With that strain of bacteria having a generation time of 6.6 generations per day, the study presently represents approximately sixty thousand generations of observation, a period equivalent to a million years of human existence, and a one-of-a-kind opportunity to study evolution in progress. Lenski's research was to assess the role of contingency in a long-term evolution experiment. Contingency in evolutionary theory means that the pathway that evolution has taken is contingent on the neutral mutation events that were consequential in the outcome. Their random occurrence established a potential outcome that would not have been possible otherwise. If starting over again, the probability that the same sequence in mutations would occur is vanishingly small.

A defining characteristic of E. coli is its inability to metabolize citrate in an aerobic environment. Lenski's study involved initiating twelve identical but separate lines of E. coli, isolating them in different flasks, and allowing them to evolve in a rich nutrient broth of glucose and citrate, with subpopulations transferred to new enriched flasks every twenty-four hours over the twenty-five-year period. Every seventy-five days, samples from each of the twelve populations were frozen for future studies and as backup to trace the occurrence of any changes. The study showed there were differences in the pathways developed to metabolize glucose among the twelve populations. But the biggest event was when one strain, after 31,500 generations, evolved the ability to use citrate as an energy source by a mutation that duplicated a section of DNA, activating a neutral gene coding for a citrate transporter across the bacteria membrane. The change was attributed to the acquisition of what they called potentiating mutations that prepared for future changes inducing citrate metabolism, referring to the event as a historical contingency. The authors suggested that the citrate-consuming bacteria had the potential of producing a new species, since it evolved a new biochemical function, consistent with Coyne's reference to what qualified for speciation in bacteria. In higher organisms, a new species would be a more extensive change that occurs at the microevolutionary level involving multipart systems.

Many other such examples of evolution potentially leading to speciation can be identified by practitioners in the field most familiar with the biology of particular organisms. For example, among the five Pacific salmon species endemic to the northeastern Pacific coast, and one of the most variable in life history, is the sockeye, *Oncorhynchus nerka*. This species resides in freshwater lake environments as juveniles, migrates to marine waters after its first year of life at approximately ten centimeters in length, and returns to freshwater to spawn at maturity when reaching approximately sixty centimeters at age four years. However, there is a resident freshwater form of the species called kokanee that remains in its lake environment to maturity, and its descendants are largely resident forms. This may be a life history strategy to sustain the population in times when its pathway home from marine waters is made inaccessible, but some biologists consider the resident form as splitting off from the anadromous counterpart through sympatric speciation; when in isolation, it would continue to deviate from its parental form, as demonstrated in some lake systems. Although the occurrence of kokanee may qualify only as microevolution, at least in the context of adaptation to totally freshwater life history, continual freshwater residence compared to those making the round trip to the marine environment is a much different selective experience involving multiple differences. At maturity, kokanee are smaller than the anadromous form, varying in size (fifteen to thirty centimeters) depending on the productivity of the lake, and consequently much less fecund, but generally much more abundant. Kokanee are not exposed to the hazards of migration and experience a much lower diversity and abundance of predators than the anadromous form. So, while both life history forms experience selective pressures, those pressures are very different, and with the near isolation on the spawning grounds, there is the potential of further separation and eventual isolation evolving as segregated species.

Ernest L. Brannon

Macroevolutionary Implications

The examples cited thus far are microevolution in character; even the complex multipart systems technically don't fall within the magnitude of what would be considered macroevolution. As summarized by Mayr,[12] in reference to the broader concept, he wrote, "Evolution is a historical process that cannot be proven by the same arguments and methods by which purely physical or functional phenomena can be documented. Evolution as a whole, and the explanation of particular evolutionary events, must be inferred from observations." Understandably, the time element over which macroevolutionary change would be recognized is too far drawn out to ever be observed as an event. Micro-change can be observed, but the accumulation of such changes is too slow to observe the culminating result that would occur above the family level, involving new archetypes and the acquisition of evolutionary novelties. There is little doubt among neo-Darwinists that accumulation of microevolutionary change is the macroevolution process, and development of complex multipart systems is an advanced part of that process. But is there evidence of actual taxonomic changes that qualify as macroevolution?

Darwinian orthodoxy on natural selection and microevolution as the sole process leading to macroevolution has been challenged. Although adamant evolutionists, Niles Eldredge and Steven Jay Gould[13] have presented the strongest opposition to that mechanism of major change. Eldredge considered stasis as a predominant pattern in the fossil record, extending millions of years in most cases, with little evidence of gradual change. Gould[14] concurred that while selection at the organismic level is an element in microevolution, the accumulation of adaptive differences progressing to macroevolution is not what the actual paleontology data show. Their observation was that evolution appears to happen abruptly, often related to major environmental disruptions, and followed by long periods of little or no change. Rapid change is also associated with small isolated populations where genetic alterations can have a major influence among the members. Mayr[15] describes the situation explicitly:

> According to Darwinian theory, evolution is a populational phenomenon and should therefore be graded and continuous. This should be true not only for microevolution but also for macroevolution and for transition between the two. Alas, this seems to be in conflict with observation. Wherever we look at the living biota, whether at the level of the higher taxa or even at that of the species, discontinuities are overwhelmingly frequent. Among living taxa there is no intermediacy between whales and terrestrial mammals, nor between reptiles and either birds or mammals. All 30 phyla of animals are separated from each other by a gap ... The discontinuities are even more striking in the fossil record. New species usually appear in the fossil record suddenly, not connected with their ancestors by a series of intermediates. Indeed there are rather few cases of continuous series of gradually evolving species. How can this seeming contradiction be explained?

Gould and Eldredge have explained the contradiction seen in the fossil pattern as punctuated equilibrium, abrupt changes, and extended stasis. Gould revives the hierarchical system of evolutionary thought with different levels of individuality: genes, cell lineages, organisms, demes, and species. He gave considerable attention to species as the unit of selection in the process of macro-change. Just as organisms are the unit of selection in microevolution within populations, species are the units of change in macroevolution, in effect disjoining microevolution as the only (or even the primary) force in macroevolutionary change. Gould and Eldredge essentially introduced macroevolutionary theory as a separate agent of change.

Gould did not consider hierarchical selection as a refutation of neo-Darwinism but only an expansion of the evolutionary convention.

He viewed macroevolution as more than a simple extrapolation of trait selection and thus change that occurred at its own level beyond microevolutionary mechanisms. His position is supported by the very numerous observations preserved in paleontological history with the absence of gradual modification. Species traits are those that emerge at the species level or are species emergent, such as schooling of fish to reduce predation, density tolerance, trait variability, drift, and reproductive isolating mechanisms. These are changes that Gould and Eldredge referred to as punctuated equilibrium characterized by rapid changes separated by long periods of stasis.

The tenet of neo-Darwinism is that mutagenic changes are random, undirected, and without purpose, but that through natural selection and great lengths of time, these accumulated micro-changes are responsible for all different life-forms that have existed through history to the present day. The difference between punctuated equilibrium and neo-Darwinian convention is that punctuated equilibrium deals with change as a rapid event in geological time. That means changes that were in response to radical environmental perturbation, such as the effects of mass extinction events where dominant life-forms were eliminated, provided the opportunity for other life-forms to flourish. The classic example is the extinction of dinosaurs that ushered in the rise of mammals. But other dramatic changes such as continental isolation that encouraged unrestrained diversity of life-forms would also fit the macroevolutionary model in evolutionary theory. Gould was careful to distinguish punctuated equilibrium from saltation, the instantaneous mutation of the archetype into a different physical form. Punctuation was the consequence of allopatric (isolation) speciation where mutations that were otherwise unsuccessful under restraint of competition or predation were free to differentiate in the absence of those effects.

Punctuated equilibrium was a proposal that fit the paleontological evidence. In that form of evolutionary theory, different life-forms were established rapidly enough in geological time to leave what would only appear as a gap in the fossil record. But Mayr countered that Gould's punctuation involving isolation and rapid evolution was only a truncation of the neo-Darwinian process. It involved separation and isolation of founder population units from their parental source long enough to accrue morphological differences that would include acquisition of complex multipart systems through natural selection, but in such a rapid fashion over geological time that it left limited fossil evidence of the transition.

There was no reconciliation between the perspectives on punctuated equilibrium and gradual microevolutionary changes as the primary mode leading to macroevolution in spite of the paleontological evidence showing abrupt occurrence of different life-forms and stasis until extinction. Mayr considered punctuated equilibrium a form of variation and natural selection at the population level and, thus, consistent with the Darwinian paradigm. That is the present view among the majority of evolutionists, which leaves macroevolution simply the extension of microevolutionary processes. Complex multipart systems are evidence of a more extreme form of variation and natural selection leading to macro-change.

Creationist Perspective

It is interesting that Mayr said both microevolution and macroevolution *should* be graded and continuous but admitted that such is not the case. Paleontological evidence shows discontinuities are the rule, intermediates are missing, and new species usually appear in the fossil record suddenly. But he then concludes that macroevolution must be inferred from observations, which appears to be inconsistent with the rationale that was just presented. This problem has intensified over the last two decades with the expansion of molecular biochemistry, and many evolutionists are now saying that the Darwinian model is insufficient to account for the complexity now apparent in life.[16]

The issue is whether such a mechanism as chance is sufficient to produce complex multipart systems that go on to define different phylogenetic lineages. It appears that proteins and macromolecules demonstrate encoded complexity so far beyond what was understood in the twentieth century that it makes believing their integration to form an organism by chance unrealistic.

So let's look closer at the ability of an organism to evolve such systems that involve two or more synchronized mutations. As noted above, Coyne and Miller point to research on bacteria that show they can readily restore biochemical functions of experimentally deleted genes that enable the bacteria to survive. The bacteria respond by recruiting other genes to develop an alternate biochemical pathway that achieves a comparable result, and the University of Rochester lactose example that was covered by Coyne and Miller was the case in point. However, design theorists insist that such complex biochemical systems will not occur by chance, because the probability that new proteins could form by such a process is so minuscule that it is virtually impossible to achieve. But as demonstrated in the laboratory study on bacteria lactose metabolism, it can occur. Therefore, if retrofitting the expression of genes for the functioning of complex biochemical systems by chance mutations is considered impossible, but it still happens, then there must be an explanation. The creationist again turns to design.

Referring to Miller's statement[17] about the Barry Hall laboratory lactose study on the evolution of complex systems at the University of Rochester, Miller said,

> By the very same logic applied by Michael Behe to other systems, therefore, we could conclude that the system had been designed. Except we know that it was not designed. We know it evolved because we watched it happen right in the laboratory! No doubt

about it—the evolution of biochemical systems, even complex multipart ones, is explicit in terms of evolution. Behe is wrong.

But what was it that they were watching in the University of Rochester laboratory? Was the laboratory study demonstrating the ability of *E. coli* to recover the lactose system by genetic-based changes in its genomic construct through the fortuitous chance of random mutations, as Miller posited? Or was it programmed by cellular feedback to meet the need? Was this chance by material cause, or was it design of molecular mechanisms through inherent predisposition by intelligent cause to meet such challenges? Creationists would suggest that in the Rochester laboratory study, they were watching the demonstration of the fingerprints of the Creator in the predisposition of the bacteria to accommodate biochemical challenges at the molecular level. If the probability of such biochemical systems occurring by chance is mathematically incomprehensibile,[18] and yet it occurs, then design must be considered as the logical alternative.

So there are two possibilities. One is that mutations are not entirely random, and thus in some cases, an alternate system is within reach to substitute for the deleted genetic constructs. Mutations during DNA transcription have been induced by stressful situations in response to circumstances challenging individuals,[19, 20, 21, 22] and thus those mutations would be nonrandom. Also, hot spots in the genome have greater tendency to mutate,[23, 24] occurring with the right mutation in specific genes to allow the cell to continue development. It has been determined[25] that the lactose-point mutations occur at a frequency of less than 10^{-8}, and the probability of the two occurring would be their multiple, and thus a highly improbable occurrence by chance. This suggests that when bacteria are environmentally challenged, there is a response induced to accommodate the need, indicating that the response is directed by feedback mechanisms within the bacteria. In some cases, information will be switched on under stress and switched off when the stress is resolved, with cells able to generate extreme variability in localized regions of their genome.[26, 27] Evidence from Hall's study was consistent with that situation. Adaptive mutations are non- or slowly dividing cells that mutate only when primarily being exposed to certain selective conditions, such as starvation. Those mutations only occur that will provide a growth benefit. Such an event demonstrates what appears to be a directed response to mitigate for the condition and thus functioning as nonrandom mutations.

Furthermore, it has been shown that in the *E. coli* experiments when the bacteria were unable to use lactose, they mutated back to the wild-type only when lactose was present in the medium, not when lactose was absent,[28] confirming the presence of a feedback mechanism. Hence, bacteria with defective or deleted lactose genes appear inclined to mutate in a manner that expresses a functioning new enzyme that breaks down lactose. This would be similar to the evidence with *E. coli* starved for inorganic phosphate that was shown to direct mutations to de-repress the phosphate-regulated suite of genes, resulting in a new high-affinity phosphate transport system that gets phosphate into the cell and activates a hydrolytic enzyme able to get phosphate from new sources.[29, 30] The findings indicate that there are inherent mechanisms at the molecular level to facilitate alternative pathways to achieve functioning systems.

The other possibility is that those scientists who claim that such complex systems are impossible to achieve by chance mutations are wrong. We are not talking about the development of an entire protein from scratch, but one that might involve the substitution of two or three alleles on the existing gene that also maintain the appropriate quaternary structure of the protein to function appropriately. Bacteria are so numerous and reproduce so frequently that chance may become a certainty in some cases. This is consistent with the position of Andreas Wagner[31] on the nearly inexhaustible library of amino acid combinations that are possible in the amino acid text of protein composition. The Wagner concept is that molecular innovations through mutation can provide the same protein fold and function, and most often they are unrelated to the specific text of the original.

However, there was more to the Hall experiments that may diminish the likelihood that the process was only chance related. The deleted site that was reactivated involved a mutation that increased the efficiency of lactose metabolism of a galactosidase enzyme gene already in the cell. The reactivated system didn't function without an artificially added inducer to the test medium in order to synthesize lactose permease that delivered lactose inside of the cell.[32] Moreover, in attempts to replicate the experiment by removing the recovered lactase gene, and although the same procedures were followed for many generations of the E. coli laboratory population, no new alternate lactase enzyme mutations arose.[33] These results suggest either insufficient time transpired, or, as discussed later, the organism reached the limit of its capacity to change. These results were also inconsistent with the Wagner concept of the unlimited amino acid library that could substitute functional amino acid alternatives.

The two possibilities are opposite tenets in how molecular evidence is interpreted in the modification and descent of organisms. Although the substitution of two or three alleles is not as improbable as developing an entire protein, their synchronization is still a very highly improbable event by chance. While an inexhaustible amino acid library may exist, most often the mutation is an alteration of an amino acid in the DNA code of the original protein. But compatible amino acid substitutions are generally not in close proximity in the amino acid library and thus would involve an entirely new protein construct. That greatly reduces the chances available for a functioning random substitution, returning to the restraints of probability.

Nonrandom mutations elevate design as the explanation of how otherwise improbable events can readily occur, effectively eliminating the time element for change. So design becomes a very plausible mechanism in the rapid construct of complex multipart systems, and we can conclude that Behe, in fact, was not wrong. The substitution of alternate lactose enzymes deleted from experimental populations of *E. coli* in the University of Rochester laboratory study fits the concept of programmed cellular feedback to meet the challenge, which implies that nonrandom mutations are potentiating changes as viable provisional strategies.

The same applies to what has been referred to as irreducible complexity. That level of complexity is said to characterize structures and functions composed of many interacting parts, the loss of any one part resulting in the dysfunction of the system. The human blood-clotting system was cited earlier as such an example. So let's look closer at the process.[34, 35] Clotting involves two soluble protein molecules in the blood plasma called fibrinogen and prothrombin. Fibrinogen has a sticky region covered by amino acid chains with negative charges that repel the fibrinogen molecules and keep them from sticking together. Prothrombin is an inactive protein-cutting enzyme called a protease. When a tissue incision or hemorrhage occurs, the prothrombin is activated to become thrombin and starts clipping off the charged amino acid chains from fibrinogen, changing it into the molecular form called fibrin. With the removal of the negative charges, the fibrin molecules start sticking together to form a clot that seals the wound. However, this is the end result of clot formation. There is a series of actions preceding the production of thrombin and fibrin, referred to as a cascade, because there are several steps required, and each step in the sequence activates the next step.

Thrombin is activated from prothrombin by other protease molecules. But in order for prothrombin to be able to change to thrombin it has to have its amino acid residues modified by another enzyme that requires vitamin K to work. Furthermore, these protease molecules must also be activated from their inactive forms, and that can occur via two different pathways, one caused by an injury such as a surface wound referred to as the intrinsic pathway, and the other is the extrinsic pathway caused by the infusion of blood into tissue, such as a hemorrhage.

When either pathway is initiated, there is a sequence in the activation of proteins by enzymes that progresses step by step, each depending on the existence of the previous activating step, with some crossover between pathway components. The clot that forms is not simply a blob of coagulated fibrin protein but rather a mesh-like formation facilitated by another activated enzyme that forms cross-links between fibrin molecules that serve as a net to prevent blood cells from passing. To limit the extent of coagulation, there are other proteins that have anti-coagulating properties that limit the activity of fibrin, preventing it from solidifying the rest of the circulatory system. And there is another protein that cuts up the fibrin, dissolving the clot upon healing, without affecting the prothrombin or fibrinogen.

Michael Behe[36] considers the blood-clotting system to be irreducibly complex, in that each step is dependent on the previous step, and all are activated from their inactive forms by different enzymes that must also be activated. Any step removed shuts down the system, in either clot formation or its control and dissolution. Kenneth Miller,[37] who proposed a stepwise sequence of how such a clotting system might evolve, based on the extensive research of Russell Doolittle, disagreed with that proposition. He proposed that a series of precursors of the blood-clotting system were recruited from other non-clotting functions and adapted for the new purpose. This is alleged to have occurred over great lengths of time as products of gene duplication, with mutations that altered amino acids in the duplicated sequence for different functions from their previous role. The system started in a simplified manner sufficient for the ancestral form and progressed as the organisms advanced in evolution.

The problem with Miller's suggestion of such a process is the probability involved in the development of such a complex system of form, function, control, and dissolution by chance. Mathematically, such a system is recognized as an impossibility. Further, there is no process described by Miller that suggests how the duplicated section of DNA is recruited as a functioning gene, or how functional proteins are co-opted for other tasks by chance processes. However, from the creationist's point of view, what is referred to as chance in evolutionary theory has a much deeper origin as intelligent cause, implicating design where impossibilities become certainties.

The question is, how does design manifest itself? In evolution theory, the general concept deals with variations of the idea that the codons co-evolved with the synthesis of each respective amino acid. But the code is much more than just the cognate amino acids, and this is the essence of the design argument. The point is that irreducible complexity is not proposed by design advocates as an appearance of a cluster of proteins in fully functioning form, instantaneously imposed by an intelligent agent. Creation theory says that irreducible complexity unfolds in a process consistent with a pattern of development that culminates with a living organism. As evidenced in all cellular functions, there is a process involved, and irreducible complexity is the product of a programmed process of differentiating parts with their separate functions embedded in the polymer language of DNA. It may have been implemented by a stepwise sequence, but it would have done so by nonrandom mutations as potentiating changes in a provisional strategy.

As observed in the examples of phenotypic modification, where some aspect of the genetic code is altered, the process works to resolve the problem. The beaks of the finch, the color morphs of the peppered moth, bacteria immunity, and the recovery of lactose digestibility in bacteria all involved molecular changes that benefited the organism. These examples of change are at the microevolutionary level, involving nucleotides as biochemical entities that are the repository of the information they transmit. The elements of the encryption are material, physical matter, but the information that is transmitted into the encrypted code is not. The evidence pertaining to that information is organized and sequential; it has product specificity, a functional outcome, a purpose, and the end point of the process is foreseeable. Those are attributes of design embedded in the cell. To the contemporary creationist, those attributes are consistent with what is expected of intelligent cause.

Archetype Stability

The long-term accumulation of random beneficial mutations through natural selection is not viewed by most creationists as a viable mechanism to achieve the programed complexity of multipart systems inherent in life. But if evolution can build such a case around random variability and selection, it would have had to accomplish such a task as part of the entire evolution of life's complexity in the six to ten million years that passed during the Cambrian period. What are the possibilities of that having occurred?

Kenneth Miller[38] pointed out that artificial selection such as those found in the laboratory or breeding programs can accelerate change ten thousand to ten million times faster than the rate of change observed in the fossil record. Consequently, selective breeding will disclose the inherent variability or the potential for variability that might be possible over much greater lengths of time for life-forms to diversify under conditions of natural selection in the wild. So the changes that pigeon fanciers produced artificially in the variety of pigeons bred for special features represented a significant level of diversity within the rock dove lineage. One can assume that some of the pigeon bloodlines have been developed over a period of at least two hundred years of intense selection (figure 1). Using Miller's figures, two hundred years of intense artificial selection, with generation times less than a year, would represent a period well over twenty million years under natural conditions. But the result of that intensive effort is that pigeon breeders have produced only pigeons when there would have been every intent by the pigeon fanciers to diversify to the greatest degree possible. Such a breeding effort should have demonstrated the formation of new archetypes, but that hasn't been the case.

Figure 1. Portrayal of pigeon diversity.

The domestic dog is another good example (figure 2), as referenced by Jerry Coyne:[39]

> Take the domestic dog (Canis lupus familiaris), a single species that comes in all shapes, sizes, colors, and temperaments. Every single one purebred or mutt descended from a single ancestral species – most likely the Eurasian gray wolf – that humans began to select 10,000 years ago. The American Kennel Club recognizes 150 different breeds, ... the Chihuahua ... the Saint Bernard ... the greyhound ... the dachshund ... and the Pomeranian. Breeders have virtually sculpted these dogs to their liking, changing the shade and thickness of their coat, the length and pointiness of their ears, the size and shape of the skeleton, the quirks of their behavior and temperament, and nearly everything else.

Figure 2. Dog diversity

The variability within the canine types is indeed astonishing, and it is demonstrative of the magnitude of what can be considered the potential genetic variability reservoir inherent within the species. Coyne[40] and a colleague calculated that it takes from one hundred thousand to five million years to evolve two reproductively isolated lineages. Differences in time would understandably depend on the rate at which the selective force of the environment would occur and the genetic variability present at the time of environmental challenge. With the ongoing efforts that have been undertaken with dogs using Coyne's less than ten thousand years of canine artificial selection, and Miller's minimum artificial selection acceleration rate, the changes observed among domestic dogs could represent something greater than one hundred million years of wild dog evolution.

However, rather than diversifying into a great variety of life-forms comparable to different body plans of the Cambrian period, they have produced only dogs. While those dogs represent an immense variety of what we refer to as breeds, they have remained entirely within their archetype and haven't even reached the point where the selected lineages are reproductively isolated, except for the limitations imposed by physical size.

Moreover, some evidence suggesting that life-forms can change from within their taxonomic archetype should be available in the extensive studies on bacteria, with their short generation time and immense numbers. The Michigan State University study by Richard Lenski[41] is the most prolonged study of its kind, looking at evolutionary contingency with *E. coli* bacteria maintained in the laboratory, allowing them to evolve in a rich nutrient broth of glucose and citrate over a period of sixty thousand generations. *E. coli* is characterized by its inability to metabolize citrate in an aerobic environment, but in this study, one population evolved the capacity to use citrate as an energy source. It was interpreted that the bacteria had experienced potentiating mutations that allowed for the contingency to metabolize citrate, and that amounted to its potential as an incipient species. Although the mutant was later shown not to be a unique evolutionary event[42] (no novel gene function evolved), and it appeared that contingency was a misinterpretation,[43] the fact remains that the ability to metabolize citrate was the only substantial change observed in the longest laboratory trial undertaken on evolution, other than grow rate, and no incipient forms occurred outside the typological lineage.

The question remains whether this evidence showing the lack of change in the taxonomic lineage of Galapagos finches, the peppered moth, pigeons, dogs, and bacteria demonstrate that the concept of macroevolution is invalid. The creationist camp is divided on that issue, but the evidence in the realm of complex multipart systems covered in this chapter goes no further than what would be attributed to microevolution. There were no trends in the examples presented that would infer that microevolutionary changes were transitioning into what would qualify as macroevolution. Those species, which had been given some of the most intense manipulation through artificial selection representing more than a hundred million years of natural selection, showed no new archetypes. There appears to be little evidence that complex multipart systems are anything more than sophisticated adaptations as design options of life-forms at the microevolutionary level. Lenski's laboratory conditions were quite uniform and did not represent the level of environmental disparity that would be expected to induce a major differential response of *E. coli*. Selection under benign circumstances would favor stasis or little change, and it is fair to conclude that is all that the Lenski study has shown.

Creation scientists posit that the complex multipart systems in the cellular domain demonstrate the comprehensive and multifarious nature of the information network encoded in the cell. It is apparent that such innovative integrated systems are beyond chance occurrence and are consistent with an intelligent cause. If the development and advancement of the different life-forms from the information network that produces the parts and machinery of the molecular multipart systems have virtually no probability of occurring by chance, then the alternative that there had to be a design element and thus a designer is not an unreasonable conclusion. This suggests that if inter-archetypical changes were a creative mechanism used by an omnipotent Creator in the establishment of different life-forms, it would have been by design rather than chance.

Conclusion

Neo-Darwinian theory purports that complex multipart systems are the combination of separate parts, each of which occurred by random variation, were honed for a certain application, and were later co-opted for a different biochemical function. The evidence presented by evolutionists for such complex systems is based on laboratory research that has demonstrated the development of such systems in real time but interpreted as the result of random mutations.

Creation scientists believe that complex multipart systems do not originate by chance, but what has been interpreted as random processes originate as part of the design apparatus within the cellular domain. In some cases, changes may be random when the option fits the design of the system, but in other cases, they are directed, nonrandom changes. These systems are molecular processes that function as feedback in response to needs within the cell and testify of an intelligent cause associated with programmed molecular systems to meet the challenges of the system.

In conclusion, studies on the re-evolution of complex multipart systems have been initiated in laboratory trials that are alleged to demonstrate the capacity of random variation and natural selection to achieve rapid restoration. The question remains, however, what in fact were researchers observing? It appears from the evidence that results were misinterpreted as chance when the restoration of complex multipart systems were molecular alterations initiated through programed cellular feedback, which accounted for rapid responses similar to cell differentiation itself. Precursors that are co-opted for new functions need a recruiting mechanism, and design is the more cogent alternative for development and application than mistaken chance assembly and use without purpose.

Endnotes

1 Behe, *Darwin's Black Box*, 24–25.
2 Miller, *Finding Darwin's God*, 134.
3 Behe, *Darwin's Black Box*, 110–11.
4 B. G. Hall, "Evolution on a Petri Dish: The Evolved B-Galactosidase System as a Model for Studying Acquisitive Evolution in the laboratory," *Evolution Biology* 15 (1982):85–150.
5 Miller, *Finding Darwin's God*, 146.
6 Miller, *Finding Darwin's God*, 151.
7 Miller, *Finding Darwin's God*, 152–58.
8 R. F. Doolittle, "The Evolution of Vertebrate Blood Coagulation: A Case of Yin and Yang," *Thrombosis and Hacostasis*, 70 (1993):24–28.
9 S. J. Gould, *The Structure of Evolutionary Theory* (2002), 875–84.
10 Coyne, J.A. 2009. *Why Evolution Is True*, 141.
11 Z. B. Blount, C. Z. Borland, and R. E. Lenski, "Historical Contingency and the Evolution of a Key Innovation in an Experimental Population of *Escherichia coli*," *PNAS* 105 (2008), 7899–7906.
12 Mayr, *What Evolution Is*, 13.
13 N. Eldredge and S. J. Gould, "Punctuated Equilibria: An Alternative to Phyletic Gradualism," In E. J. M. Schopf, ed., *Models in Paleobiology* (San Francisco: Freeman, Cooper & Co., 1972), 82–115.
14 Gould, *The Structure of Evolutionary Theory*, 579–84.
15 Mayr, *What Evolution Is*, 189.
16 Stuart Kauffman, Stuart Newman, Gred Muller, Andreas Wagner among others.
17 Miller, *Finding Darwin's God*, 146.
18 Bernhard R. Heresy in "The Halls of Biology: Mathematicians Question Darwinism," *Sci Res* (New York, 1967), 2:5–66.
19 Cairns J. Overbaugh and S. Miller, "The Origin of Mutants," *Nature* 335(1988), 142–45.

20 R. S. Gallhardo and P. Hastings, "Mutation as a Stress Response and the Regulation of Evolvability," *Crit Rev Biochem Mol Biol* 42950 (2007), 399–435.

21 A. B. Williams and P. L. Foster, "Stress-Induced Mutagenesis," *EcoSal Plus* 5, 1 (2012).

22 H. Martincorena, A. S. N. Seshasayee, and N. M. Luscombe, "Evidence of Non-Random Mutation Rates Suggests an Evolutionary Risk Management Strategy," *Nature* 485 (2012), 95–98.

23 S. Benzer, "On the Topography of the Genetic Fine Structure," *Proc Natl Acad Sci USA* 47 (1962): 487 – 493.

24 C. Shee, J. L. Gibson, and S. M. Rosenberg, "Two Mechanisms Produce Mutation Hotspots at DNA Breaks in E. Coli," *Cell Reports* 2 (2012), 714–721.

25 J. R. Roth and others, "Origin of under Selection: The Adaptive Mutation Controversy," *Annual Review of Microbiology* 60 (2006):477–501.

26 Freeman, *Biological Science*, 274–86.

27 W. K. Smits, O. P. Kuipers, and J. W. Veening, "Phenotypic Variation in Bacteria: The Role of Feedback Regulation," *Nature Reviews Microbiology* 4, 4 (2006):259–71.

28 G. Purdom and K. Anderson, "Analysis of Barry Hall's Research of the E. coli efg Operon: Understanding the Implications for Bacterial Adaptation to Adverse Environments," *Proceedings of the Sixth International Conference on Creationism* (2008), 149–63.

29 B. E. Wright, "Mini Review: A Biochemical Mechanism for Nonrandom Mutations and Evolution," *J Bacteriol* 182 (2000):2993–3001.

30 B. E. Wright, K. H. Schmidt, and M. F. Minnick, "Kinetic Models Reveal the *in vivo* Mechanisms in Mutagenesis in Microbes and Man," *Mutat Res* 752, 2 (2013): 129–37.

31 A. Wagner, *The Arrival of the Fittest: Solving Evolution's Greatest Puzzle* (New York: Penguin, 2014), 4.

32 Purdom and Anderson, "Analysis of Barry Hall's Research," 149–63.

33 B. G. Hall, "Evolutionary Potential of the *ebg* A Gene," *Molecular Biology of Evolution* 12 (1995): 514–17.

34 Miller, *Finding Darwin's God*, 152–56.

35 Behe, *Darwin's Black Box*, 79–90.

36 Behe, *Darwin's Black Box*, 86.

37 Miller, *Finding Darwin's God*, 157.

38 Miller, *Finding Darwin's God*, 110.

39 Coyne, *Why Evolution Is True*, 136–37.

40 Coyne, *Why Evolution Is True*, 194.
41 Blount, et al., "Historical contingency," 7899–906.
42 D. J. Van Hofwegen, C. J. Hovde, and S. A. Minnich, "Rapid Evolution of Citrate Utilization by *Escherichia coli* by Direct Selection Requires *citT* and *dctA*," *J. Bacteriol.* 198:7 (2016), 1022–34.
43 J. R. Roth and S. Maisnier-Patin, "Reinterpreting Long-Term Evolution Experiments: Is Delayed Adaptation an Example of Historical Contingency or a Consequence of Intermittent Selection?" *J. Bacteriol.* 198:7 (2016), 1009– 1012.

CHAPTER 8
The Fossil Record

We now turn to the fossil record, considered by Darwin to be some of the best evidence of evolution. Fossils are the remains of organisms that have been preserved or mineral casts of the deceased organism that resulted from being impregnated and replaced with minerals forming a rock caricature of the original form. Fossils that occur in the rock layers in which they were encased can be dated based on the age of the rock layer. Circumstances that formed the fossils meant the organisms that died were covered with materials soon enough to keep them intact and free of major deterioration effects and then to have experienced sufficient pressure to induce petrification. In many cases, fossils on land have been found in concentrated densities, indicating that death was caused by major perturbations of the local environment, such as ash deposits from volcano eruptions, floods, and land-mass movements, and thus largely limited to such catastrophic circumstances.

In contrast, marine plankton remains have some of the best information on evolutionary lineages. They have an exoskeleton and upon death fall to the bottom of lakes or the sea, where they are subsequently covered with silt and debris, which allows the layers to build up as a sequence, providing a record of change over time. Plankton fossils representing time frames ranging in the millions of years have been traced in silt cores taken from the ocean floor.

Fossils provide a mixed historical picture, and even the existence of a sequential record of change at the macroevolutionary level is debatable. Mayr[1] says, "Evolution as a whole, and the explanation of particular evolutionary events, must be inferred from observation ... However, most inferences made by evolutionists have by now been tested successfully so often that they are accepted as certainties." Although inference must be made in most cases, there are certain aspects of the fossil record that show definite evolutionary change. Recent fossils appear almost indistinguishable from living species, and as one goes further back in time in older rock strata, greater differences from living representatives can be observed. This is some of the best evidence of the pattern of changes that have occurred from the ancient past. Most of those ancient types have been extinct for millions of years, although bacteria, sponges, and worms, which were the earliest fossilized remains, have persisted to the present in nearly their original form.[2, 3]

In general, an unbroken series of fossils showing the gradual change in a species back through time is very rare.[4] As a common occurrence, new types often appear suddenly, without any earlier relatives found in older rock strata. The changes in the horse over the last fifty-five million years is one of the exceptions. When fossils of the horse family are placed in sequence, a pattern of microevolution can be shown, with many dead-end extinct side branches, but progressing from smaller four-toed forms to the present diversity observed in these magnificent animals (figure 1). There have been some challenges to the sequence, since some members of the assembled sequence have been found in the same strata, indicating they existed at the same time.[5] However, except for size and foot structure, their morphology has remained much the same, as evidence of their typological lineage.

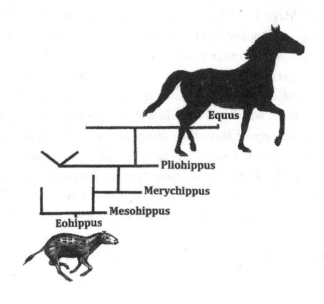

Figure 1. Horse archetype

Perhaps the biggest mystery in the fossil evidence is what is called the Cambrian explosion, estimated to have occurred 543 million years ago. Prior to that period, single-celled organisms existed for about three billion years, with no other forms appearing until the late Precambrian era 560 million years ago. That period was followed by the Cambrian explosion, so named because of the sudden appearance of all animal body plans and many phyla that still exist today. Fossils found in the famous Burgess Shale of Canada and the Maotianshan Shale of China occurred over a time period of only six to ten million years in duration. Moreover, there is no evidence of intermediate or ancestral forms that would link the various and novel phyla, and they were further distinguished by the near lack of diversification within phyla.[6] Diversification in lower taxa didn't appear until later. The absence of the transitional forms has heightened the mystery around the Cambrian fossils, especially with the scarcity of precursory fossils in the earlier Precambrian era. The later Precambrian fossils, the

Ediancaran fauna, showed no relationship to the many forms and novel features of the Cambrian fossils that demonstrated complexity in appendages, body segments, and the exceptional eye innovation.

There are three facts shown by the fossil record that are cause for serious deliberation. The first is the time span of hundreds of millions of years associated with the age of fossils. But one must also acknowledge the presence of rooted upright fossil trees that penetrate diverse layers of coal, interpreted to span geological ages, which raises questions about the assumed geological time scale. The second is the extreme diversity that exists among fossils, both in size of the life-forms and in their complexity. Life has occurred in nearly every form imaginable. And finally, the extinction of 90 percent of life that ever existed, the near extinction of life itself, and the manner in which those that survived were able to sustain themselves. These facts are the foundation from which analysis of the worldviews must take place, and they underscore the multiplicity and antiquity of life itself.

Evolutionist Perspective

There is abundant evidence of evolution in the fossil record. Fossils have been found that can be placed in a sequence that falls into the pattern that neo-Darwinian proponents would anticipate under the theory. Other trans-taxa arrangements of fossils have been assembled based on anatomical similarities of those thought to be transitional forms in proposed lineages. The evidence is inferential but is considered so strong that evolutionists feel confident that the fossil record reveals the changes that occurred in organisms over time, all of which are alleged to have descended from a common origin, as originally proposed by Darwin and now the basis of evolutionary theory.

This is called the theory of common descent, initially based on anatomy and most recently on molecular evidence. Mayr[7] wrote,

Indeed, paleontologists have succeeded in showing that all carnivores descended from the same common ancestor type. The same descent from the common ancestor is true for all rodents, all ungulates, and for all other order of mammals. Indeed this principle of common descent also holds true for birds, reptiles, fishes, insects, and all other groups of organisms ... This joint ancestry is the reason why the members of a taxon are so similar to each other.

Although Mayr was referring to descendants within types, Coyne[8] took the analysis of the fossil record to the next level and put it in the evolutionist's perspective of the big picture, with simple photosynthetic bacteria appearing in sediments estimated 3.5 billion years ago and continuing as the only detectable forms for the next two billion years. Then came the eukaryotes, the first true cell with a nucleus. Between five hundred and six hundred million years ago, many multicellular forms appeared suddenly, including worms, jellyfish, and sponges, which have persisted from their beginning to the present. The multicellular forms diversified, with fossils of terrestrial plants, four-legged animals, reptiles, mammals, and birds occurring over the succeeding four hundred million years. True amphibians appear, and then the reptiles are found, with the first mammals evolving from reptiles two hundred fifty million years ago, and birds, also from reptiles, fifty million years later. These forms became more diverse with time, to the point that in the most recent strata, the fossils increasingly come to resemble living species. Humans are recent, with the lineage branching off from other primates only about seven million years ago.

That series of events is what is portrayed in evolutionary theory as the tree of life (figure 2). It shows that once initiated, life diversified from a simple one-celled life-form, seen as the trunk of the tree, to more complex descendants, slowly advancing in gradual step-by-step changes that accumulate to form other kinds of life, seen as branches on the tree. The process continues, causing greater diversity within kinds, and forming other life-forms that pass through transitional states, eventually producing the plethora of variation seen in the fully expanded phyletic tree of life. Those descendants and transitional forms that have been preserved in the fossil record are what Mayr considers some of the best evidence of Darwinism.

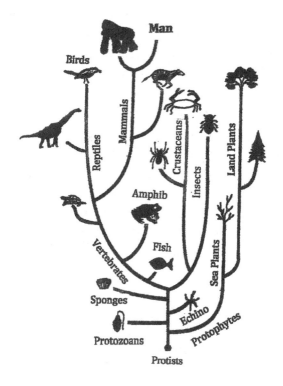

Figure 2. Tree of life

Mayr[9] shows a persuasive diagram of the pathway proposed for the evolution of mammals from reptiles. Mammals are thought to have derived from the therapsid reptiles based on anatomical similarities, with some intermediates that could be classified as either reptile or mammal based on comparative relationships. The most remarkable similarities other than their overall skeletal form are the forelimbs. This is most evident in the outstanding displays of the Chicago Museum of Natural History, where the forelimb joints and bone structure appear to the novice as almost identical among reptiles and mammals.

Another impressive rendering of the fossil evidence is the evolution of the whale, which was a mystery until the late 1980s, when Phillip Gingerich,[10, 11] University of Michigan, made expeditions to the prehistoric Tethys ocean floor, now called the Egyptian desert, where remains were found and identified as an ancestral whale. The ancestor of the whale has been traced to an even-toed ungulate, and among living forms today most closely related to the hippopotamus. Whale emergence started fifty-two million years ago, with the now-extinct form of *Pakicetus,* a terrestrial animal about the size of a German shepherd (figure 3). The fossil was only the head of the animal but had cetacean-like inner ear bones in the skull structure, previously found only in cetaceans (whales, dolphins, and porpoises). A more complete skeleton was found in 2001, indicating that *Pakicetus* was fully terrestrial.

Figure 3. *Pakicetus*

Fifty million years ago, there was a creature called *Ambulocetus* that was partly aquatic dwelling and possessed whale-like structures, but had short, hoofed sturdy limbs, indicating its ability to transport itself on land. Then came *Rodhocetus* forty-seven million years ago, with more characteristics of a whale, showing an elongated head, with nostrils moving backward and a stout backbone. It had strong forward limbs but a small pelvis and hind limbs, indicating it spent most of its time in water. There was a burst of diversity in whale-like forms at that time, some weighing up to sixteen hundred pounds and some with heads like crocodiles showing gaping mouths. At about forty million years ago, *Dorudon* and *Basilosaurus* appeared that were up to fifty feet in length, with blowholes, eyes moving to the side of the head, flippers replacing forward limbs, and hind legs further diminished. The pelvis separated from the spine, and their tails formed broad horizontal flukes that provided the thrust to move their larger bodies. After another six million years, thirty-four million years ago, the *Balaenidae* family of whales evolved, along with other cetaceans. The fossil evolutionary pathway was based on morphological characteristics, using whale-like features and the unique characteristic of even-toed ungulates, a double-pulley shape of the anklebone called the astragalus in those fossil forms five million years prior to what evolved into the legless whale.

On an expedition to the Egyptian desert in 2004, I was impressed with the extent of the marine fossil evidence on the ancient Tethys ocean floor. The sands were swept away from an area covering about fifty acres, and the ground was covered with ancient shells and carapaces of ancient life long past. It was a sobering experience to see the remains of organisms millions of years old that appeared much as their recent descendants do today. Most impressive were the numerous sand dollars, the bleached endoskeleton of the echinoderm's body called the "test," which visually displayed the same five pedal-like pattern on the body surface, indistinguishable from the tests found on beaches today.

Coyne[12] presented other impressive evidence of fossilized evolution and speciation that is evident among marine plankton. Upon death, generations of plankton fall to the bottom of the water column and over time are covered with layers of silt, providing the ability to show changes over the time frame of millions of years that are apparent in silt cores taken from the ocean floor. In one case, a small marine protozoan showed changes in the number of chambers of its spiral shell, with the number dropping from 4.8 to 3.2 chambers over a period of eight million years.

Another case is with the trilobites, an ancient arthropod numbering over twenty thousand species that went extinct but existing in large numbers during the Cambrian period, 543 million years ago. Trilobites had a hard exoskeleton, made up of fifteen or more body segments. In a two-hundred-meter-long silt core taken from the ocean floor, Coyne[13] showed five species evolving, with an increase in an irregular fashion from one to three body segments over a three-million-year period.

Transitional Forms

In the last few years, fossils have been discovered as transitional forms that fit well into what the neo-Darwinian evolutionary theory predicts. The recently discovered fossil intermediates leading to the whale are considered transitional forms. Another interesting transitional form is a fossil that is intermediate between fish and amphibians, called *Tiktaalik roseae*.[14] In 2004, it was found on Ellesmere Island in the Canadian Artic by a team led by Neil Shubin from the University of Chicago, an expert in the evolution of limbs from fins. They discovered it in a location and time frame that they believed would be most logical for the search. The fossil was found among a group of like forms that ranged from one to three meters in length, stacked together in sedimentary rock from an ancient stream. It was said when Shubin saw the fossil face sticking out of the rock, he knew he had at last found his transitional form. Coyne[15] states,

Tiktaalik has features that make it a direct link between the earlier lobe-finned fish and the later amphibians. With gills, scales and fins, it was clearly a fish that lived its life in water. But it also has amphibian-like features. For one thing, its head is flattened like that of a salamander, with eyes and nostrils on top rather than on the sides of the skull ... The fins had become more robust, allowing the animal to flex itself upward to help survey its surroundings. And, like the early amphibians *Tiktaalik* has a neck. Fish don't have necks—their skull joins directly to their shoulders.

Other traits were also present that helped *Tiktaalik's* descendants invade land. It appeared to have lungs as well as gills. It had sturdy ribs that helped support its form in shallow water and would facilitate pumping air to primitive lungs. It had fewer bones in its fins than observed in fish, and the bones described by Coyne as part fin, part leg were very sturdy, similar in number and position to those of land animals. An important point in the discovery was that *Tiktaalik* was found in exposed strata 375 million years old, which coincided with the time period evolutionists believe the transition link between fish and terrestrial vertebrates occurred.

One of the most well-known transitional-related fossils is *Archaeopteryx lithographica*. It was discovered in 1860 and at that time was considered a link between birds and reptiles. *Archaeopteryx* was found in the upper Jurassic, placed 145 million years ago. Coyne[16] considered *Archaeopteryx* the transitional form between birds and theropod dinosaurs, commenting, "*Archaeopteryx* is really more reptile than bird. Its skeleton is almost identical to that of some theropod dinosaurs.... The reptilian features include a jaw with teeth, a long bony tail, claws, separate fingers on the wing ... and a neck attached to its skull from behind (as in dinosaurs) instead of from below (as in birds)."

Mayr considered *Archaeopteryx* as the undisputed bird fossil. But rather than linking it to theropod dinosaurs, he placed it with a theropod ancestor. Mayr favored the view that *Archaepoterix* originated from the archosaurian reptiles. The most similar theropod dinosaurs were more recent in their evolution, occurring between eighty and a hundred and ten million years ago, approximately thirty-five million years later than the age of *Archaeopteryx*. Also, *Archaeopteryx* had different numbered hand digits from that of theropods and peg-like teeth, also very different from the serrated teeth of theropods. The forward extremities and pectoral girdle of the theropod dinosaurs were too small and weak to support the wings that could lift the ancestral bird off the ground.

However, *Archaeopteryx* as the ancestor of birds is disputed by other evolutionists, with the more recent discovery of Bambiaptor as the feasible link with birds. Some have indicated that *Archaeopteryx* was simply a feathered dinosaur, and others also reject the idea that birds evolved from theropod dinosaurs.[17, 18, 19, 20, 21] It is suggested that fossils such as *Archaeopteryx* were the manifestation of the variation that exists among the dinosaur taxa and was mistakenly classified as a transitory intermediate. But flying reptiles were well represented by the diverse pterosaurs that flourished over two hundred million years ago.

Evolutionists recognize the Cambrian explosion that began five hundred sixty million years ago as a major event in the fossil record that has yet to be explained. It was an abrupt appearance that was sustained for a relatively short period in the geological time frame, with no additional body plans occurring after 543 million years ago to the present. Mayr said, "This period of seemingly exuberant production of new structural type (phyla) soon came to an end. Although some 70 to 80 different structural types (body plans) appeared in the late Precambrian and early Cambrian, no new ones originated at any later period." The neo-Darwinian position is that the gap between the scant fossil evidence of Precambrian and the burst of the numerous different body plans of the Cambrian period is an artifact of circumstance, because they were either too small or soft bodied to be vulnerable to fossilization, or fossil formation didn't occur because conditions weren't conducive for preservation. Neo-Darwinists believe that at least two hundred million years of major evolutionary events must have been involved during the Precambrian prior to the Cambrian period in order for such an advance of different body forms to be present during the latter period, but those events haven't yet been observed.

Creationist Perspective

It is important to understand that the evolutionist's position is limited within the concept of the Darwinian model that prescribes how fossil evidence must be interpreted. There are two assumptions that are considered givens in evolutionary theory. The first is that only natural phenomena are involved in the origin and diversity of life. Observations in all of nature must be understood and explained as natural cause. Metaphysical influences associated with intelligence are simply not an option. If something is not yet understood, research will eventually reveal the testable explanation.

The second is that of common ancestry or common descent. It is believed that all of life, in all of its diversified forms, has descended from one original form of life, a basic principle of naturalism. It is stipulated that starting with a species and following its history of change back in time will reveal an ancestor from which it and at least one other species were derived. If it were possible to continue the process further back in time, it would reveal other branching forms from which different types of organisms evolved, and eventually passing through hundreds of millions of years, the original progenitor would be found, and probably in a form of photosynthetic bacteria.[22]

Those two assumptions in the evolutionist's position establish the working hypothesis that is followed in how observation and research are approached and within which all scientific information will be interpreted. Given those limiting criteria, it is clear that no conclusion other than evolutionary thought would be reached as an explanation as to why the fossil evidence confirms evolutionary theory. Those assumptions in the working hypothesis were clearly demonstrated in the discovery of *Tiktaalik*. They were looking for a transitional form, and that was how the finding was interpreted, even before it was analyzed. But is *Tiktaalik* really the transitional form between fish and tetrapods? A paper published in 2010[23] presented evidence that tetrapods existed long before *Tiktaalik*. Paleontologists discovered numerous tetrapod trackways and footprints in the Zachelmie quarry in Poland, a time that preceded the age of *Tiktaalik* by approximately twelve million years.

Their conclusion renders *Tiktaalik*[24] as a life-form with intermediate characteristics of fish and terrestrial vertebrates, but not the first alleged transitional form, and perhaps little more than a life-form similar to the mudskipper, which also shows adaptive pectoral fins with hinge joints to assist in walking and the ability to breathe through the skin when out of water. As Mayr indicated, interpretation of the fossil evidence is inferential. In other words, while it is important not to minimize the constructed fossil lineages that have resulted from years of study by many paleontologists, without experimental evidence in which such evolution across taxa can be demonstrated, that linkage has to remain as an implied relationship.

When evolutionists are attempting to assemble lines of relationship, inferential interpretation is also a factor when a fossil possesses the same anatomical structure as another fossil. But homology does not prove relationship, nor does it establish common descent. It allows only inferences but is routinely used to establish what they consider as evidence in line with evolutionary theory. When two unrelated fossils show the same or similar morphological feature, they call it convergent evolution, indicating that development among what is considered unrelated organisms underwent independent evolutionary pathways that acquired the same feature. However, convergent logic can be used just as well as an alternative explanation to explain homologous-like features among fossils that are used to allege ancestral relationships.

The evolution of the whale is a good example. The ancestor of the whale was an enigma until morphological characteristics associated with the whale were found in the ancient fossil of *Pakicetus,*[25, 26, 27] a land-dwelling animal the size of large dog. The defining feature was a small bone in the inner ear called the involucrum, also present in the whale skull domed with thick bone, the edge of which is the involucrum that encloses the inner ear. The projected ancestry assembled thereafter are fossils associated with a series of intermediate morphological similarities thought to represent what the whale paleontologist Philip Gingerich believes to characterize the evolution of the whale from land to marine habitat over the last fifty million years. But that ancestry is only hypothetical. The involucrum of *Pakicetus* could have been the result of convergent evolution, especially when the other features are so unlike whale morphology. Moreover, the cetacean-like inner ear involucrum bone used to identify whale ancestry has also been found in fossils of another land-dwelling animal, *Indohyus,*[28, 29] a small deer-like mammal. Because of that feature, *Indohyus* has been considered related to the ancestor of the whale, but the fact that the feature has been identified in another terrestrial mammal tends to question whether it represents a more independent convergent occurrence rather than such a diverse linkage with whale ancestry.[30]

There are other uncertainties about whale evolution. The published series is an assembly of fossils selected based on the Darwinian model of evolutionary theory. The actual fossils of whale evolution that would follow the concept of continuous incremental changes over time have yet to be found. Recent analysis of whale evolution by Jonathan Wells[31] is also illuminating about the problem. Based on the ages of the fossils used as evidence of the above ancestral trail, the Darwinian evolutionary time line wouldn't be sufficient for such extreme morphological changes involving anatomical transformation of tails to flukes, legs to fins, nostril relocation, acquisition of a unique blood circulation system, a collapsible chest diaphragm, nursing adaptations, and the extreme diversifications in form by chance.

So in the case of *Pakicetus*, as well as with *Archaeopteryx* and *Tiktaalik*, were they really transitional forms in the evolution of mobility on land, air, and water, or were they independent life-forms that displayed rather extreme variability confined within their typological taxa in response to environmental opportunities or challenges? *Tiktaalik* and the others may well be legitimate transitional forms, but that remains an uncertain inference that is based on how evolutionists interpret paleontological data consistent with the Darwinian evolutionary model.

Other fossil evidence reinforces that uncertainty. The lungfish, *Protopterus*, is a good example. It originated three hundred forty million years ago, and except for variability within its kind, there were no substantive changes in its morphology, even though it was stressed by severe environmental changes that were responsible for dehydration, lack of food, and vulnerability to predation. It is justifiable to think that over such a long period of time, mutations would have provided other morphological changes to cope with those challenges. The changes that were made were adaptations within their taxon to accommodate some of the environmental conditions lungfish were confronted with, but they were left to struggle in face of other trials that were apparently beyond the limits of their adaptability. Lungfish remained as lungfish and didn't transition much beyond their original form for over three hundred forty million years.

Similarly, the walking catfish, *Clarias batrachus*, has struggled to maintain itself in limited habitat and to translocate to new opportunities. It too has adapted to breathe air, and ridged spines have adapted from pectoral fin rays as walking canes to help function in mobility on land. But it has to exercise itself with extreme swimming bodily flexures to make such crawling possible. One would expect significant mutations accumulating to at least alter fins into stout appendages to assist in moving on land, but that hasn't happened. The changes have been within the taxon, and the walking catfish has remained a walking catfish.

Mayr[32] explains such situations as a normal pattern in evolutionary processes, where a large percentage of life-forms have been shown in the mode of stasis for millions of years, in part from environmental stability but also from the absence of innovative mutations that would make an improvement in their state. In referring to the situation where there is a lack of change, he says, "All mutations of which this genotype is capable and that could lead to an improvement of that standard phenotype have already been incorporated in previous generations. Other mutations are apt to lead to a deterioration and all of these will be eliminated by normalizing selection."

The lungfish and the walking catfish are examples of life-forms that have not acquired further morphological features that would have facilitated their ability to respond more effectively with the environmental conditions defining their general habitat. It appears they have reached the point in their pathways where mutations may no longer provide improved performance and have experienced the limitations of their typological kinds.

Succession

There are other issues that are also problematic. As discussed earlier, the hypothesis that life started as a simple organism that diversified into many and complex forms traced over time is contrary to what the fossil evidence actually shows. Evolution under the neo-Darwinian theory is that life should start as the ancestral form and through a gradual and continuous process become more diversified over time, as depicted in the standard evolutionary tree of life. But as Mayr, Gould, and Eldredge have noted, that is not what has been observed in the paleontological evidence. Five hundred million years ago in the Cambrian period, there was the abrupt appearance of all animal phyla known today that have not altered their body plans in any revolutionary manner. Vertebrates were thought to have been absent during that period, but Shu, et al.[33] has since reported the discovery of two vertebrate genera from the Lower Cambrian Chengjiang Formation (the Maotianshan Shale) in South China.

So the evidence from the Cambrian period has been characterized by what Wilson[34] and others have portrayed as an orchard rather than a tree, where the many different body plans appear abruptly, without intervening forms that would bridge the gaps among them (figure 4), and novelties in form including appendages, segments, and complex eyes appear suddenly as fully formed features. Many body plans associated in the Cambrian period are now extinct, with no relationship to body plans in evidence today. The life-forms fossilized during the Precambrian period were bacteria, algae, and sponges, none of which were associated with the fossils that appear to have originated during the Cambrian explosion.

Figure 4. Orchard type origins

Evolutionists contest such conclusions. As discussed above, they believe that Cambrian ancestors existed during the millions of years of the Precambrian period, but because of alleged small size or soft tissues were not susceptible to fossilization forces and disappeared. However, evidence shows that cyanobacteria and green algae colonies, worms, jellyfish, and comb jellies representing small and soft-bodied forms were well preserved in the fine, small-grained sediments in both the Precambrian and Cambrian periods, contrary to the neo-Darwinian allegation. So small size and the lack of hard body parts of the earlier fauna assumed to have existed during the Precambrian period doesn't appear to reconcile their absence.

The evolutionary pattern since that time is not entirely unlike that of the Cambrian period. The big picture in the fossil record is that new forms generally appear suddenly and then continue in stasis for long periods of time, disappearing in extinction. Even Niles Eldredge,[35] a committed evolutionist, confirms those observations. He says, "No wonder paleontologists shied away from evolution for so long. It never seems to happen. Assiduous collecting up cliff faces yields zigzags, minor oscillations, and the very occasional slight accumulations of change over millions of years, at a rate too slow to account for all the prodigious change that has occurred in evolutionary history."

This contrasts with what Coyne[36] portrays when he describes the fossil pattern. "Simple organisms evolved before complex ones, predicted ancestors before descendants.... And we have transitional fossils connecting many major groups." But there is no disputing what the fossil evidence shows. Most certainly the record of Cambria with all major animal body plans suddenly appearing, with no connecting ancestors or linkages among the groups and no revolutionary changes since, is directly the opposite from what Coyne has promoted as the bottom-up pattern of the continuously branching evolutionary tree of life.

Granted, creationists are as guilty as evolutionists in defending their interpretation of the evidence, but the Cambrian fossil record thus far has shown the top-down pattern of major body plans suddenly appearing, and diversity within those lineages occurring thereafter. Even the more recent fossil evidence that Eldredge refers to does not conform to the idea of an incremental, evolutionary bottom-up tree of life. The observations of Gould and Eldredge of the comparatively rapid change followed by long periods of stasis and often followed by extinction were the basis of their proposed hypothesis of punctuated equilibrium. Admittedly, large complex life-forms came later in the fossil pattern, but the general pattern in the fossil record, beginning with photosynthetic bacteria, followed by the burst of all animal phyla, and extinction of many forms thereafter, is more consistent with Creation theory than with that of neo-Darwinism.

It is also important to understand something seldom mentioned in evolutionary literature, and that is the organism's limited capacity for change. Mayr[37] pointed out, "This background extinction has been going since the beginning of life. The reason for it is that every genotype seems to have limits to its capacity for change and this constraint might prove fatal under certain environmental changes, particularly sudden ones." Therefore, it is recognized that organisms have limits in their capacity to change, exhausting themselves of beneficial mutations, and at the same time are prone to selection that stabilizes the genome. These factors encourage species stasis and contribute to Eldredge's view that the gradualness of microevolutionary changes of neo-Darwinian theory occur at a rate too slow to account for the macro-changes observed over evolutionary history. But more importantly, it suggests that macroevolution requiring a plethora of mutations at the microevolutionary level may be constrained by the organism's genomic limitations.

The possibility of sudden major genetic mutations has serious problems. Rapid changes at that magnitude are potentially lethal. Mayr,[38] referring to sudden major morphological alteration, said,

> Since it was known that potential mutations at most gene loci have deleterious or lethal effects, how could a massive shake-up of an entire genotype by a major mutation possibly produce a viable individual? ... But where are all of these millions of failures resulting from such a macromutational process? They have never been found because, as is now quite obvious, such a postulated macromutational process does not occur.

But that is true of macroevolution in general. Where are the many millions of intermediate forms that would have had to occur during the process of accumulating massive microevolutionary changes? So evolutionary theory is that change occurs by gradual microevolution, but as Mayr pointed out, the capacity of the genotype to continually make changes is limited, and the absence of abundant evidence of progressing intermediates leaves neo-Darwinism in a dilemma.

The point is that such limits to the genotype's ability to change fits very well in the concept of reproducing after their own kind, in essence being limited by the genetic boundaries of their typological lineage. Limitations on the extent that genotypes can change at the microevolutionary level leave the concept of accumulating such changes over millions of years that eventually lead to macroevolution contrary to the evidence. Creation scientists are divided when it comes to the origin of different forms of life with regard to common descent, but they do not question such change within the various lineages of different kinds of animal and plant life. For example, the fossil evidence of the changes that occurred in the horse family over the span of fifty-five million years up to the present shows the horse remained within its typological lineage in spite of significant alterations. This is the pattern of fossil evidence in general, that shows most changes used as evidence of evolution are in fact confined after their own kind.

Variation and natural selection are rational explanations for ongoing changes witnessed in adaptation that can lead to speciation within kinds. This becomes a bit confusing when one considers the somewhat arbitrary definition of species. Depending on the organism, a species can be identified by as little as a change of a single allele, all the way up to the standard of actual reproductive barriers. The question in the creationist's camp is, how did the different kinds of life come to be? Were there multiple forms coming forth at the beginning of life that henceforth diversified along typological lineages, as proposed by some contemporary creationists, or were life-forms created from a common ancestor, consistent with theistic evolutionary theory?

New Genes and Information

The significant element of the Cambrian period was the time frame of only approximately six million years, in which the concentration of most new body plans occurred. The process would require the acquisition of new genes that would contribute to the development of different body-plan morphologies. New genes can occur by point mutations of preexisting genes, but that doesn't increase the number of genes and hence contribute to the explosive increase in life-forms during the Cambrian period, where a mega-increase in the critical information responsible for the production of the different body plans had to occur. Large numbers of new genes were required, and the most common building process is said to be the duplication of sections of DNA sequences of existing genes.[39] Because it is a duplicate, it would be bypassed by RNA polymerase, and thus free to independently accumulate altered nucleotide mutations that would not be subject to natural selection, until eventually being recruited for a new function.

However, that is also the problem. Without the refinement of natural selection, the duplicated DNA sequences would accumulate random mutations, most of which would be deleterious when transcribed or result in nonfunctional proteins. Moreover, the functional element of the protein requires a precise tertiary or quaternary structure in the folded shape to succeed in its utility, and it will require the right combination of amino acids to form the specific folds to function in an innovative application. The improbability of forming a stable functioning protein by random mutations would increase by the number of amino acid substitutions required for the new function. These problems would be an inhibiting force for chance to provide the diversity of life-forms[40] and would be compounded by the relatively brief time frame of the Cambrian explosion.

Other scenarios to build new genes have been suggested, such as the fusion of two genes into one, lateral gene transfer common in bacteria, reverse-transcriptase, and other models. But the resolution of how the mega-amount of information necessary to achieve such an objective is gained, as well as the uncertainty of what causes a duplicated section of DNA to be recruited as a functional gene, remain elusive. This is problematic for neo-Darwinian theory, because the rapid increase in new body plans during the Cambrian period would require a mega-increase in the demands to build the number of new genes, new cell types, and the protein systems to meet those needs. Most of those changes would require multiple mutations in the amino acid sequence of a new protein, and many of those would require coordination to act in concert before becoming functional. Behe[41] determined that to develop immunity in mosquitoes that required two coordinated mutations, it would take millions of years. In applying a similar model to humans, given known generation times, Rick Durrett and Deena Schmidt[42] concluded that it would take more than a hundred million years to acquire one pre-specified pair of mutations, the first of which inactivates an existing transcription factor binding site and the second of which creates a new one. Although these models have been challenged, the point is that the studies demonstrate the unlikelihood of random chance mutations accumulating to the point of becoming effective. The implausibility of chance variation and natural selection sufficient to account for such a rapid pace of change during the Cambrian period or the burst of new information associated with the different life-forms and structural novelties that were apparent in that period is again unlikely.

The fossils of the Cambrian period show no cross-phyla morphological similarities that could be associated with macroevolution. This indicates that a different model from that of slow and continuous change needs to be considered. The fossil evidence shows that stasis will persist, unless there is a significant change in the environmental conditions that will induce an abrupt change or a series of abrupt changes in the organisms to meet environmental challenges. It appears that traumatic environmental events would have had to occur during the Cambrian explosion to induce such a surge in morphological innovation, but it is inconceivable that the variety and complexity of the body plans were produced in such a short time frame by any other means than abrupt and substantial constructs in form and function.

The creationist's interpretation of the fossil evidence is that the Cambrian explosion is associated with the creation of animal life, and the high degree of variability observed over the subsequent time thereafter was the branching of forms along those typological lineages. The fossil record shows that the appearance of animal body plans occurred in a short geological time frame, with no indication of a common ancestor from which they evolved. The evidence suggests, therefore, that the appearance of those archetypal forms either occurred as separate events or were derivatives of an ancestral prototype that differentiated with extreme rapidity as kinds along separate trajectories of diversification.

Creationists tend to dismiss the evolutionary perspective on the source and diversity of life. That is a mistake. The extensive scientific research that has transpired over the last century has expanded our understanding of life from the fossil evidence, its extreme diversity, and its history of form. Creationists differ with neo-Darwinists on the interpretation of paleontological data, but the evidence from the past is the foundation on which that interpretation rests. Because the fossil record is incomplete, the possibility of all of life originating from a common descent cannot be dismissed. However, if in fact that occurred, Creation theory would consider it as a historical contingency from which change progressed, but under design by an omnipotent agent. If some of what has been thought of as typological variation is in fact transitional forms traversing the parental taxon of kind, as alleged by evolutionary theorists, then the creationists would have to look carefully at major progressive changes as the result of an omnipotent creative plan that promoted involuntary diversification.

Conclusion

Fossil discoveries are not consistent with the neo-Darwinian evolutionary theory. Fossil evidence started in geological time referred to as the Precambrian period and took the form of photosynthetic bacteria and other simple life-forms, including algae and sponges, ending five hundred forty million years ago. It was followed by the Cambrian explosion, a crucial period of the ancient world five hundred forty to four hundred eighty-six million years ago, as a burst of animal life that included all body plans existing today as well as many other forms no longer in existence. There was no evidence of a common ancestral life-form and no linkages between body plans; diversity within archetypes occurred well after those original life-forms first appeared.

The single-celled cyanobacteria of the Precambrian period, and the explosive appearance of fully formed body plans in the Cambrian period, established the foundation on which subsequent fossil evidence has to be assessed. It would be fair to conclude that the big picture portrayed by the fossil evidence is contrary to the neo-Darwinian bottom-up model of the tree of life. Fossil evidence supports the top-down model of the sudden appearance (in geological time) of all known animal body plans that subsequently diversified within intraspecific lineages. Although there are no specifics about how the formation and diversity of the Cambrian body plans occurred, the fossil evidence is more consistent with the rapid appearance of major phyletic forms that diversified thereafter, rather than with the gradual advancement of a simple life-form that henceforth diversified into more complex plants and animals over geological time.

Endnotes

1   Mayr, *What Evolution Is,* 13.
2   Coyne, *Why Evolution Is True,* 28.
3   Mayr, *What Evolution Is,* 47.
4   Mayr, *What Evolution Is,* 14.
5   Mayr, *What Evolution Is,* 18.
6   Mayr, *What Evolution Is,* 58–63, 209.
7   Mayr, *What Evolution Is,* 22.
8   Coyne, *Why Evolution Is True,* 28–30.
9   Mayr, *What Evolution Is,* 15.
10 P. D. Gingerich, "The Wholes of Tethys," Natural History, 1994, www.
    personal.umich.edu
11 Mayr, *What Evolution Is,* 17.
12 Coyne, *Why Evolution Is True,* 30–32.
13 Coyne, *Why Evolution Is True,* 34.
14 Coyne, *Why Evolution Is True,* 38.
15 Coyne, *Why Evolution Is True,* 40.
16 Coyne, *Why Evolution Is True,* 43.
17 Mayr, E. 2001. *What Evolution Is,* 65–68.
18 D. Naish, "Birds," in M. K. Brett-Surman, T. R. Holtz, and J. O. Farlow
    (eds.), *The Complete Dinosaur* (Second Edition) (Bloomington &
    Indianapolis: Indiana University Press, 2012), 379–423.
19 A. Feduccia, *The Origin and Evolution of Birds* (Yale University Press,
    1999).
20 L. D. Martin, "A Basal Archosaurian Origin for Birds," *Acta Zoologica
    Sinica* 50 (2004), 978–90.
21 J. E. Quick and J. A. Ruben, "Cardio-pulmonary anatomy in theropod
    dinosaurs: Implications from extant archosaurs," *J. of Morphology* 270
    (2009):10.
22 Coyne, *Why Evolution Is True,* 28–29.

23   G. Niedźwiedzki and others, "Tetrapod Trackways from the Early Middle Devonian Period of Poland," *Nature* 463, 7277 (2010): 43–48.

24   E. B. Daeschler, N. H. Shubin, and F. A. Jenkins, "A Devonian tetrapod-like fish and the evolution of the tetrapod body plan," *Nature* 440, 7085 (2006): 757–63.

25   P. D. Gingerich and D. E. Russell, "*Pakicetus inachus:* A New Archaeodete (Mammalia, Cetacea) from the Early-Middle Eocene Kuldana Formation of Kohat (Pakistan)." Contributions from the Museum of Paleontology, University of Michigan, 1981, 25:235–46.

26   P. D. Gingerich and others, "New Protocetid Whale from the Middle Eocene of Pakistan: Birth on land, Precocial Development, and Sexual Dimorphism," *Plos One* (2009).

27   Gingerich and others, "Origin of Whales from Early Artiodactyls: Hands and Feet of Eocene Protocetidae from Pakistan," *Science* 293 (2001):2241.

28   K. Sanderson, "The Land-Based Ancestor of Whales," *Nature* (2007).

29   H. G. M. Thewissen, *The Walking Whales: From Land to Water in Eight Million Years* (University of California Press, 2014).

30   H. G. M. Thewissen and others, "Whales Originated from Aquatic Artiodactyls in the Eocene Epoch of India," *Nature* 450 (2007):1190–94.

31   J. Wells, "Zombie Science: More Icons of Evolution" (Discovery Institute Press, 2017).

32   Mayr, *What Evolution Is*, 135.

33   D. J. Shu and others, "A Lower Cambrian Vertebrates from South China," *Nature* 402 (1999):42–46.

34   Wilson, *The Riot and the Dance*, 191, 193.

35   N. Eldredge, *Reinventing Darwin* (New York: Wiley, 1995), 95.

36   Coyne, *Why Evolution Is True*, 30.

37   Mayr, *What Evolution Is*, 199.

38   Mayr, *What Evolution Is*, 79.

39   M. Lynch and J. S. Conery, "The Evolutionary Fate and Consequence of Duplicate Genes," *Science* 290 (2000), 1151.

40   R. Bernhard, "Heresy in the Halls of Biology: Mathematicians Question Darwinism," *Sci Res* (New York, 1967) 2:5–66.

41   M. J. Behe, *The Edge of Evolution: The Search for the Limits of Darwinism* (Free Press, 2008).

42   R. Durrett and D. Schmidt, "Waiting for Two Mutations: With Application to Regulatory Sequence Application and the Limits of Darwinian Evolution," *Genetics* 180(2008): 1501–509.

CHAPTER 9
Embryology

Embryology has been considered an important source of evolutionary evidence. Embryological development is an amazing series of events where a single cell is transformed into a multicellular organism, with billions of cells specialized as unique structures of tissues, organs, limbs, and a nervous system that controls the functions of life. It is a miracle-like event that happens almost before our eyes. In mammals, two haploid gametes join to form a zygote that immediately starts the developmental process of cell division, referred to as cleavage. One cell becomes two, two become four, four become eight, and so on to the multiple cellular stage of a blastula, a single layer of several hundred cells shaped like a round or flattened fluid-filled vesicle.

The mass of cells then forms the gastrula, where the vesicle begins to fold back on itself through a furrow or a spot on its surface called the blastopore. This results first in two cell layers that start differentiation into interior and exterior tissue layers, and where presumptive specialized cell components start forming as ectoderm (exterior), mesoderm (intermediate), and endoderm (interior) tissues. The embryo now starts to take an asymmetrical shape. A neural tube that becomes the brain and spinal cord forms along what will be the back of the embryo, establishing its dorsal/ventral orientation. Neural tube formation is the beginning of organogenesis, where the body, organs, and limbs take shape. The ectoderm becomes the epidermis and nervous tissue. Mesoderm gives rise to muscles, internal organs, connective tissue, and the somites that eventually become the vertebrae and ribs. The endoderm forms the digestive track and associated organs. Multiplication of the cell types continues growth until the embryo becomes a fetus up to the time of birth. Cell differentiation, organogenesis, and growth are marvelous events that unfold in a programmed epigenetic manner, engaged by control genes.

The issue in embryology that has made it so pertinent in evolutionary theory is the relationship and the developmental sequence of different life-forms, concentrating mostly around the vertebrates. Embryology was well on its way to becoming a science by the beginning of the nineteenth century. Darwin[1] considered embryology as the strongest evidence in support of his theory of descent with modification. This was in part from the level of understanding available about embryonic development at that time, which involved the sequence of events and similarities of attributes of different life-forms, but also from the influence of Ernst Haeckel, a contemporary of Darwin and a strong supporter of Darwin's theory.

As a scientist in the areas of zoology and anatomy, Haeckel made use of embryology in the evidence he gathered in defense of Darwin. In 1866, he proposed the concept around the motto "ontogeny recapitulates phylogeny," where ontogeny was the name he gave the series of developmental stages that the embryo advanced through, and phylogeny was the line of descent from the common ancestor. As embryonic development unfolded, the differentiation of morphological features of the more advanced life-forms were said to pass through or recapitulate the phase of the less advanced ancestors and proceeded on to further modify those features. Consequently, embryos of more advanced vertebrates passed through the miniature facsimile of the ancestral adult stages of the proposed evolutionary sequence. Amphibian embryos passed through the fish adult stage, reptile embryos passed through the fish and amphibian adult stages, and mammal embryos passed through the fish, amphibian, and reptilian adult stages, and so on. This was considered strong inferential evidence of a common ancestry, and Haeckel called the principle of recapitulation his "biogenetic law."

Haeckel studied embryos of vertebrate life-forms and printed copies of the drawings he made of those embryos as they advanced through stages of development (figure 1). His conclusions about embryo development and his drawings were influential on embryology, and their impact lasted for well over a century. However, Haeckel's drawings were deceptive.[2] He included only the most similar vertebrate embryos of fish, reptiles, birds, and mammals, and then made them look even more similar in the stages of development depicted in the drawings to fit with Darwin's theory of common descent. He even used the same woodcut in printing the images of some of the different embryos and didn't present the actual earliest stages of development that were quite dissimilar to one another, contrary to his claim. Moreover, using much later stages of development in his drawings, he represented the embryos as though they were the same size, when size differed tenfold. The deception was so obvious that some of his contemporary scientists accused him of fraud, even in that era where there was a general effort by other scientists to interpret biological phenomena in line with Darwin.

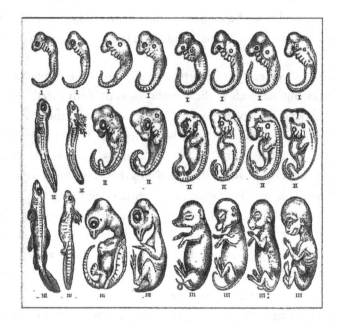

Figure 1. Haeckel compared eight vertebrate embryos; fish, salamander, tortoise, chicken, pig, cow, rabbit, and human. All stages were altered in an attempt to represent similarity among embryos, but the earlier stages shown in the upper line were altered the most. Images from George Romanes' 1892 book, *Darwinism Illustrated*.

Jonathan Wells[3] has researched the story of Haeckel's embryos and gives a revealing account of the problem. The general motif fits well into evolutionary theory, and Haeckel's drawings have prevailed in textbooks even to the present, regardless of their inaccuracy. But the most curious aspect of Haeckel's legacy is that his general philosophy on recapitulation still has an influence on evolutionary thinking. A less extreme form of recapitulation that describes the development of embryos of invertebrates as passing through embryonic stages of their evolutionary ancestors is how embryogenesis is interpreted by many evolutionists.

Evolutionist Perspective

Embryology is used as one of the current pieces of evidence supporting evolutionary theory, primarily on the principle of common descent. Although Haeckel's biogenetic law has been discredited insofar as recapitulation of embryos passing through ancestral adult forms, it has had a major influence on present evolutionary thinking. Mayr[3] recognized the exaggeration of Haeckel's drawings but used his term *ontogeny* and, to some extent, accepted recapitulation, indicating that during development, the anatomy of an embryo passes through the embryonic stages of the series of ancestral forms that have preceded it in the history of life. He wrote,

> In certain features, such as the gill pouches, the mammalian embryo does indeed recapitulate the ancestral condition ... and embryonic structures are found in thousands of cases to be indicative of their ancestors, but these same structures are absent in the adult life-forms. The embryologist could not escape the question of why in these cases ontogeny followed such a roundabout way to reach the adult stage.... The reason was eventually discovered by experimental embryologists, who found that these ancestral structures serve as embryonic "organizers" in the ensuing steps of development.... This is the same reason why all terrestrial vertebrates (tetrapods) develop gill arches at a certain stage in their ontogeny. These gill arches are never used for breathing, but instead are drastically restructured during later ontogeny and give rise to many structures in the neck region of reptiles, birds, and mammals. The evident explanation is that the genetic development has no way of eliminating the ancestral stages of development and is forced to modify them during the subsequent steps of development in order to make them suitable for the new life-form of the organism.

Mayr understood that the embryo in line of succession does not pass through the adult stage of its ancestors but believed it passed through early developmental stages of its ancestral embryonic forms, because particular organs appear to have evolved from such structures in their ancestral history.

A similar commentary on embryology is given by Coyne,[4] where he describes recapitulation in development:

> Let's start with that fishy fetus of all vertebrates – limbless and sporting a fish-like tail. Perhaps the most striking fish-like feature is a series of five to seven pouches, separated by grooves, that lie on each side of the embryo near its future head. These pouches are called the branchial arches, but we will call them arches for short. Each arch contains tissues that develop into nerves, blood vessels, muscles, and bone or cartilage. As fish and shark embryos develop, the first arch becomes the jaw and the rest become gill structures: the clefts between the pouches open up to become gill slits, and the pouches develop nerves to control the movement of the gills, blood vessels to remove oxygen from water, and bars of bone or cartilage to support the gill structure.... The really curious thing is that, as our (human) development proceeds, the changes resemble an evolutionary sequence. Our fish-like circulatory system turns into one similar to that of embryonic amphibians. In amphibians, the embryonic vessels turn directly into adult vessels, but ours continue to change—into a circulatory system resembling that of embryonic reptiles. In reptiles this system then develops directly into the adult one. But ours change further, adding a few more twists that turn into a true mammalian circulatory system, complete with carotid, pulmonary, and dorsal arteries.

Coyne then asks why vertebrates that wind up looking very different as adults begin development looking like a fish embryo. His answer was that each vertebrate undergoes the evolutionary sequence of it ancestors' development in a series of stages, and the sequence of those stages is the pattern of recapitulation. The reason is that which was given by Mayr: evolution builds on previous structures because of its inability to start from scratch to build new structures. So the fish developed directly into the adult form, but amphibians pass first through the embryonic fish stage and then on to amphibians, while the reptile starts with the embryonic fish stage, passes through an embryonic amphibian stage, and then to the adult reptile stage. Mammals also start with the fish embryonic stage and pass through the embryonic amphibian and reptilian stages, before developing into the adult mammalian stage. This is viewed as substantial evidence of common descent in the succession of life-forms.

Coyne[5] felt that Haeckel was accused unjustly in making his embryos look more similar than in reality, because embryos do show a form of recapitulation. He said that human fetuses never resemble adult fish or reptiles, but in certain ways they resemble embryonic fish and reptiles. Although he admitted that recapitulation is neither strict nor inevitable, not every feature of an ancestor's embryo appears in its descendants, nor do all stages of development unfold in a strict evolutionary manner.

Coyne[6] went on to point out that during development, human embryos go through a stage of ontogeny that retains the membrane equivalent to the membrane surrounding yolk material in egg yolk embryos, even though human embryo development is not associated with yolk at any time during incubation. Human development builds on the genetics of their ancestral legacy during differentiation of embryonic structures.

So Mayr and Coyne believe that recapitulation of the evolutionary sequence of development is not mistaken and is most apparent among evolutionarily more advanced embryos because of the apparent stages they pass through. Their view is that while it does not occur to the extent that Haeckel claimed, the influence of ancestral genetic features remains as the foundation on which more advanced structures are built. Their position is that recapitulation is the evidence of embryos associated with the historical evolutionary sequence of embryos progressing from the universal common ancestor.

Creationist Perspective

Contrary to Haeckel's misrepresentations, embryogenesis among the various animals early in development is very different.[7] The earliest stage of development in vertebrate embryos, starting with the zygotes or the fertilized single cell stage, shows major differences in cell size and the subsequent pattern of cell division, as well as the development through the blastula stage. Vertebrate embryos appear most similar midway in development, and that was the stage selected by Haeckel in support of his hypothesis on recapitulation. The alleged similarity of the midstages of the different embryos, however, was only present in Haeckel's drawings. The differences are demonstrated in current drawings by Jody Sjogren of Metamorphosis Studios, Ohio, representing the same stages that Haeckel claimed were the early stages of development[8] (figure 2), and most recently in actual photos of the embryos. The comparative examination of the two sets of drawings make it quite apparent that vertebrate embryos are very different.

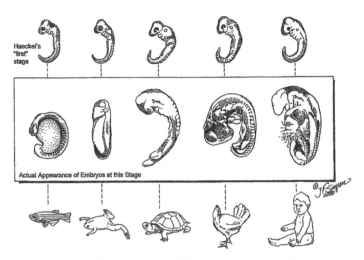

Haeckel's "first" stage

Actual Appearance of Embryos at this Stage

Figure 2. Comparison of five vertebrate embryos from Haeckel's fraudulent drawings with the actual appearance of the embryos at the same stage of development, from Wells 2000, *Icons of Evolution*.

Jonathan Wells[9] reviewed the extent of that difference in gastrulation, which is the beginning of cell differentiation:

> At the end of cleavage, the cells of the zebrafish embryos form a large cap on top of the yolk; in the frog they form a ball with a cavity; in the turtle and chick they form a thin, two-layered disc on top of the yolk; and in humans they form a disc within a ball. Cell movements during gastrulation are very different in the five classes: In the zebrafish the cells crawl down the outside of the yolk; in frogs they move as a coherent sheet through a pore into the inner cavity; and in turtles, chicks and humans they stream through a furrow into the hollow interior of the embryonic disc.

It is apparent that evolutionists had persisted with the proposition of recapitulation because the idea validated the Darwinian model. When recapitulation of vertebrate embryos passing through the adult stage of their ancestors was shown to be false, the assumption that embryos at least pass through their ancestral early embryonic stages persevered because it served as evidence of common descent. Although Coyne admitted that not every feature of an ancestor's embryo appears in its descendants, nor do all stages of development unfold in a strict evolutionary manner, he had been explicit in describing the evolutionary sequence of embryonic development passing through ancestral embryonic forms and presented it as strong evidence of neo-Darwinian common ancestry, although Coyne is not an embryologist and apparently depended on others for information.

Since this has been a source of much interest in developmental mechanisms during embryonic differentiation, a research team[10] undertook a re-examination of the extent of variation in vertebrate embryos. They reviewed the external morphology of embryos at the tailbud stage, thought to represent the most conserved phase of vertebrate embryos. Contrary to claims of embryo recapitulation, they concluded there is no highly conserved embryonic stage in the vertebrates. They summarized the observed differences: body size, body plan (for example, the presence or absence of paired limb buds), number of units in repeating series such as the somites and pharyngeal arches, pattern of growth of different fields (allometry), and the timing of development of different fields (heterochrony). These observations from the most comprehensive study on comparative morphology of invertebrate embryos since Haeckel postulated his principle of biogenetic law discredit the lingering embryonic recapitulation model endorsed by Darwinian evolutionists. Mammalian embryos may show greater similarity among themselves than with more distant life-forms, which is only expected, but their differences set them well apart from each other. The fact that all embryos start out as a single cell makes it apparent that even though unrelated, the embryos will have some similarities as they differentiate into multiple-celled forms.

However, the development and subsequent loss of some features during embryogenesis has been observed to occur within some phylogenic lineages, such as the baleen whales, which are said to show tooth formation in earlier stages of the embryo,[11] and that subsequently are lost with more advanced development and absent in the adult form. This has been portrayed as recapitulation, but such evidence does not support the case. Whales would have a common ancestry with the cetacean archetype, and in that category, there are currently existing toothed and baleen whale members that could show embryonic relationships along that lineage. But it is hypothetical to suggest there are ancestral relationships with some earlier form, since the anatomy of such an embryo is unknown, and there is no evidence that whale embryos pass through fish-like, amphibian-like, and reptile-like embryonic forms in their developmental progress.

One of the most common arguments used in support of recapitulation is what has been described as gill slits or pouches in mammalian embryos, alluding to their origin as gill structures in fish embryos and said to recapitulate the ancestral condition of the more primitive ancestor.[12, 13] The argument is that gill arches have been maintained in the more advanced vertebrate embryos that evolved much later and are morphological remnants on which the advanced changes were built. But these formations are in fact not gill arches.[14] They are presumptive tissue folds that differentiate into different structures, depending on the animal. In fish, the tissue develops into gill arches, on which gill tissue differentiates at a later stage. In humans, the tissue folds develop into pharyngeal tissue, parathyroid gland, middle ear, and the thyroid gland. These tissue folds have been misidentified as being associated with gills because of their superficial appearance and because in fishes, they eventually development into gills. But the tissue has different destinations in mammalian development. Having subscribed to the Darwinian model, the protagonists will always interpret such features in light of that paradigm.

Another example is the membrane in human embryos, referred to by Coyne as remnants of the genetic code for yolk-sac formation in ancestral life-forms.[15] That is also conjecture based on the Darwinian model. The human yolk sac is not a vestigial remnant. It is not even associated with yolk. It is a crucial membrane-lined umbilical vesicle outside the embryo connected by a tube called the vitelline duct though the umbilical opening.[16] It provides nourishment in the early stages of the embryo development, takes part in the formation of blood, and is the rudimentary circulatory system before the embryo is able to circulate blood internally. As the embryo develops, parts of the vesicle are incorporated into the embryo as the foregut, midgut, and hindgut, and eventually the vitelline duct is engulfed by the umbilical cord, replacing its function.

Conclusion

Since 1866, when Ernst Haeckel fashioned his biogenetic law, the concept of recapitulation has persisted in the scientific literature and textbooks, in spite of the evidence that Haeckel's data bordered on fraud. It has persisted as part of evolutionary theory because it fit so well with the philosophical context of evolution, but the evidence that embryos pass through ancestral embryonic stages is in dispute.

Given that there is morphological similarity among some life-forms, it is reasonable that their embryos would show similarities in their pattern of differentiation that could be misinterpreted as recapitulation. Without further evidence, however, the conclusion that embryos pass through the alleged evolutionary sequence of embryonic ancestral forms that preceded them appears to have originally been an interpretation to underwrite the evolutionary model and passed without verification because it was contrived to support the concept of Darwinism. The conclusion that all mammalian embryos develop gill arches at a certain stage in their embryogenesis is an example of such motivational interpretation, when what is observed is the transformation of tissues below the head region that differentiate independently in different animal forms.

Recent studies by embryologists indicate that there is no validity to the claim that invertebrate embryos build on the evolutionary sequence of their alleged distant ancestors. These are the most comprehensive comparative re-examinations of invertebrate embryo morphology since Haeckel first proposed recapitulation, and the results indicate there is no conserved embryonic stage in vertebrates.

Endnotes

1   Darwin, *The Origin of Species*, 419.
2   Wells, *Icons of Evolution*, 93–94.
3   Wells, *Icons of Evolution*, 81–109.
4   Mayr, *What Evolution Is*, 30.
5   Coyne, *Why Evolution Is True*, 78–80.
6   Coyne, *Why Evolution Is True*, 83–84.
7   Coyne, *Why Evolution Is True*, 76.
8   Wells, *Icons of Evolution*, 95.
9   Wells, *Icons of Evolution*, 96.
10 M. K. Richardson and others, "There Is No Conserved Embryonic Stage in the Vertebrates: Implications for Current Theories of Evolution and Development," *Anatomy and Embryology* 196 (1997), 91–106.
11 Darwin, *The Origin of Species*, 428.
12 Mayr, *What Evolution Is*, 29–30.
13 Coyne, *Why Evolution Is True*, 79.
14 Wells, *Icons of Evolution*, 105–106.
15 Coyne, *Why Evolution Is True*, 76–77.
16 A. C. Enders and B. F. King, "Development of the Human Yolk Sac," in F. F. Nogales (eds.), *The Human Yolk Sac and Yolk Sac Tumors* (Berlin, Heidelberg: Springer, 1993).

CHAPTER 10
Morphological Similarity

Morphological similarities have been the foundation for developing general categories of different forms of life. The comparative anatomies of all identified life-forms were classified along lines of taxonomic similarity by Swedish botanist Carolus Linnaeus in 1735. Plants and animals were placed in categories that were classified as species, genera, family, order, class, and phylum. Where all members of a particular category had virtually the same features, they qualified as a single species. Based on similarities of broader morphological characteristics among the species, they were then grouped into what were called genera, and the genera that shared certain features were joined in the next larger category that was called the family, and so on, forming a hierarchical pattern from species to phylum. All phyla were then placed in either the plant or animal kingdoms. Categories were later refined, and all kingdoms were separated into three domains identified as bacteria, archaea, and eukarya. Those possessing a nucleus in the cell, including plants, animals, and fungi, all fell within the latter.

Richard Owen[1] was a contemporary of Darwin and was a morphologist of considerable fame as an expert in plant and animal classification. Skilled in the anatomy of different organisms, he developed the term *homologous* to describe a feature of an organism that was shared by other organisms. So the liver in a fish would be considered homologous to a liver in a dove, or the forelegs of canines would be homologous to the wings of birds. Homology in life-forms was a well-recognized feature used in determining relationships among plants and animals within the different categories of the

Linnaean classification system. While that system was meant to be a classification arrangement of living organisms, it was adopted as the foundation for the interpretation of evolutionary relationships.

Evolutionist Perspective

Upon the publication of Darwin's *Origin of Species,* the Linnaean hierarchical classification system was unhesitatingly reinterpreted as the history of life, demonstrating what Darwin postulated as descent with modification, and thus the basis of evolutionary theory and the primary evidence in support of common descent. The categories centered on the anatomical similarity of existing groups of organisms from species up to phylum are seen as phylogenic relationships, presented as a branching tree of descendants. Hypothetically, each group of organism could be traced back to their nearest common ancestor, and that corresponded with the concept of descent based on morphological modification within what is considered the line of descendants. Darwin's theory fit very well into the hierarchical Linnaean classification relationship, and that is why it soon became the model that was revised to represent evolutionary theory.

Darwin[2] redefined homologous characters to be those of two or more organisms that were derived by evolution from an equivalent feature of the nearest common ancestor. Homology is used as some of the strongest morphological evidence supporting Darwin's theory of common ancestry, and it is readily apparent in the forelimbs of vertebrates (figure 1), a subphylum of Chordata. The wing of a bat, the fin of a dolphin, the foreleg of a cat, and the arm of a human are made up of the same bone structure. Alterations in length of bone have evolved corresponding to the application of the feature in sustaining the function of the specific animal's limb. For example, the relative proportions of the femur and phalanges are different in the different life-forms, but they essentially have the same anatomy. The conclusion is that these are all homologous structures that evolved from an ancestral archetype of the original vertebrate, and that this body part is thought to have originated from the pectoral fin of the fish.[3]

Evolutionists consider the morphological similarities described as homologous structures as supportive evidence of common descent[4] and thus is presented as evidence of Darwinian evolution. Moreover, these morphological similarities, derived from an ancient common ancestor, even in isolation, are not the result of alterations in a couple of amino acids but involve many changes in the genetic code and epigenetic influences. In evolutionary theory, this is considered macroevolution,[5] especially when one recognizes that the changes demonstrated in the limbs of all animals were commensurate with other major changes that had to occur in the anatomy and behavior of the organisms as unique characteristics of the different life-forms.

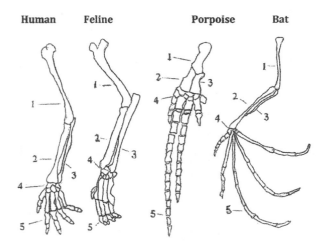

Numbers indicate the same bone among forelimb examples.

Figure 1. Homology of forelimb structure in universal among mammals, although function of the forelimbs is quite different. Hoofed animals and birds show greater structural diversity.

Creationist Perspective

Although the assuming principle of homologous structures in evolutionary theory is that they represent the common origin from a single ancestor, application of the concept combining all vertebrates must remain inferential.[6] The vertebrates include mammals, amphibians, reptiles, birds, and fish, embodying an extreme diversity of life-forms for which there is no living evidence demonstrating transitional intermediates of the five different kinds of animals. While kinds are thought to represent categories above family, at least as far up the taxonomic lineage as class, they remain within their typological identity. Moreover, there is no paleontological evidence of a series of steps suggesting a pathway taken in the gradual evolution of any of the homologous features of the vertebrates.[7] While each shows modifications of their typological kind and thus demonstrate variation within their respective archetype, the allegation of overall common descent is not the only possibility regarding origin of homologous features.

In Creation theory, an alternative to common origin is that morphological similarity among vertebrates would be a matter of optimum design. The structural disposition of homologous features is the same among all vertebrate life-forms because that design addressed the most effective anatomical engineering regardless of archetypical origin. Therefore, homology of limbs among mammals, amphibians, reptiles, birds, and fish occurred as the optimum design for mobility in spite of being different typological kinds. However, if the origin of vertebrate homologs occurred from a common ancestor, it would not negate design from consideration. The manner in which creation unfolded in an unknown and common origin should not be summarily dismissed as the mechanism of intelligent cause in the phenotypic legacy of kinds when so much is indeterminate.

Design requires a mechanism through which a phenomenon comes to pass, just as chance requires a mechanism in order to materialize. For example, in the Genesis account, when God said, "Let there be light," science has shown the mechanism was the nuclear furnaces of the stars emitting energy that transformed the cosmic dark ages[8] following the Big Bang. In like manner, genetic recombination, mutations, and natural selection are mechanisms that can result in homology among different kinds of vertebrates when optimum function is contingent on a given structural design.

As mentioned earlier, typologists of the nineteenth century viewed the synchrony between form and place as preordained, saying in essence that life-forms were created to match their environment. The design paradigm through natural selection is an alteration of Owen's structuralism.[9, 10] The difference is that the organism is endowed with adaptive ability to accommodate environmental diversity that provides an ongoing process of synchronization, which is a much more omnipotent provision by intelligent cause than fixation of type. In the case of homology of features, it is the provision of the optimization that results in the most efficient function of structural form. From the perspective of the creationist's camp, that is not the result of blind chance but the consequence of design, precisely what would be expected in the omniscient plan of the Creator. Synchrony in form by altering nucleotide sequences in the genetic code is a very ingenious way to implement optimization and the most innovative way of achieving it.

Darwin got it right when he concluded that adaptation was the result of variability and natural selection, but he mistakenly associated it entirely with chance. Understandably, creation unfolding over a time frame of events in the formation of life would be interpreted as natural processes under the constraining principles of naturalism, but that is because the analysis isn't taken to the next stage, where natural processes are simply shown to be the tools of the Creator, consistent with the physical, chemical, and biological laws that were established in the beginning. This equates with James Watson, the co-discoverer of DNA structure, who claimed that he had revealed the secret of life,[11] when in reality, he only discovered the blueprint and didn't recognize the architect.

Conclusion

Richard Owen referred to features of an organism's anatomy as "homologous" when they were shared by other organisms. Darwin redefined homologous characters to be those of two or more organisms that were derived by evolution from an equivalent feature of the nearest common ancestor. That can apply in the case of diversity within an archetype, but it is only inferential to apply it to a grand ancestor of all life-forms. How Creation was accomplished has not been described, nor has the process been recorded in scripture. From the creationists' point of view, homologous features among the vertebrates can be interpreted as evidence of optimum design emanating from the plan of an omniscient Creator either in the progressive creation from a common origin or implemented as a common design of form in separate creations.

Endnotes

1 R. Owen (1804–1892), Wikipedia, the free encyclopedia.

2 Darwin, *The Origin of Species*, 415–19.

3 Coyne, *Why Evolution Is True*, 28–29.

4 E. Mayr and Ashlock, *Principles of Systematic Zoology* (New York: McGraw-Hill, 2001), 1991.

5 Mayr, *What Evolution Is*, 188–90.

6 Mayr, *What Evolution Is*, 27.

7 M. Denton, *Evolution: Still a Theory in Crisis* (Discovery Institute Press, 2016).

8 C. Q. Choi, *The Universe's Dark Ages: How Our Cosmos Survived* (Science & Astronomy, 2011). Space.com.

9 S. J. Gould, *The Structure of Evolutionary Theory* (New York: Belknap Harvard Press, 2000), 251–341.

10 Darwin, *The Origin of Species*, 14–18.

11 J. D. Watson and A. Berry, *DNA The Secret of Life* (Knopf, 2003).

CHAPTER 11
Vestigial Structures

Vestigial structures are defined as structures no longer necessary in sustaining the life of the organism. They are considered to be either no longer functional or altered characteristics that in time past were fully functional in an organism's ancestor. There are many examples such as the remnant eyes in cave-dwelling organisms, the human appendix, and the pelvic bones of some whales. Vestigial structures have not been entirely eliminated by natural selection, but nearly so in many cases, such as the wings of the kiwi in New Zealand, which are very small and hidden by its feathers. The ostrich has wings that are used for display and balance, and may even assist in mobility, but they are not able to lift the bird in flight (and perhaps never were). The evidence of so-called vestigial structures testifies that change has taken place over the history of a particular life-form.

Evolutionist Perspective

Vestigial structures are considered important evidence that shows the previous course of evolution. Such structures are not rare. Coyne[1] writes,

Whales are treasure troves of vestigial organs. Many living species have a vestigial pelvis and leg bones, testifying ... to their descent from four legged terrestrial ancestors. If you look at a complete whale skeleton in a museum, you'll often see the tiny hind limb and pelvic bones hanging from the rest of the skeleton, suspended by wires. That's because in living whales they're not connected to the rest of the bones, but are simply imbedded in tissue. They once were part of the skeleton, but became disconnected and tiny when they were no longer needed.

The small remnant hind legs that can occur on some whales indicate that the ancestor of the whale was a land-dwelling tetrapod. The legs also provide a clue towards identifying the intermediate life-forms that progressed in macroevolution of the ancestral lineage.[2]

That is the story of some structures in a host of animals. The cavefish lost its functional eyes that were no longer needed when living in total darkness. Flightless ducks, the kakapo parrot, and penguins haven't lost their wings, but don't fly because their adopted or altered biosphere no longer required it. This too can be the result of natural selection. Flightless birds have usually been associated with areas where predator mammals were absent or in lower numbers, and where flight to escape danger was no longer necessary.

In such cases, where organisms have migrated into areas where the need for certain features were downgraded or changed, such specialized features became superfluous and even selected against. Eyes, limbs, and other novelties require maintenance energy, and when no longer used, they atrophy to reduce the unnecessary cost of sustaining the feature. Whatever the cause for eliminating a feature, such as change in structure or function, it is evidence of evolution along the line of descent. Douglas Futuyma has stated that vestigial structures make no sense without evolution.[3]

Creationist Perspective

The presence of vestigial structures is not contrary to Creation theory as defined in chapter 2. Vestigial structures have always been used in support of change, but that is justified only as microevolution and thus relevant within archetypes. Eyeless organisms whose ancestors were sighted or birds that lost the ability to fly are considered descendants of the same life-form that historically used those features for the presumed purpose. The need to maintain those features under circumstances where they were no longer necessary is consistent with degeneration or adaptive forfeiture of a structure.[4]

In many cases, the term *vestigial* is mistaken. The penguin's ability to maneuver in the sea would suggest a very appropriate adaptation of the wings and body structure that enhanced their ability to survive in that environment. Such a structure is considered an exaptation, where a structure has been modified for a new function. Some structures assumed to be vestigial are actually functional, such as tonsils and the appendix in humans.[2] Then there are the cases where the use of a structure has been reduced in function, such as the wings of the ostrich that has become too large to fly but are still used for display and balance.

The other consideration is that what is assumed to be vestigial may only be a mistaken alteration of embryonic differentiation, where cells that specialize to form a structure suffer an abnormality. During embryogenesis, in the formation of organs and skeleton tissue, mutations can alter such physical structures. Congenital abnormalities occur, and they are often associated with a form of dysmelia, where an extra appendage develops, which is usually deformed, or amelia, where the birth defect results in absence of one or more limbs.

The point that is relevant about vestigial structures is that they are always remnants of features degenerated through adaptive alteration, but the archetype doesn't change. Such adaptive changes would be expected to occur as organisms invade new habitat. For instance, flightless ducks still represent their original *Anatidae* lineage, but the more persuasive characteristic is that after invading environments where flight is no longer necessary, or where genetic alterations no longer permit flight, their anatomy has not changed substantially from that of their flying progenitors. The basic body plan associated with the physical structure of their limbs and beak hasn't changed from that of the archetypical form, suggesting again that genetic variation is limited within certain constraints.

The whale as envisioned by evolutionists is an interesting matter. The small hind legs are considered vestigial structures that point to functional legs in the historical past. If the various fossils assembled to depict the hypothetical lineage, beginning with the small dog-like *Pakicetus*[5] and advancing to its present morphological form, are correct, as discussed in chapter 8, that would be regarded as significant evidence regarding Darwinian macroevolution as defined by Mayr.[6] But was that in reality the evolutionary pathway? And if it were, can we conclude that the sequence of forms alleged to have occurred were by chance, or were the changes the result of inherent natural processes in the advancement of design of structural form?

The fact that cetaceans occasionally sport small remnant legs is considered evidence of a major change having occurred in that life-form from ancient times, but could these occasional dysfunctional small legs simply be the proclivity of cetaceans to be susceptible to congenital limb dysmelia, where a functionless limb develops as a structural anomaly? Whales have a pelvic girdle as an anchor on which certain muscles are attached, and their pectoral flippers show the same bone structure as other mammals consistent with their lineage, but the occasional markedly diminished hind limbs may be the result of a congenital anomaly in their genetic code.

While it is assumed that cetacean hind legs were present and functional in the distant past, when that particular life-form most likely weighed much less and could be supported by legs, the actual scenario of what transitional life-forms occurred from that tetrapod ancestor to the present is unknown. The series of intermediate fossil forms that have been assembled by evolutionists to represent the cetacean ancestral lineage have been organized to conform to the

Darwinian model, but the members of the assembled sequence show other major differences in size and structure that leave the alleged relationship only as an inference. Vestigial structures, in general, represent a level of microevolution within the archetype that show a regressive alteration of form, but those life-forms have remained within the typological lineage.

Conclusion

Vestigial structures represent a regressive change in the form of an organism, most often at the level consistent with degeneration of a feature that is no longer an advantage or even necessary for the survival of that particular form of life. Vestigial transformations have been alleged as evidence in support of macroevolution by evolutionists because of the level of change that has occurred with evolutionary novelties or structures of that life-form. But such vestiges are not evidence that life-forms have transgressed beyond their archetypical kind. Flightless ducks remain as ducks. Blind cave-dwelling fish are still that life-form. Although the vestigial structures indicate that changes have occurred in a life-form, those changes are degenerative and are expressed at the microevolutionary level.

Endnotes

1   Coyne, *Why Evolution Is True*, 64.

2   A. Reeder, "Evolution: Evidence from Living Organisms" (Bioweb, 1997). Retrieved October 16, 2008.

3   D. J. Futuyma, *Science on Trial: The Case for Evolution* (Sunderland, MA: Sinauer Associates Inc., 1995), 49.

4   Mayr, *What Evolution Is*, 30–31.

5   Coyne, *Why Evolution Is True*, 54.

6   Mayr, *What Evolution Is*, 188.

CHAPTER 12
Biogeography

The distribution of plants and animals across the continents was of great interest to nineteenth-century naturalists. Similar plants and animals had been found on different continents that were separated by extensive ocean barriers. Fossils of the same freshwater reptile had been found in Brazil and South Africa, and a land reptile fossil found in rocks of the same age in South America, Africa, and Antarctica heightened the mystery of origins.

Biodiversity within island communities was also the focus of much of that interest, and birds are one of the most diverse organisms associated with island communities. Nearly sixty species of honeycreepers had been recorded on the Hawaiian Islands, thirteen to twenty species of finches on the Galapagos Islands, and the many flightless birds of New Zealand, including the extinct giant moa. These are oceanic islands and an oceanic continent, well separated from the other continents, and generally absent of amphibians, reptiles, and land mammals. Madagascar is an exception with the most primitive primate, the lemur, arriving on the island sixty million years ago and diversifying into what has been thought to represent seventy-five endemic species.

These distributions were puzzling until biodiversity was related to the physical geography of the landmasses. Mayr[1] retrospectively wrote,

Evolution also helped explain another great puzzle of biology, namely, the reasons for the geographical distribution of animals and plants. Why are the faunas of Europe and North America on both sides of the North Atlantic so relatively similar, whereas those of Africa and South America on both sides of the South Atlantic are so very different? Why is the fauna of Australia so strikingly different from that of all other continents? Why are there normally no mammals on oceanic islands? Could these seemingly capricious patterns of distribution be explained as the product of Creation?

The resolution of those questions was the evidence on continental drift, where the continents were once joined in what was called Pangaea[2] and separated about two hundred million years ago (figure 1). Similar forms of endemic flora and fauna exist on continents in areas originally adjacent that subsequently were isolated from one another after continents separated sufficiently to create barrier seas between them. Camels are an example of such a form that evolved across continents but became extinct in what is now North America after continental separation. Madagascar separated from Africa as part of the continental drift and had drifted far enough by the time the lemurs[3] diversified that they were isolated from other primates in Africa.

Figure 1. Map of Pangaea with six landmasses separating south of the equator during continental drift, including Madagascar.

Evidence of biogeographical differences in the phenotypes of animals and plants that are no longer contiguous because of mountain or sea barriers in essence represents allopatric speciation. For example, when a taxon colonizes an island isolated from the mainland, it will go on to microevolve differently under the pressures of each new environment. This is the situation with the birds in Hawaii and the Galapagos. The isolation is sufficiently distant from the continents that amphibians, reptiles, and mammals have not made the journey, but those particular birds did, and then subsequently speciated into extensive varieties.

There are only a few marsupials outside of Australia and New Guinea, but many mammals in Australia bear incompletely developed infants that they carry and suckle in a pouch. These animals cover a range of types from the cat-like, mouse-like, flying squirrel-like, and wolf-like phenotypes, and others that have similar counterparts without pouches on other continents. How does one account for this? It was found that marsupials originated in North America and subsequently expanded south and onto Antarctica and Australia before the landmasses separated. Fossil species of marsupials have been found in Antarctica,[4] and they went on to colonize Australia, where they were isolated and free to speciate in greater diversity.

Evolutionist Perspective

Coyne's discussion about oceanic island biodiversity is given as some of the best evidence for evolution. Certain native freshwater fish, amphibians, reptiles, and land mammals common on the continents are absent on oceanic islands because they were unable to migrate across such distances. In contrast, native birds, plants, and insects that were able to negotiate such distances are found in large numbers and have diversified into many different species. Even some weed-like plants that made the transition to the islands have, in the absence of continental trees, adapted and assumed the role of trees in the absence of competition, filling the niche that would have otherwise been occupied by trees. In his explanation, Coyne wrote,[5]

> To sum up, oceanic islands have features that distinguish them from either continents or continental islands. Oceanic islands have unbalanced biotas – they are missing major groups of organisms, and the same ones are missing on different islands. But the types of organisms that are there often comprise many similar species – a radiation – and they are the types of species, like birds and insects, that can disperse most easily over large stretches of ocean. And the species most similar to those inhabiting oceanic islands are usually found on the nearest mainland, even though their habitats are different.

How do these observations fit together? They make sense under a simple evolutionary explanation: the inhabitants of oceanic islands descended from earlier species that colonized the islands, usually from nearby continents, in rare events of long-distance dispersal. Once there, accidental colonists were able to form many species because oceanic islands offer lots of empty habitats that lack competitors and predators. This explains why speciation and natural selection go wild on islands, producing "adaptive radiations" like that of the Hawaiian honeycreepers. Everything fits together if you add accidental dispersal, which is known to occur, to the Darwinian processes of selection, evolution, common ancestry, and speciation. In short, oceanic islands demonstrate every tenet of evolutionary theory.

Coyne presented such biographic information as conclusive proof of evolution. He also alleged that Creation couldn't explain such distribution, because why would a Creator not create the same species to inhabit continents and islands alike? Mayr concurred that for a creationist, there is no rational explanation for distribution irregularities of the same species widely separated in different locations, but such distribution patterns are completely compatible with historic evolutionary explanations.

Creationist Perspective

Selective immigration to oceanic islands from the continents is not contrary to Creation theory. It would appear that the thoughts of Mayr and Coyne about what creationists believe or don't believe about life-forms replenishing the Earth only demonstrate their parochial thinking. Mayr and Coyne have both equated Creation with the idea that life-forms were created instantaneously as species, immutable in phenotype, and distributed universally with no geographic disparities. But just as in the scientific arena where genetics and molecular biochemistry have matured well beyond the interpretation of Lamarckism, science has also enhanced our understanding of the Creation events beyond the seventeenth-century computations of the Irish bishop Ussher.

Distribution, isolation, and speciation as discussed throughout the previous chapters are part of the microevolutionary process that is recognized by creationists as patterns in animal life that are consistent with their history. The composition of island immigrants determined by their ability to make such a trip across barrier spans of ocean is only reasonable and in no way refutes Creation logic. Creation theory recognizes the natural processes that have been shown to have occurred over great lengths of time, such as continental drift and migration of life-forms, and whether based on theory as outlined in this manuscript or interpretation of scripture, there is no problem with biogeographic information on fauna distribution and diversification.

What biographical studies have made abundantly clear is the magnitude of life's extreme ability to diversify. The potential in the genome of life-forms is absolutely beyond imagination, and the diversity it has produced and the mechanisms that induce such change are phenomenal. The Madagascar evidence on lemur diversity is astonishing. Although much reduced from habitat loss and human encroachment, the diversity that microevolved to fill the niches on a land mass that lemurs were free to exploit shows the extensive genetic potential that exists in how one form of life can adapt and specialize. That potential is built into the genome, and in the case of the Madagascar lemurs, it is in the blueprint for their life-form, with impending diversification unleashed through microevolutionary processes when unrestrained in open habitat.

Coyne stated that oceanic islands demonstrate every tenet of evolutionary theory. But is that true? Oceanic islands demonstrate microevolution as in adaptive radiation, but there are no new body plans appearing, no new novelties forming, only diversification within the typological format. In the case of Madagascar, over a period of sixty million years,[6] the lemur isolated from other competitive primates, diversified into a radiation of many species, but remained within its archetype. There were no other forms of life that evolved from the lemur body plan over that extensive time period in an environment that encouraged many varieties of the originating lemur form (estimated by some to represent as many as a hundred species[7]). The evidence indicates that while lemurs have diversified to such a phenomenal extent, they have reproduced only after their own kind.

So the evidence is actually contrary to Coyne's allegation that oceanic islands demonstrate every tenet of evolutionary theory. When birds arrived on the islands, there were no changes to anything that resembled acquiring a new archetypical form, even though a foreleg and hand would have proven most beneficial, especially when flight was no longer necessary or possible. Although flightless birds adapted with larger, more robust legs or altered wings or bill morphology to accommodate different feeding strategies, there were no changes that went beyond the form of their typological limits. The problem that Coyne has with oceanic island accounts of colonization and diversification is that the evidence is insufficient to validate anything beyond microevolution.

As Mayr[8] wrote about the limits of change, "The reason for it is that every genotype seems to have limits to its capacity for change and this constraint might prove fatal under certain environmental changes, particularly sudden ones." In biogeographic isolation, there is abundant evidence of diversification of species and, in some cases, regression in form, but no evidence of major transformations. The life-forms that colonized oceanic islands have remained within their general life-form for millions of years, which is contrary to what would be anticipated in neo-Darwinian evolutionary theory. Nothing beyond adaptive radiation of the given life-form has occurred. This is particularly relevant to the controversy because diverse open habitat is the condition under evolutionary theory that would generate allopatric transformation of a taxon into new archetype life-forms, but changes that occurred on oceanic islands after millions of years were limited only within types. The island biodiversity evidence provides no support for evolutionary theory regarding taxonomic transformations.

Conclusion

Biogeography evidence in support of neo-Darwinian evolutionary theory is missing beyond microevolution. Colonization of oceanic islands with certain animal life and the absence of others is only a logical consequence of distance from the continents. Amphibians, reptiles, and land mammals would have a lower probability of traversing great reaches of the ocean separating the landmasses and islands than would birds and flying insects. Contemporary Creation science recognizes biodiversity, geographic distribution, and microevolutionary processes that are evident in biogeographic patterns of life-forms around the planet. Biogeography shows evidence of change, but not at the level that would result in transformations of kinds, and implies nothing that is inconsistent with Creation theory.

Endnotes

1   Mayr, *What Evolution Is,* 34.

2   M. Romano and R. L. Cifelli, "100 Years of Continental Drift," *Science* 350:6263 (2015), 915–16.

3   "Evolution of Lemurs," Wikipedia, free encyclopedia.

4   M. O. Woodburne and W. J. Zinsmeister, "Fossil Land Mammal from Antarctica," *Science* 218(1982):284–86.

5   Coyne, *Why Evolution Is True,* 116.

6   M. Godinot, "Lemuriform Origins as Viewed from the Fossil Record," *Folia Primatologica* 77, 6 (2006): 446–64.

7   R. A. Mittermeier and others, "Lemur Diversity in Madagascar," *International Journal of Primatology* 29, 6 (2008): 1607–56.

8   Mayr, *What Evolution Is,* 199.

CHAPTER 13
The Alternative Models

The two different models on the origin and diversity of life were established at very different times in history. The Creation model originated as the account of life's beginning at the time of Moses, centuries before Christ, and the traditional interpretation of the narrative since that time made the assumption that the events presented were meant to be taken literally as six twenty-four-hour days, that different kinds appeared spontaneously, and they were relatively fixed morphologically. Up to the mid-nineteenth century, that was the generally accepted interpretation of the Genesis account, although there was dissent parallel to that view throughout that time.

Darwin's theory as the preeminent alternative model on diversity wasn't established until 1859 with publication of *The Origin of Species*, and was delineated by his statement,[1] "I should infer from analogy that probably all the organic beings which ever lived on this Earth have descended from one primordial form, into which life was first breathed." The Christian community objected to Darwin's model, but the objection wasn't based on the science, rather it was the implication that God was being dismissed and Genesis relegated to myth. Darwin's advocates defined the controversy as science against religion, creating a false dichotomy, as though scientific truth discredited religion. That has persisted to the present, most apparent in the writings of ardent evolutionists such as Jerry Coyne, who believes that Creation is a discredited religiously based theory. Although such a position is consistent with many in the scientific arena, their argument is based primarily on the philosophical rejection of anything that would imply

Ernest L. Brannon

intelligent cause. But if there is to be any reconciliation, the issue clearly must be kept in the realm of the comparative interpretation of the scientific evidence.

Theistic evolutionists fall victim to the same error in differentiating between the Creation narrative and science. Kenneth Miller[2] puts the argument in the context of two alternatives, one as magic and the other as reason. Either the new species appears in a literal puff of smoke, or it occurs as the offspring of another species. But again, the rationale driving those alternatives is based on the same nineteenth-century argument. First, there is nothing that suggests Creation materializes as a puff of smoke. That is an archaic concept in how critics of Creation view the issue, as though no process is involved. Life just appears. In reality, there is always a process when something is created, and that process involves mechanisms, because that is how the natural world has been designed to function. Just as in the formation of a life. The process starts from a single cell and advances into a functional adult form by cell multiplication, differentiation, and growth.

The second is the implication that life-forms were created as species. The word used in scripture was after their own "kind," for which "species" has been substituted because of their intraspecific reproductive limitations. But species as a synonym for kind takes some liberty in the translation of the Hebrew word *miyn*, meaning to portion out or sort, and not necessarily as a narrow category. Species is a human-derived classification that designates the smallest taxonomic unit in the Carolus Linnaeus classification system originating in the 1700s. Life-forms in scripture were to bring forth after their own kind, and kind is not exclusive of diversity. Salmon are a kind of fish but include different species; ducks are a kind of bird but include different genera; marsupials are a kind of animal but include many families. In terms of its use in scripture, the meaning of the phrase "after their own kind" is determined by the object of the noun. If the reference is to a particular animal, such as in Leviticus 11:15, where eating certain animals was forbidden, it says "every raven after his kind" was to be forbidden. A raven would be limited to the genus *Corvus* made up about fifty species, or perhaps to the 120 members of the Corvidae family. Genesis 1:24, where reference was made to the living creature after its kind, suggests a much broader reference to related life-forms. Based on the nearly sixty distinct and unrelated animal body plans that first appeared in the short time frame of the Cambrian explosion, it is suggested that the term "kind" would be a reference representing a level above family as an archetype and perhaps in some cases even above class at the phyletic level of differentiation, under the Linnaeus classification system. Kinds are said to have been created, and their adaptive diversification thereafter could have been much expanded, but reproduction within that expanded diversity would still be considered within the archetype of their own kind.

Those details are not disclosed in the Holy Scriptures. The author of Genesis wrote for the audience to know only of the Creation account in a manner current for all time. Science has shown evidence of the fingerprints of the Creator, but how life was started, how the digital genetic code was established, how the complex and specific molecular machines involved in life came about, are yet unknowns in spite of the scientific rigor given to the search of life. Consequently, notwithstanding their commitment, Christian theorists know nothing about the manner of how Creation unfolded, or how long the Creation events were drawn out after they were initiated.

The two models differ in how the scientific evidence is interpreted. As discussed repeatedly, the foundation on which neo-Darwinists base their model of material cause, compared to the creationist's model of intelligent cause, differs in how natural phenomena are assessed. Neo-Darwinists contend that design is only an illusion thought to be the result of the fine-tuning of variability through natural selection over millions of years. They believe variation is caused by random genetic mistakes in the reproductive process. In contrast, the creationists believe design is real and variation has purpose in the blueprint of life. Creationists posit that much of variation is a genetic adaptive mechanism, including epigenetic processes in design to meet environmental challenges and induce diversity. So the task is to see how these two models can be reformed around the current understanding of scripture and scientific advancements, and to find common ground on the conception and diversity of life.

Reformation of the Neo-Darwinian Model

The neo-Darwinian evolutionary model has been the biological standard since the 1940s, and its proponents have resisted any reform. Their basic tenet is that everything in the universe was the outcome of natural processes, referred to as material cause or naturalism. But there is a growing point of view among scientists that the precepts of Darwinism are incomplete.[3, 4, 5] That is the first matter that needs attention. Natural phenomena occur within the standards of physical, chemical, and biological laws, and it is inconceivable that those laws were established by happenstance. They testify of a potent origin that needs to be part of the reassessment. That origin of the standards inherent in our universe has a major influence on the rendition of the model and will alter chance from its role as the predominating influence of change.

As Gred Muller and Stuart Newman[6] posited, evolutionary theory has concentrated almost exclusively on diversification of life-forms through variation and natural selection. In their assessment, a major element that needs to be addressed is origination of organismal form and structure. They make the distinction between innovation and diversification, where emphasis now needs to be given to the former. What is the theory on how phenotypes and their accompanied functional machinery were first established? What was it about the genotype that resulted in a particular phenotypic form, or a particular organ or tissue? These unknowns leave the proposition under the canopy of random variation and natural selection problematic. Such a sophisticated and complex system is nearly impossible to explain by traditional evolutionary theory as an incremental continuum of small changes and has to be given attention in reformation of the model.

The origination of mega-changes should be part of that effort. Steven J. Gould and Niles Eldredge[7] proposed punctuated equilibrium as the vehicle for an abrupt major change, because that is what the evidence shows, and the standard neo-Darwin theory has not been convincingly demonstrated as a process resulting from the gradual accumulation of microevolutionary changes. If microevolution is the only feasible pathway to macroevolution, it will be important to include a realistic time-sensitive trajectory that would involve both the number of minor progressive changes and the probabilities associated with those changes occurring as random events to provide a more robust inference.

However, the problem is exacerbated in that the present version of neo-Darwinism based on incremental functionalism is challenged by the inability of the concept to provide rational explanations about the existence of many different novelties. Michael Denton[8] has addressed this in detail in his book *Evolution: Still a Theory in Crisis*. Most apparent in this category are Open Reading Frame (ORFan) genes that have no antecedent source. In line with neo-Darwinian principles, new genes have been considered to occur by evolving gradually from pre-existing genes, but contrary to evolutionary theory of gradual incremental changes, functional ORFan genes appear to have occurred abruptly. They are found in the genomes of many different organisms, with no evidence that they were actualized gradually by functional continuums, leaving the notion that origination of these genes resulted from intrinsic developmental cause.

The origin of vertebrate limb structure is another mystery. Tetrapod limbs have no predecessor in form, and no evidence of gradual adaptation for their functions.[9] The bony elements of the fins of a fish are alleged to have been the antecedents of tetrapod limbs, but as Denton summarized the evidence on limb structure, specifically the hand and wrist or foot and ankle have no homologous structure in fish, except perhaps some similarity with the lobefins of lungfish and coelacanths. The evidence supports the position that tetrapod limbs were an emergent natural form that occurred suddenly in vertebrate origin as a result of internal cause rather than by a continuum of incremental advancements.

Another is the translation system in protein formation that seems inconceivable except by a saltation featuring both the protein and the translation mechanism as coordinated sympatric events. Proteins are formed as products of the mRNA decoding in the ribosome by tRNA, translating the polymer series of codons on the mRNA molecule into a linked series of amino acids via peptide bonds. But the translation phase of the complex protein building involves proteins as activators. They are part of the ribosome complex, and those proteins must be formed by translation in the tRNA system and thus represent an irreducible complex system, suggesting intrinsic structural organization.

Then there is the appearance of the flowering plants, the angiosperms, that have no antecedents that would fit the neo-Darwinian model of a continuous series progressing from an ancestral phylogenetic form. Denton[10] points out that none of the taxa-defining characteristics of angiosperms, including the key novelties of the flower—sepals, petals, stamens, carpels—are found in any other group of plants, extant or fossil. The absence of transitional candidates, the structure of the flower, the unique sequence of cytological events, the megaspore components, development of the embryo sac, and the double fertilization events isolate angiosperms from all other plant forms. These phenomena are explained far better as internal structural origination.

There are other challenges covered in earlier chapters that need to be addressed. How does evolution reconcile the evidence of the sudden appearance of the multiplicity of all animal body plans during the Cambrian explosion five hundred million years ago, with the absence of intermediate and ancestral forms, and no apparent linkages between phyla? What was the origination of the polymer language of the genetic code? How can long-term stasis of life-forms in the fossil record, as described by Mayr[11] and Gould,[12] be rationalized with multiple changes in form by chance in the time frame available? And how effective are chance mutations in forming complex protein structures, given the low probability of functional substitutions? Axe[13] has demonstrated that a protein of even modest length being formed by chance is so minuscule that it defies reality. Durrett and Schmidt's model[14] on the length of time for coordinated mutations of a new protein to occur by chance in humans was calculated to take millions of years. Even the addition of Andreas Wagner's concept[15] of an unlimited library of protein options requires that such textual changes in protein formation must have a synonymous construct to continue the same function. His research has shown that the library of synonymous amino acid texts is rare in a given protein neighborhood. That means the chance that a particular amino acid of the original protein text will have a readily positive substitute is unbelievably small.

What about the research that shows that not all mutations are random?[16, 17] Mutations can be induced by stressful situations,[18] and there are genome hot spots with greater tendency to mutate[19] with the right mutations in specific genes to facilitate survival. *E. coli* experiments[20] have shown feedback systems to direct mutations that allow these bacteria to utilize nutrient sources previously unavailable to them. The findings suggest that there are numerous mechanisms for the cell to induce and direct mutations to specific genes and specific sites in those genes to meet a need. Neo-Darwinian orthodoxy recognizes only random mutations, and by that predisposition, achieving complete understanding of molecular mechanisms may be circumvented.

These are possible avenues for reform that would expand the neo-Darwinian model to be consistent with more recent advancements in science that are beyond random variability and natural selection. The traditional theory is based on what Darwin proposed, but science has progressed to a level of understanding that is far in excess of what could have been imagined in the nineteenth century, and that should be reflected in a more comprehensive evolutionary model directed at macro-changes. Natural laws are standards that have been shown to exist in all of life. The universality of DNA as the blueprint for protein assembly and much of cellular function, with ATP as the stored chemical energy system, are well-recognized standards, but origination of organismal form and structure, origination of the genetic code, and origination of highly improbable events are options that should be addressed in evolutionary theory to achieve credibility in the science arena. These standards imply design, and while the proponents of evolution theory are not ready to accept the concept of a designer, consideration of design in the origin of life and its diversity in the multiplicity of forms should not be dismissed. Life itself is a feature that implies an intelligent source. The problem is that neo-Darwinism has no alternative to incremental functionalism to explain different archetypical origins, and it is left as an incomplete model to resolve the issue of diversity beyond adaptation.

Reformation of the Creation Model

Contemporary Creation is an update of the original Creation model, but Creation scientists are not unified in the details of the contemporary view. Those who adhere to Creation having occurred in six twenty-four-hour days feel that they are faithful in reverence to the wording of the Bible, and that is commendable, but in truth, they are faithful to the interpretation of the wording as found in the King

James translation by the Church of England at the beginning of the seventeenth century. Reformation must consider pertinent evidence corroborated by what has been learned through twenty-first-century science. At the other extreme, theistic evolution seems to attribute material cause apart from the Creator, disregarding the thought that material cause is simply part of the Creator's tool kit. Reformation of the Creation model has to be based on the reexamination of the assumptions that have been associated with the Mosaic narrative. While that narrative is considered the inspired word of God written in a form that is current for all time, its interpretation has been made with assumptions about the meaning of the message that conforms to the bias of the reader or is consistent with the popular trend prevalent in the era of its reading.

So let's put this in terms of the contemporary time frame, recognizing that intelligent cause is considered by all in the Creation camp as the source of the universe and is directly or indirectly responsible for all that exists. Scientific revelations on the age and composition of the universe, history of the Earth, diversity of fossils, and geographic distribution of diverse life-forms support such a restructured paradigm.

Reformation of the original model recognizes that preparation of the Earth for life has been shown to occur over great lengths of time in human terms. It involved bringing forth the composition of matter with the right elements to ensure molecular structure and to combine in certain tertiary and quaternary compounds to form the inorganic and organic material from which life would emerge. Life came even in its most basic form as a creation of a complex prototype of cell form, with its development programmed in polymer language to differentiate and function as the foundation that defines the organism and its behavior. That prototype disclosed the process by which life reproduces, adapts, and expands through the genetic code as the storehouse of information.

Through that construct of the basic unit of life among all creatures, the common standards of the cell, its division, differentiation, replication, and the bioenergy systems are viewed as evidence of a pragmatic cause-and-effect process culminating from an ingenious, omnipotent creative plan. That plan allowed life to flourish in an inexhaustible diversity, facilitated by adaptive radiation throughout Earth's dynamic environmental panoramas. The process was elaborated through alterations of those structural plans, with some adaptive changes occurring to accommodate environmental challenges that would otherwise threaten life's existence. Those processes should be viewed as mechanisms established by life's architect in his creative system of order, demonstrated by the magnitude of life's multiplicity and the functional ecological enterprise that exists in the realities of the physical world. All life-forms, from bacteria to plants to the largest mammals, are interrelated in that community, and each contributes to the symmetry of the system.

The fossil evidence indicates that when animal forms first appeared, they were morphologically distinct from one another. Such an abrupt appearance of all animal body plans that occurred during the relatively short period of the Cambrian explosion, and the absence of linkages, supports the theme that mega-differences in animal body plans occurred upon their origination. The lack of living examples that show progressive intermediate stages of life-forms also support the concept that Creation took form as separate kinds. However, reformation is to recognize that the creative time frame revealed through science is far beyond the traditional interpretation of the Genesis account. Changes in the multiplicity of life-forms ever since they first appeared indicate that microevolution has been an ongoing mechanism, stimulating diversity within typological lineages after their origination. Further, the fossil evidence suggests that such a novel mechanism included involuntary diversification determined by circumstance rather than simply a wish list of the Creator, but by design, confined within the molecular potential of the respective lineages. So reformation of the

Creation model among much of the Creation camp is to recognize the role of microevolution over time as the engine of the diversification process manifest as adaptive radiation, but within the typological lineages among distinctly created archetypes.

However, among the more theistic evolutionary-oriented scientists within the creationist camp, there is a slightly different reformation approach. Rather than first creation occurring as multiple life-forms, they consider the creative strategy to have been the creation of the original form of life, from which all other life-forms were brought forth through the process that is referred to here as creative progression. Creative progression means that Creation proceeded through a process not unlike an evolutionary sequence of life-forms in a primal plan of succession. Creative progression would have been the innovative plan and could have occurred in a relatively short geological time frame, forming the distinct archetypes, which diversified thereafter through adaptive radiation. In this manner, the different life-forms would have arisen as archetypes, but having come forth via developmental prefigured mechanisms[21] or internal causal factors from the original life-form endowed with such potential. Creative progression engenders a level of support in the Genesis account, where it is said that the waters and the Earth brought forth the moving and living creatures.[22] The wording implies that after creation of certain forms of life, it was from within the waters and from the land that subsequent life-forms were brought forth as God's creative strategy. Therefore, first life could have been endowed with a unique inherent primal structure from which all other diverse archetypes would come forth, through creative processes unfolding by intrinsic primal mechanisms within the cell machinery of that ancestral form.

Creative progression as a mechanism of mega-changes that result in the transformation of different kinds of life-forms, such as birds from dinosaurs or mammals from reptiles as a matter of design, is very controversial within the Creation camp. But the possibility that first life was created as the template on which the Creator brought forth archetypical diversity should not be dismissed. Scripture does not identify how Creation was accomplished, nor have Creation advocates been given insight as to what processes were used in the creative labor of God, except that the material of life-forms came from the dust of the ground. Given the omnipotence of the Creator, mega-changes implemented through alterations of the DNA digital code and homeotic genes controlling anatomical features of an organism could have been the forum through which Creation unfolded by divine intent, as displayed in the creation of Eve. Creative progression may have been an innovative process in the Creation paradigm, but such options have to remain as unknowns in the undisclosed details of the omnipotent Creator's strategy.

Understandably, such mega-change hypotheses are still inferential. As Ernst Mayr[23] indicated, genotypes have limits to their capacity for change. Major transformations of life-forms implied by the creative progression narrative would not be considered possible through the chance occurrence of mutations, but it would be possible through design-driven alterations of the original primal structural plan of life. Such a model is exemplified in embryogenesis. The primate embryo starts at the initial combination of gametes to form a single cell, progresses on through the multiple-cellular stage, differentiates into a recognizable fetus, develops into a functional juvenile, and grows into the ultimate mature form. That process represents the progress of a lesser to a more advanced life-form in real time. Other such tutorial models are the metamorphoses of a caterpillar into a butterfly or a tadpole into a frog as examples of mega-changes in form. Granted, such a change is the manifestation of a program in the genetic code of the larvae, but metamorphosis represents a major change of one life-form into another as a demonstration that such transformations can occur and can progress through markedly different body plans at those stages. To suggest that such mega-changes could not occur in the creation of different organisms along the lines of such a model would have to deny what can be observed in a short time frame of metamorphic transformations.

The Design Paradigm

The challenges that the neo-Darwinian model faces in reformation do not surface with the contemporary Creation design paradigm. Evolutionists allege that it is because creationists simply attribute the unknown to the supernatural. That is true to some extent, but it is not without evidence. Creation scientists are just as obligated as evolutionists to explore cause and effect, and by the evidence it is apparent that there is a universal code in the function of life-forms, that the cell works in an orderly fashion, that the complex mechanisms such as transcription and translation follow prescribed dispositions, that vesicle transport along microtubule tracks by motor proteins as well as a host of other such evidences all imply design.

Obviously, the design concept is not new. At the turn of the nineteenth century, William Paley[24] told of how one would immediately recognize design if he came across it, represented in his example by a watch lying in a field compared to a simple rock resting along the path. Paley articulated a novel perception about the design of God's hand in nature. Richard Dawkins[25] attempted to discredit Paley's insight with today's enlightened scientific understanding, but he failed to eclipse Paley's great truth about the evidence of design that is apparent to the observer. Richard Owen's nineteenth-century concept of primal order[26] was also in effect design preordained by natural laws of the Creator. So the concept is not new but is revived by the evidence of design that advancements in science have revealed. Evolution is credited as the result of natural processes, but the design paradigm identifies the source of those processes as the endowment of the Creator.

Ernest L. Brannon

Intelligent design (ID), as advocated by Meyer, Denton, and Wells of the Discovery Institute, is the most recent rendition of the design paradigm. Their concentration is on the science, and they do not identify with religion or endorse God as the agent. Their argument is that apart from the other evidence, chance cannot address the requirements of life. The origin of the encoded information system by itself is an insurmountable challenge to evolutionary theory, but not to design implemented by intelligent cause. Behe[27] explains how decoding the DNA information of a section of a polynucleotide strand and transcribing the message so it can be translated into the polypeptide language of proteins demonstrates processes that cannot be interpreted apart from the concept of design.

If the evidence favors design as the source of diversity and function of life-forms, how is design transcribed from the plan of God into the cell? Contemporary Creation posits that the cell was endowed with design functions at conception, and either through transition via creation of different typological models or through progression from an original life-form, the potential is passed on in each generation as the natural law of inheritance in the same manner as cellular differentiation is passed on. Most of the variability in the genetic code occurs as a function of genetic recombination, and that function is considered a design attribute that provides diversity within the given population.

Variation via mutation is a more enduring change in the genotype. Mutations may occur randomly and may or may not be deleterious. When mutations are artificially induced in laboratories, they are generally deleterious, but the laboratory process may cause a higher rate of negative effects than what occurs naturally. In Creation theory, randomness of mutations is also considered a design mechanism that allows the phenotype to respond to some unpredictable challenges. Such a low-cost system, that doesn't require genomic maintenance and functions by natural selection, is a mechanism of change that can markedly increase diversity beyond the scope of recombination.

Creation theory also considers what has been cited as nonrandom mutations to readily fall within the concept of design. These would be alterations that represent a specified change in response to a stimulus or to an anticipated condition. The research showing nonrandom mutations suggests that when an organism is confronted with certain challenges, there is a response at the cellular level to induce adaptive alterations of their molecular systems through micro-changes of the genotype.[28] Nonrandom alteration would be implemented by feedback in response to needs, for which genetic processes have been endowed to respond to such circumstances. Feedback systems would originate in the genetic code established at conception of the archetype.

Some genes are more susceptible to mutations than others. There are other very stable functions of the organism that appear not as prone to change, such as cell division, cell differentiation, transcription, and protein building. These processes come with the development of the system and are regulated by promoters, repressors, and controlling enzymes programmed for specific functions. The genes associated with these responses tend to be more stable because they are critical elements sustaining the phenotype.

Mutagenic mechanisms are reported the same in all cells,[29] and a biochemical mechanism for nonrandom mutations in microevolution suggests that while randomness may characterize the occurrence of many mutations, when there is a pertinent need or environmental stress, a nonrandom or directed response adjusting the genotype with a functional alteration[30] arises. The reformed system appears to be hierarchical, based on the type of challenge faced by the organism to provide the necessary flexibility and increased rate of adaptation required in the dynamic nature of the biosphere. Design implements random and nonrandom alterations of the genetic code as programmed molecular processes in situ, with specificity that promotes the alteration. However, there are limitations to such changes that are beyond the ability of the molecular system at a given time and may be beyond the options available to the typological form. For example, after Barry Hall[31] deleted the second biochemical pathway in *E. coli* that had rapidly replaced the first deleted system, no new pathway evolved after many generations of trial, indicating that there are limitations in the options available.

The hypothesis of nonrandom mutations is much in conflict with neo-Darwinian theory because nonrandomness indicates control and hence opens the prospect of an intelligent agency. Control would mean the cell has some means of identifying the gene or even the appropriate alteration necessary within the nucleotides to address the need. Cellular systems make use of feedback circuits to achieve a range of needs,[32] and there may be such feedback sensitivity-inducing transcription base substitutions. *E. coli* starved for inorganic phosphate that was shown to direct mutations to de-repress the phosphate-regulated suite of genes to get phosphate from new sources[33] is an example of such alteration. Nonrandom mutations decrease the time required for change and would facilitate mega-change in a much-reduced time frame. Such a system would still be subject to natural selection, but its pivotal role would be much reduced, given the specificity of cellular responses.

It is important to recognize the implications of the design paradigm. What neo-Darwinists cite as evidence in support of their model of chance evaporates when recognizing design as the alternative rationale. The thought that chance mutations and natural selection are sufficient to form very complex multipart biochemical systems for a particular cellular function is simply the forgone conclusion emanating from the neo-Darwinian model. The citation of the *E. coli* University of Rochester study by Berry Hall is a good example, where the deleted gene that produced the galactosidase enzyme was rapidly replaced by a new biochemical pathway to recover the bacteria's ability to metabolize lactose for food. However, laboratory demonstrations that multipart biochemical systems in bacteria can supposedly occur to meet metabolic-expressed functions doesn't mean that, in fact, the luck of the draw was responsible. When considering the improbability of such happenstance events, design as the alternative explanation becomes infinitely more logical. That alternative is simply not given consideration by the neo-Darwinian community, because they are not open to anything that has the potential of implicating intelligent cause. The result is that evidence underpinning design as the functional element in complex cellular constructs is misinterpreted by evolutionists as chance occurrence and has been reported as proof of their evolutionary model. The fact of the matter is that design cannot be eliminated as the more legitimate alternative to the basic concept of chance under Darwinian theory.

Some of the most phenomenal evidence in the Creation scenario is the manner in which the DNA double helix is designed. As reviewed in chapter 5, the partner strands of the double helix are antiparallel alignments, with adenine and guanine of one strand always paired with thymine and cytosine of the other strand. That means the nucleotide configuration of one strand obligates the antiparallel components of the partner strand, each exemplifying a different sequence of amino acids comprising a specific functional protein configuration or part thereof. So while random chance consistent with neo-Darwinism appears inconceivable as the origination of the genetic code on a single strand of DNA, the fact that the obligated nucleotide sequence of the antiparallel partner strand also has a specific but different function makes its origin by chance utterly incomprehensible.

Another example is the often-debated rotary motor of the bacterial flagellum.[34] Intelligent design enthusiasts point out that there is no logical sequence of intermediate evolutionary stages that would explain the occurrence of the drive shaft, rotor assembly, universal joint, propeller, and sealing bushings through the outer membrane of the bacteria having occurred by stepwise chance advancements. The contemporary Creation perspective is that the system is irreducibly complex and functions as a complete operational unit, fated at conception and assembled in a predetermined manner for such utility. The concept of random chance consistent with neo-Darwinism in assembling such complex and interrelated structures is implausible, but that doesn't mean the system wasn't assembled consistent with an innovative design algorithm. Science has yet to recognize any algorithm associated with form and function conceived by the omnipotent force. And because such a force is rejected by neo-Darwinists, there is no alternative they can turn to other than chance. But even if one could explain what design enthusiasts consider irreducible by progressive alterations of other systems recruited for such purpose, the concept that the assembly occurred by chance rather than by design is incredible.

Conclusion

The neo-Darwinian model is a paradigm of chance based on random variation and natural selection leading to macroevolution. It is incomplete in that it does not deal with origination of organismal structure, the genetic code, development, differentiation of cells, cell machinery, or perceived saltations. These are deficiencies that impact the credibility of the model and must be addressed in terms of twenty-first-century science. That is true also for the Creation model. Reformation must recognize scientific detail about the age of the universe, the Earth, fossil evidence, and the role that adaptive radiation had in the diversification of life-forms over time. It is acknowledged that details of the recorded Genesis account do not specify the manner in which creation was performed, nor does it reject the possibility that creative progression may have been the manner in which the assembly of those life-forms was facilitated. The evidence provides a more inclusive design paradigm consistent with the broader category of kind forthcoming from both scripture and scientific research, and this needs to be applied in the reconciliation of the worldviews. Both worldviews need to recognize that the omnipotent force is beyond human intelligence and understand that the omnipotent plan of life is manifest largely as an unfolding of involuntary processes.

Endnotes

1   Darwin, *The Origin of Species*, 455.
2   Miller, *Finding Darwin's God*, 99.
3   S. A. Kauffman, *The Origin of Order: Self-Organization and Selection in Evolution* (Oxford: Oxford University Press, 1993).
4   Wagner, *The Arrival of the Fittest*.
5   G. B. Müller and S. A. Newman, Eds., *Origination of Organismal Form: Beyond the Gene in Developmental and Evolutionary Biology* (Cambridge, MA: MIT Press, 2003).
6   Müller and Newman, *Origination of Organismal Form*.
7   S. J. Gould and N. Eldredge, "Punctuated Equilibrium Comes of Age," *Nature* 366 (1993):223–27.
8   Denton, *Evolution: Still a Theory in Crisis*.
9   Denton, *Evolution: Still a Theory in Crisis*, 157–69.
10 Denton, *Evolution: Still a Theory in Crisis*, 145–56.
11 Mayr, *What Evolution Is*, 278–79.
12 Gould, *The Structure of Evolutionary Theory*, 749–65.
13 D. Axe, "Estimating the Prevalence of Protein Sequences Adopting Functional Enzyme Folds," *Journal of Molecular Biology* 341 (2004): 1295–315.
14 R. Durrett and D. Schmidt, "Waiting for Two Mutations: With Applications to Regulatory Sequence Evolution and the Limits of Darwinian Evolution," *Genetics* 180 (2008), 1501–509.
15 Wagner, *The Arrival of the Fittest*.
16 Barbara E. Wright, "A Biochemical Mechanism for Nonrandom Mutations and Evolution," *Journal of Bacteriology* 182, 11 (2000) 2993–3001.
17 Martincorena, Seshasayee, and Luscombe, "Evidence of Non-Random Mutation Rates," 95–98.
18 Cairns, Overbaugh, and Miller, "The Origin of Mutants," 142–45.

19 Shee, Gibson, and Rosenberg, "Two Mechanisms Produce Mutation Hotspots," 714–21.
20 Waldherr, Eissing, and Allgower, "Analysis of Feedback Mechanisms."
21 Denton, *Evolution: Still a Theory in Crisis*, 115–17.
22 King James Bible. Genesis 1:22, 24.
23 Mayr, *What Evolution Is*, 199.
24 Paley, *Natural Theology*.
25 Dawkins, *The Blind Watchmaker*.
26 R. Owens, *On the Nature of Limbs* (London: John VanVoorst, 1849).
27 Behe, *Darwin's Black Box*, 286–92.
28 Wright, Schmidt, and Minnick, "Kinetic Models Reveal the *In Vivo* Mechanisms," 129–37.
29 Wright, Schmidt, and Minnick, "Kinetic Models Reveal the *In Vivo* Mechanisms," 129–37.
30 Wright, Schmidt, and Minnick, "Kinetic Models Reveal the *In Vivo* Mechanisms," 129–37.
31 Hall, "Evolutionary Potential of the *ebg* A Gene," 514–17.
32 Smits, Kuipers, and Veening, "Phenotypic Variation in Bacteria," 259–71.
33 K. Makino, M. Amemura, S. K. Kim, A. Nakata, and H. Shinagara, "Mechanism of Transcriptional Activation of the Phosphate Regulon in *Escherichia coli*," in A. Torriani-Gorini, E. Yagil, S. Silver S, editors, *Phosphate in Microorganisms: Cellular and Molecular Biology* (Washington DC: ASM Press, 1994) 5–12.
34 Behe, *Darwin's Black Box*, 69–73.

CHAPTER 14
The Genesis Account

Genesis is the book of beginnings, the beginning of heaven and Earth, the beginning of life, and the beginning of human institutions. The Genesis account of Creation contained in the first book of the Bible was the source of debate about the origin of life long before Darwin published *On the Origin of Species*. When Darwin attributed the diversity of life to the happenstance of a common ancestor that evolved into the multiplicity of forms rather than to Creation by God, it caused a firestorm of controversy, because it was dismissing God as Creator. Early in the nineteenth century, the traditional view of Creation was the literal six twenty-four-hour-day events, and that interpretation is still claimed by some Christians, including Young Earth Creationists (YEC),[1] where the Earth and all of its life-forms were brought into existence less than ten thousand years ago. As the natural sciences progressed into the twenty-first century, scientific orthodoxy made clear that such a traditional position was contrary to how science was interpreted, and as a result, Genesis was rejected by the proponents of evolution and viewed simply as a religious myth.[2]

But those opponents are wrong on two accounts. First, the Creation account is not contrary to scientific evidence. The opposition base their argument against the secularist's view of Creation that had its origin long before the nineteenth century and is as obsolete as Thomas Huxley's nineteenth-century scientific description of the cell.[3] Second, it is the anti-theists' interpretation of Genesis that is contrary to scientific evidence. Naturalism recognizes no God, and from that perspective, the anti-theistic view of origins would certainly be contrary to the Creation message and simply attributed to material cause. Consequently, with such a view, there would be no other option but to believe that life was happenstance, that it had no purpose and no direction. Given that perspective, naturalism's allegation is that the Genesis account of Creation has no scientific merit.

We are reminded that Genesis was not meant to be a scientific document. It gives the description of the beginning and outlines the sequence of events associated with that beginning. But the issue addressed in this treatise comes down to the question of whether it is scientifically credible. Genesis is attributed to Moses, who wrote the book several thousand years ago, long before scientific knowledge was acquired about the universe or the biological details of life. Christians consider Genesis either as allegorical or the literal, inspired, inerrant word of God, but in either case, it should be consistent with the evidence that has been acquired about those beginnings and thus scientifically relevant. There are significant differences in the interpretation of Genesis by theologian scholars, who emphasize the deeper spiritual implications of the Hebrew text, but that is beyond the task at hand. This review will concentrate on the scientific perspective of the written message and its scientific credibility.

The Creation Narrative

The first verse of Genesis says, "In the beginning God created heaven and earth." "Created" is the translation of the Hebrew word "*bara*," meaning to create or make as in the formative process. It is apparent that Creation was not instantaneous, since the Genesis account was spread over six phases during which the sequence of events was described. This is significant, because it gives insight to the manner in which God proceeded to accomplish his creative objectives to prepare the Earth for habitation. Genesis 1:1 doesn't say what mechanisms were involved, only that there was a beginning. Nor does it say anything about the length of time involved in the processes related to that beginning. It just says that there was a beginning of heaven and Earth, as the first recorded creative act of God.

Hubble's scientific analysis confirmed that there was a beginning of our universe. No longer is the universe thought to be eternal by the scientific community but rather that there was a point in the past where everything we observe today progressed from what has been referred to as the Big Bang, when out of nothing, the universe sprang forth. But science has revealed much about that beginning placed approximately 13.7 billion years ago, the pathway of elements being formed, the sequence of cosmic events, and the appearance of Earth. Science has not yet discovered what mechanisms were involved in initiating the Big Bang beginning, only the progressive series of events that occurred thereafter. The point is that science agrees with the message of scripture that there was a beginning, and there is nothing that science has concluded that is contrary to the first verse of Genesis.

The second verse tells about the condition of Earth in that process. It says, "And the earth was without form, and void, and darkness was upon the face of the deep. And the Spirit of God moved upon the face of the waters." This verse says that there was a point after the beginning when the Earth, as the object of creation, was yet without form. The condition of the Earth was represented as a void. Further, that darkness was upon the face of the deep, which is interpreted here as the description of darkness in deep space. And the Spirit of God, or the formative cause, is said to have moved or hovered over the waters. Waters is translated from the Hebrew word *mayim*, but depending on its use, mayim has different meanings in both the spiritual and physical realms. It represents water in liquid form, and it can also have the connotation of a liquid mixture of gases and elements. In the second verse of Genesis, it appears that the latter, the primordial liquid of gas and elements, best describes the intent of how the word is to be understood in that message. Nothing more is given in scripture than that statement about the condition of Earth that was involved in the subsequent formative process.

How is this reconciled with the scientific account following the beginning? Astrophysicists tell us that after the Big Bang, the cosmos was filled with ironized gases. Those neutrons, protons, and electrons spewed forth from a singular point in the extreme temperatures of the explosive beginning and immediately thereafter started to cool as they spread out. Upon reaching < 3000° Kelvin, hydrogen was formed and later helium. These elements absorbed photons, so the universe was opaque, and darkness characterized that period referred to as the cosmos dark age,[4] which is said to have lasted four hundred million years. The scientific data is consistent with scripture in describing the conditions in the universe before the solar system was formed, and darkness was upon the face of the deep.

After the formative cause moved upon the face of the liquid mixture of elements and atomic particles massing after the Big Bang, the first formative day is recorded in the third through fifth verses of Genesis 1, which mention the appearance of light.

> And God said let there be light: and there was light. And God saw the light, that it was good: And God divided the light from the darkness. And God called the light Day, and the darkness he called Night. And the evening and the morning were the first day.

This describes the first event that came to pass after the beginning, and it is said to have constituted the first day of the formative sequence.

The word "day" has been a major source of controversy from the time of the traditional interpretation of six twenty-four-hour days of Creation. However, as Kenneth Miller[5] concluded, even a literal reading of Genesis does not require the believer to subscribe to the six twenty-four-hour-day instantaneous Creation. Reverend C. I. Scofield of the Scofield Reference Bible[6] would have agreed. At the end of the nineteenth century, he was careful to interpret the original scriptures with his consulting editorial board, all doctors of divinity, in a manner more consistent with Saint Augustine's *The Literal Meaning of Genesis*[7] (AD 415), where days were metaphors for the separate phases in the Genesis narrative, and the origin of the day-age concept where days were interpreted to represent ages. The day-age interpretation was challenged by the traditionalists, who considered day simply as a twenty-four-hour period, and that version is still advocated by the Creation Institute of the YEC.

However, there are three meanings to the word "day" in scripture, two of which are used in this passage. Day is the English translation of the Hebrew word *yowm*, and as described in verse 4, its meaning is light. "And God called the light Day, and the darkness he called Night." Here, "Day" describes light as visible radiance, in contrast to "Night," which means darkness, or the absence of light. In this usage, there is no time element associated with the word. This is an important distinction, because day is a reference to the general phenomenon of the appearance of light, often a synonym of truth.

The second meaning of *yowm* refers to a period or a phase or a process during which the purposes of God are to be illuminated or accomplished, such as the day of the Lord in Zachariah 14:1. Again, in this application, "day" is not an expression of time but a consummate declaration of a phenomenon, such as a specific formulation of a major creative event in the Creation account that continues onward. This is believed to be the meaning of *yowm* as it is used to express the formative events of Genesis, representing six phases associated with the readiness of the Earth for the presence of man. Each phase represents a process beginning in the ancient past and culminating with the final state or advancement expressed by the author. "And the evening and the morning" are metaphors referring to the culmination of that action as evening, and where significant events blossomed forth described as the morning, the dawning of a truth.

The third meaning of *yowm* is in reference to that part of the twenty-four-hour day when sunlight shines forth, as in Matthew 25:13: "Ye know not the day or the hour." In this case, it is reference to a specific source of light, the sun, and the duration of the light as daytime. Sunlight has an hourly time element associated with it, but sunlight isn't mentioned until the fourteenth to nineteenth verses of Genesis.

Astrophysicists have determined that there was a four-hundred-million-year dark age of the universe after the beginning. During that time, no stars or galaxies were forming until the latter part of that period, but as they coalesced, their light was absorbed by hydrogen and helium and some of the other elements being produced. However, at the end of the four-hundred-million-year period, re-ionization was initiated and had advanced to the point where the universe became translucent, allowing the light from the forming massive molten nuclear furnaces in galaxy clusters to be transmitted unrestrained. The cause of re-ionization has not been determined, but the visibility of that light is what is thought to have represented the first event recorded in scripture after the beginning. "Let there be light" is consistent with the scientific evidence about when light would first have appeared in the universe. Stars that formed during the latter part of the dark age as an ongoing process were the source of light early in the evolving universe.

The words "Let there be light" do not imply a creative act but rather the appearance of light as the consequence of the aftermath of the Big Bang beginning. When God gave that command, it is associated with the subsequent appearance of light, but there had to be a mechanism through which light was generated. Science indicates that light was first shown forth when re-ionization changed the universe from opaque to translucent, allowing starlight to pass freely. While it qualifies as a onetime continuing event, it involved a process described by science that was responsible for it happening, which is how intelligent cause would have functioned. There is always a process through which the Lord works out everything in conformity with the purpose of his will, and as science discovers the process, it is discovering the fingerprints of God.

The second day or phase is recorded in Genesis 1:6–8:

> And God said, Let there be a firmament in the midst of the waters and let it divide the waters from the waters. And God made the firmament, and divided the waters which were under the firmament from the waters which were above the firmament: and it was so. And God called the firmament Heaven, and the evening and the morning were the second day.

This refers to the formation of heaven from the Hebrew *shameh*, meaning the observable arch of the sky, which would include the celestial bodies of our galaxy, the Milky Way. At this point, our galaxy was forming and separated from the mayim or liquid mixture of gases and other star clusters of the universe. Earth as a planet had not yet solidified, but the solar system was forming as part of the firmament. To what extent the planets had developed at this point is uncertain, but they would appear as the sun was forming in its role as the major presence in the arch of Earth's sky.

Here again, the formation of our galaxy in preparation for the existence of life was a process so important that it is dealt with as a separate phase in Creation's account. How long that preparation phase lasted is an unknown but appears to have involved billions of years, if the astrophysicists are correct. The process set the stage for the formation of planet Earth with all the chemical constituents, water, and the atmosphere required for an inhabitable environment. "And

God called the firmament Heaven, and the evening and the morning were the second day."

The third day is referred to in verses 9–13, involving the appearance of dry land, the seas, and plant life:

> And God said, let the waters under the heaven be gathered together unto one place, and let the dry land appear: and it was so. And God called the dry land Earth; and the gathering together of the waters called he Seas: and God saw that it was good.

So the third phase is when the Earth, previously mentioned as being without form, now solidified to become a planet, described as dry land, Pangaea, when the liquid elements (mayim) were gathered together, forming the solid state, and the accumulation of surface waters. The "gathering together" indicates that these events were processes, rather than sudden existence or spontaneous creations, and as processes, they involved a time element of some unspecified length.

Science indicates that when the Earth had its beginning 4.5 billion years ago, it was in an amorphous state that coalesced as hot magma from the debris of materials involved in forming the sun. It was in that condition for nearly a billion years, during which major changes took place, and during the aftermath of its formation those changes involved cooling, solidification, and a shroud of atmosphere, including water vapor. The source of liquid water was thought by some scientists as having originated from asteroids transporting water that subsequently reached the Earth, but it has been suggested that such events would not account for the entire magnitude of water present. And thus it is thought that much of the water must have been present as a dense atmosphere of vapor originating as a component of mayim, the gaseous elements that solidified as Earth was formed. When Earth solidified, the water vapor condensed into its liquid state and was then supplemented with water from asteroids during the billion years thereafter. Scripture is consistent with such an account.

The third phase also included the first appearance of plants:

> And God said, Let the earth bring forth grass, the herb yielding seed, and the fruit tree yielding fruit after his kind, whose seed is in itself, upon the earth: and it was so. And the earth brought forth grass, and herb yielding seed after his kind, and the fruit tree yielding fruit, whose seed is in itself, after his kind: and God saw that it was good. And the evening and the morning were the third day.

Several things are significant in these verses about plants. Plants were brought forth from the Earth. They were brought forth as the first form of biological life on the planet, and there was a diversity of plant forms involved. The word "created" was not used for this third formation process, but rather the phrases used were, "whose seed is in itself," and "the earth brought forth." This is noteworthy. A plant coming forth from a seed is the most descriptive reference to explain life's beginning from the first functional biochemical construct that was formed from earthly matter. How else would the ancient commentator describe such a revelation before scientific terms had even arisen? A seed is the basic unit from which development progresses to the more advanced form, and in this application, it refers to the beginning of the first living organism.

The statement that "the earth brought forth" describes a process rather than reference to a spontaneous creation. That process is not described, but reference to the Earth bringing forth a variety of plant forms implies that plant variety was brought forth as events unfolded over the third formative phase. This suggests that the Earth bringing forth was an ongoing process, indicating that the third formative phase was the beginning of plant life that is ongoing to the present, with different varieties of plants brought forth, ultimately forming what is referred to as grass, herb-yielding seed, and fruit trees in reference to the variety of plants originating from seeds or first cells, such as algae in the seas.

Finally, the plants were generated from seed "after his kind." This is a statement consistent with what is known about life's generation. The statement that plants were to generate fruit after their kind delineates a limitation that is observed in the reproduction of life-forms. Reproductive limitations confine plants to reproduce within their typological lineage or archetype. The word "kind" is from the Hebrew word *myin*, meaning to portion out or sort, as a category of life-forms. As discussed in chapter 13, it has mistakenly been referred to as species, because that is the scientific classification of a category that is confined within the limits of reproductive success. Genesis does not limit kinds to species. As covered previously, kind includes a range of varieties above the species level. Plants also are more prone to hybridization than animals, and the hybrid can maintain both sets of parental chromosomes (polyploidy), giving it a new form, but still considered within its own kind.

The takeaway message of the multifaceted third day is that the primordial elements gathered to form the Earth and the seas, and plant life was brought forth from seeds that originated upon Earth. Plants were before animals, which is consistent with the fossil record and scientific reasoning, since plant respiration is a source of oxygen for animal life, and plants are photosynthetic, producing carbohydrates and other nutrients necessary to sustain animals. Scripture and science are consistent about first life, but the details about the mechanisms are not provided in either the message or the science.

Verses 14 through 19 of the fourth day involve the celestial bodies: sun, moon, and stars:

And God said, Let there be lights in the firmament of heaven to divide the day from the night; and let them be for signs, and for seasons, and for days, and for years: And let them be for lights in the firmament of heaven to give light upon the earth: and it was so. And God made two great lights; the greater light to rule the day and the lesser light to rule the night: and he made the stars also. And God set them in the firmament of the heaven to give light upon the earth, And to rule over the day and over the night, and to divide the light from the darkness: and God saw that it was good. And the evening and the morning were the fourth day.

Here is where the sunlight is first identified as the source of the twenty-four-hour day. Reference is made specifically to the kind of light that comes from the sun, and its role in determining the twenty-four-hour day, the timekeeper, the determinant of the seasons, and the calendar.

However, the issue here is not the content of the verses in the description and function of the sun, moon, and stars, but rather the chronological disparity between the preparation of the Earth in the third formative day, and the description of these celestial bodies in the fourth formative day. Science contends that the first stars were formed chronologically long before our solar system, and the moon appeared well after the Earth was formed. Are these verses in Genesis contrary to science? Three related points address that issue.

First, God brought forth light on that first formative day, the galaxy was present in the arch of the sky during the second formative day, and during the third formative day, the Earth took on its solid state, and life in the form of plants was initiated. These verses imply that the requirements for plant life were present, and that would have included the substrate, atmosphere, and at least diffuse light, indicating that the sun was present when the galaxy was formed, as were most of the stars we now observe. The moon is thought to have been formed when a large asteroid struck Earth, causing a shattering of part of the planet, the debris from which coalesced into the moon early after the Earth was formed, so the reference to the sun, moon, and stars doesn't refer to the creation of these celestial bodies during the fourth formative phase. Star formation has been an ongoing process through time.

Second, the words used by the ancient commentator do not imply a creative act. Create in Hebrew is *bara*, as used "In the beginning God created." But that was not the word used in these verses of the fourth phase. The words used were descriptive, saying, "Let there be lights in the firmament of heaven," indicating the appearance of light as observed from Earth. And the word "made" used in the phrase "And God made two great lights," is *a'sah* in Hebrew, meaning to bring forth or make visible. It is believed that when the Earth was formed, the atmosphere around the planet was very dense, much like that which is observed around the other planets of the solar system. But when the asteroid struck Earth and the debris coalesced, forming the moon, it is thought that the dense atmosphere that had engulfed the Earth dissipated, and the celestial bodies then became visible from Earth.

The third and most germane point to this understanding is that these verses apply to the role of the sun, moon, and stars with respect to Earth as the center of God's plan involving humankind. The verses were not meant to represent their chronological creative order, but rather to represent their role in support of Earth in the creative exposition. The Earth was made ready for the introduction of life during the third phase, and during the fourth phase, the light of the celestial bodies was rhetorically described as the luminaries, the *ma'ohr*, shining upon Earth, and thus their function for order on Earth. So what appeared as an incongruity in the chronology of events is amended by the understanding that their order in the formative sequence was reference to their purpose centered on Earth.

The next event set is the fifth formative day; the creation of animal life in verses 20–23:

And God said, Let the waters bring forth abundantly the moving creatures that hath life, and the fowl that may fly above the earth in the open firmament of heaven. And God created great whales and every living creature that moveth, which the waters brought forth abundantly, after their kind, and every winged fowl after his kind: and God saw that it was good. And God blessed them, saying be fruitful, and multiply, and fill the waters in the sea and let fowl multiply in the earth. And the evening and the morning were the fifth day.

Several things are significant in the fifth phase. First, the word "created" was used the second time, following God's creation of heaven and Earth in the first verse. The second point is that animal life followed after plant life. Again the sequence is noteworthy, because animals must depend on plants to exist. Third, animal life first took form in or on the water, not on land. Fourth, the creation event was not spontaneous, because it says the "waters brought forth abundantly," interpreted to mean a process was involved, consistent with animal life occurring in two of the six phases of the Creation saga. The fifth point is that the word "creatures" indicates that the bringing forth included a diversity of different animal forms over that continuing period of time. And finally, the fowls of the air were brought forth to multiply in the Earth, as the last-mentioned kind of animal life, and all were brought forth after their kind.

In the description of the fifth day of the Creation narrative, there is a significant commonality of events between scripture and science. Based on the fossil record, animals followed the appearance of plants. Animals first appeared in the water, consistent with the fossil evidence. They were brought forth abundantly, as testified by the extreme number of different fossils and the diversity of living biota. Animal life occurred over a period of time, and they reproduced after their own kind. The mention of whales indicates that bringing forth was a process that was the culmination of a typological lineage, which by the scientific determination of succession agrees that they were the most recent within their lineage, and the plural form of the noun indicates there was a diversity of forms represented. Although "whale" was translated from the Hebrew word *tanniyn*, it can refer to great sea serpents as well as whales, and that too would be consistent with fossil evidence. Finally, every winged fowl indicates that more than one kind was implied. They were the last animals mentioned, which corresponds with their more recent appearance in the fossil evidence.

The last event set is the sixth formative day in verses 24–31:

> And God said, Let the earth bring forth the living creature after his kind, cattle, and creeping thing and beast of the earth after his kind: and it was so. And God made the beast of the earth after his kind, and cattle after their kind, and everything that creepeth upon the earth after his kind: and God saw that it was good."

Several significant points are made apparent in that ancient scripture, meant to provide an overview of the creation and diversification of life.

A major point is that after God created all living creatures in the fifth formative period, in the sixth phase, he says, "Let the earth bring forth the living creature after his kind." The words used indicate that the sixth phase was not a creative process the same as before, but rather the continuation of the bringing forth of life's diversity among the "living" creatures that invaded the land. This suggests that during the sixth phase, animal life that had begun in the waters expanded their range to living on land and diversified into many forms within their archetypical kinds, indicated by the classes articulated as the beast (reptiles?), cattle (mammals?), and creeping things (invertebrates?). The description of bringing forth types indicates that the second stage of diversification was a process of expanding into new habitat that involved diversification of animals from those remaining in the waters. The process of bringing forth is not specified, but it resulted in a variety of animal life on land over that formative period.

In essence, the sixth formative period represents the time in which all life-forms were brought forth by natural processes as God ordained after the events of the fifth formative period. Animal forms were created in the water and then brought forth or expanded throughout the waters, while other life-forms were brought forth from the waters through diversification to flourish thereafter on the land. It is apparent that animal life made a transition from water to land, but how that transpired is not explained. Moses was inspired to provide the history of life that preceded him, and his reference was based on animals of his day. He referred to the beasts, cattle, and creeping things that came forth "after their kind," which means they came forth from life-forms that preceded them, indicating they were descendants of their archetypical ancestors, which is also consistent with scientific reasoning. They were descendants of life-forms that were not necessarily the identical morphological form of that ancestor, but they were after their kind. It is apparent upon looking at the skeletal morphology of amphibians, reptiles, and mammals that they share a common skeletal anatomy in the structure of vertebrae and limbs that testify of similarities in design. There is nothing inconsistent in these verses with what observation and science have disclosed in the laboratory and the field.

The verses of the sixth phase then go on with the most critical aspect of the Creation narrative:

And God said, Let us make man in our image, after our likeness: and let them have dominion over the fish of the sea, and over the fowl of the air, and over the cattle and all of the earth, and over every creeping thing that creepeth upon the earth. So God created man in his own image, in the image of God created he him; male and female created he them. And God blessed them, and God said unto them, Be fruitful, and multiply, and replenish the earth, and subdue it: and have dominion over the fish and the sea, and over the fowl of the air, and over every living thing that moveth upon the earth. And God said, Behold I have given you every herb bearing seed, which is upon the face of all the earth, and every tree, in the which is the fruit of tree yielding seed; to you it shall be for meat. And to every beast of the earth, and to every fowl of the air, and to everything that creepeth upon the earth, wherein there is life, I have given green herb for meat: and it was so. And God saw everything that he had made, and behold, it was very good. And the evening and the morning were the sixth day.

These last verses of the first chapter of Genesis say that humankind was created, and as male and female, they were created in the image of God. When God said, "Let us make man in our image, after our likeness," it was a decisive declaration. God is a spirit,[8] so when the narrative says that man was created in the image of God, it means that man was created in the spiritual image of God, not the physical. God is spirit, and man was to have the likeness of God's spirit. That spiritual image means God-consciousness, the discernment of spiritual things, and the level of understanding that is apart from worldly knowledge and the other intellectual qualities of humankind.

Genesis 2:7 says, "And the Lord God formed man of the dust of the ground and breathed into his nostrils the breath of life, and man became a living soul." When God breathed into the nostrils of man the breath of life, it was at that moment that man was made in the spiritual image of God, and that spiritual transformation was the *foremost* event in all of creation, in effect underpinning our spiritual status that set us apart from all other creatures. Although man's body was fashioned from the same Earth substance as other life-forms, man was absolutely unique by the act of being made in God's spiritual likeness. Up to that moment in time, all of creation was in the physical realm. Even the body of the one who was created from the dust of the ground was only in the physical realm until the moment that God breathed into his nostrils. At that moment, man became a new creation; he became a living soul, a child of God. That man was Adam, and that event demarks the moment of Adam's spiritual creation: the spiritual foundation of humankind.

With that distinction, the verses above express God's intent for humankind, and that was to multiply and to be endowed with the responsibility to exercise dominion over all of creation, over all of life on Earth, and in essence to care for the living resources that God provided in life's ecological networks. Plants were recognized as food resources for humankind and for all animal life-forms, as well. Caring for those living resources was the provision that would sustain humanity on Earth.

The end of the first chapter concludes the six phases of the Creation narrative and completes the creative and formative events of the Genesis account. The prominent aspect of the narrative is its parallel with the scientific evidence accrued about the beginning of the cosmos, the formation of the earth and the life that arose thereafter. Although written thousands of years ago, the general narrative is consistent with what scientists have concluded about the beginning and the sequence of events culminating with the existence of humans.

The Seventh Day

Following the Creation events of the first chapter was the seventh day recorded in verses 1–4 of the second chapter of Genesis, which summarized the account of Creation, saying,

> Thus the heavens and the earth were finished, and all the host of them. And on the seventh day God ended his work which he had made; and he rested on the seventh day from all his work which he had made. And God blessed the seventh day, and sanctified

it: because that in it he had rested from all his work which God created and made. These are the generations of the heavens and the earth when they were created, in the day the Lord had made the earth and the heavens.

The seventh day is significant in both the discussion of its purpose and the time element covered in the Genesis Creation account. It is here that the meaning of the day, as it was used in chapter 1 of Genesis, is better understood. The seventh day represents God's rest, in essence the completion of God's preparation for his redemptive relationship with man. The seventh day was "sanctified," which in the Hebrew is *godesh*, meaning to consecrate, dedicate, make holy, or set apart for the service of God. That finished work of the seventh day was the "rest" that continues to the present time. The point is clarified in the fourth chapter in the book of Hebrews,[4] where God's rest is perpetually available to the people of God. Therefore, the seventh day, the day of rest, is a state of being, and thus not a twenty-four-hour day, but a phase that started at the point when God entered his rest and has continued to the present time, as indicated by the invitation to enter for those who choose to accept his grace. His redemptive invitation to enter God's rest remains open to us all, a period of time covering thousands of years, but referred to as the seventh day.

The evidence that the word "day" represents a creative phase in the Genesis account of Creation is further verified by the last verse presented above. "These are the generations of the heavens and the earth when they were created, in the day the Lord had made the earth and the heavens." Here it is very apparent that "day" refers to the whole period of time when the Lord made the Earth and the heavens. The verse speaks of the generations of the heavens and the Earth, in the day the Lord made them, referring to the Creation saga of the heavens and Earth, and thus "in the day" has no relationship to a twenty-four-hour day, but rather to the enlightenment of the events of God's Creation.

As demonstrated throughout this interpretation of the Genesis account, there has been an integration of scientific information with a contemporary Creation narrative. But there is more to that story as a final note related to the six formative phases. All ended in the statement, "and God saw that it was good." This shows that Creation was an assembly of events, each of which satisfied God. Those phrases signify that the Creation was something we would call perfect. But just as the world we witness today is imperfect, it means that a transition from perfect to imperfect occurred at some point after the Creation events. While this has spiritual implications that are not addressed in this analysis, it does imply that some of what is observed as imperfect functions of the organism, cellular components, and man himself were the result of that transition from perfection to imperfection. That situation is addressed in scripture in much detail, but suffice it to say that while the design of life was perfect, the offset in imperfection thereafter had repercussions that have continued throughout all of creation.

Interpretative Alternatives

The scientists of the Creation camp agree that God created man, but the membership will differ in how these details are deciphered, as demonstrated by the differences in the interpretation of the meaning of "day." It is here that we see where judgment is much influenced by one's theology. The fact is that the scriptures do not describe the creation phenomenon, so the members of the Creation camp are left with a significant unknown when contemplating what was involved in the creation of life. It can be interpreted as a spontaneous event where an object or life-form is brought instantly into existence, but it can also be interpreted as the product of an assembly process. An engineer can invent a new apparatus by assembling the mechanisms that make it function, and it would be said he created the apparatus, even though it was worked through a process. In reality, it makes little difference whether the formative events were instantaneous by God's command or were to unfold progressively by an inherent design endowed by an omnipotent Creator. In either case, life-forms were brought forth or were created and were to reproduce within the limitations of their kind.

Although the traditional interpretation of the Creation saga appeared to assume that plants, animals, and humans were created in a spontaneous manner, that perspective is quite different from the concept of the creative progression. This latter view is that God created first life as the prototype endowed to diversify into many different life-forms. Recall that the term "creative progression" is used to distance the discussion from secular evolution and to emphasize that God may have designed life-forms to advance in diversity beyond what is recognized as adaptive changes, changes at the mega level that have mistakenly been interpreted by evolutionists as the culmination of chance events. These differences in interpretation point out the absence of sufficient descriptive explanation of the Creation phenomenon in scripture to indicate how creation unfolded. Most certainly an omnipotent Creator could create plants, animals, and humans in any manner that he willed. However, we can gain some insight about the nature of life's creation events by concentrating on some of the details as they are revealed to us in scripture.

The first point is man's physical origination. The scriptures say man's physical body was formed from the dust of the ground, the same for all animal life as stated in Genesis 2:1. Man's flesh and bone are largely proteins composed of carbon, nitrogen, oxygen, and phosphorus. It is the same as with nucleotides that make up DNA, the universal genetic code in nearly all of animal life. The composition of the cell's machinery originates from Earth's substance, and those materials are fashioned into sustaining mechanisms and the functional molecular complexes they are part of. So man's body and the creatures brought forth before him are all made up from the elements of matter, the dust of the ground. This is consistent with how science identifies the origin of life.

The second point in ascertaining God's creative approach is that it can be described as having unfolded through processes. His laws are processes that we see functioning in the cosmos, in the workings of this world, in life, and in bodily development, just as an embryo develops by the process of differentiation progressing on to maturity. The declarations of the formative events involved processes described by terms such as gathering together, bringing forth, appearing, and yielding. So the manifestation of the labor of God can be said to involve processes, which provide a more pragmatic view of the Creation phenomena and can be better understood through scientific reasoning when contemplating how the six major events of the Creation narrative might have unfolded.

More specific detail about the creative process is found in the description of the creation of the first woman. We are told in Genesis 2:21 that God took from the side (*tsalah*) of Adam and created Eve. In other words, God took cellular material from Adam as the donor, apparently components containing the X chromosome construct of DNA, and formed the woman, Eve. In retrospect, while Eve's physical being was of the material that originated from the dust of the ground, as with all other life-forms, her creative pathway was initiated from donor materials well advanced in molecular form. The significant aspect of that revelation is that Eve was not created from scratch. Her creation phenomenon involved taking cellular material from one life-form to create another life-form, a process not unlike the demonstrated potential of cellular material in cloning experiments.

That description of God's creative labor provides considerable latitude in contemplating the Creation saga of humankind. Creative progression would imply that the description of Eve's creation leaves the possibility that Adam too was created using the DNA template of life-forms that had preceded him. Some might ask, was the description of Eve's creation given to provide insight in the manner that God implemented the creative process? Rather than the creation events occurring as repeated duplications of nearly the exact structure of the genetic code, cellular machinery, and the supporting energy system independently for each kind of life from scratch, Creation by the more omniscient approach of our God may have created archetypical life-forms by using the constructs of his previous creations in the process of bringing forth the different kinds of life. The cellular material still originated from Earth substance, the dust of the ground, and life was thus created, but the pathway through the creation events illuminated by the creative description of Eve opens the door to the possibility that the method of "bringing forth" the subsequent life-forms identified as cattle, creeping things, beasts of the Earth, and ultimately man was not each from scratch, but by a progressive development of life-forms from molecular components of those that preceded them. Such a Creation process could be the plan of an omnipotent Creator and accomplished involuntarily as a matter of design to provide the diversity necessary to sustain what scientists refer to as the world's ecological communities.

The third point of reference is the dual nature of man's creation. The second chapter of the narrative gives insight into that creation event. When combining the verse[9] that says, "God formed man of the dust of the ground and breathed into his nostrils the breath of life," with the verse[10] that says, "Let us make man in our image, after our likeness," it underscores the fact that man's creation involved both a physical and a spiritual process. The spiritual process covered previously was an instantaneous event identified as the moment when God breathed into the nostrils of man the spiritual image of himself. That spiritual birth recorded in the Creation narrative was when spiritual man was created. But that does not mean the physical and spiritual creation events were necessarily simultaneous. Genesis 2:7 suggests a time component in the development of the life-form of man when it says, "and man became a living soul." That phrase that man became a living soul suggests there was a physical aspect of man before God breathed into him the spiritual image of himself. So it appears that the making of the physical and spiritual aspects of man may have been temporally separate events.

If we pursue the line of reasoning that man's physical being existed prior to his being made in the spiritual image of God, then some element of time would have transpired between the physical and spiritual events. That element of timing difference might have been no more than the moment between having been formed from the dust of ground and God having breathed into the nostrils of the one who became Adam. But what if the time difference between the physical formation and the spiritual creation were much longer, say a hundred thousand years? Such a view would be consistent with the fossil record of the appearance of *Homo sapiens*, the hominid form of modern man. This would be a different matter and would fit more in line with what the theistic evolutionists might propose, but it is certainly consistent with what anthropologists have proposed about the physical origin of humans.

Anthropology as the study of humankind applies evolutionary theory in assimilating the lineage of man. Some advocates of intelligent design and most theistic evolutionists agree with the anthropologist's conception that physical man evolved from some form of an archetypical primate[11] that was also the common ancestor of the ape and chimpanzee. Anthropologists have assembled a sequential series of primate fossils that progress in skeletal structure towards a human-like form. But they were not human, nor is the sequence anything more than conjecture[12] that fits the pattern posited by those scientists based on their interpretation of the fossil evidence in line with evolutionary theory. The ultimate form placed at the end of that sequence is the hominid fossil called Cro-Magnon, the most recent member of the alleged primate lineage culminating with the likeness of modern man forty-five thousand years ago. Cro-Magnon[13] is not hypothetical but a real fossil category, essentially appearing the same as modern man and represented in scientific publications and shown in college textbooks as one of the first *Homo sapiens.*

Most lay Christians reject the idea that such a succession of primate forms evolved into *Homo sapiens,* and they may be correct. There is no evidence that the evolution of the primates actually occurred as posited, and certainly no evidence that man was the end point of such evolution rather than the culmination of a common design. The entire conceptual series is simply putting fossil skeletons of primates in a sequence representing what anthropologists imagine as the pattern of descent, when in fact they are independent discoveries well separated geographically and inconsistent with what can be contrived from geological time. The series is purposely assembled to conform to the Darwinian model of man's evolution based on the theory of primate succession, when they could just as well represent a series of fossils unrelated to man that demonstrate the diversity of primate life-forms that have existed.

But for the sake of an open mind, let's look at the anthropologist's perspective that the origin of man was the result of primate evolution through a series of advancing primates, culminating with Cro-Magnon. If we build on that conjecture as though the anthropological sequence has some validity, which in essence is the view of theistic evolution, then we can see whether or not the Creation narrative still remains cogent. Under such reasoning, when God said,[14] "Let the earth bring forth the living creature after his kind," the hominid creature of the anthropology series with the physical likeness of man was brought forth among the other creatures that were the forerunners of the cattle, creeping things, and beasts of the Earth. The hominid creature brought forth would have become the template of man's physical form in the Genesis narrative, to be made ready for the endowment of God's likeness. Under such reasoning, this means that after the physical likeness of man had advanced to the level of *Homo sapiens*, it was at that point that God said,[15] "Let us make man in our image." In other words, from among the hominid population that had already advanced in physical form of the *Homo sapiens*, it was a matter of taking a member of that population and breathing into his nostrils the breath of spiritual life to transform him into the likeness of God, educing man's spiritual creation, and thus the creation of a new life-form in the spiritual likeness of God called Adam, the first of his kind as the child of God.

Technically, such a scenario would have resulted in two lines of the man creature, those of the Adam lineage as the children of God, and those representing the descendants of the unspiritual hominid population from which the one chosen for the likeness of God was taken. Hypothetically, that would have been God's reason for creating the sanctuary Garden of Eden[16] for Adam and Eve. The garden would separate them from the influence of unspiritual man and would provide an ideal environmental sanctuary to advance in spiritual fellowship. Why else would a garden sanctuary have been established if it wasn't to separate the children of God from the trials of the world beyond the garden? But after their disobedience, Adam and Eve were ejected from the garden, exposed to the maladies of the world, and forced to live with whatever existed in that world.

Genesis 6:2 could be considered by some to even support such a scenario when it says, "That the sons of God saw the daughters of men that they were fair; and they took them wives of all which they chose." If the "sons of God" refers to Adam's lineage, then the daughters of men must refer to the other hominid lineage, suggesting it is a possible reference to the unspiritual humankind. Those verses have been the subject of much theological discourse over the ages, involving very different perspectives on who were being referred to. But if man's physical origin was among the creatures that were first brought forth from the Earth, and the sons of God related to the children of the man

Ernest L. Brannon

Adam made in the spiritual image of God, it might fit in this case with what anthropologists have hypothetically assembled on hominoid evolution from fossil evidence.

Admittedly, such an interpretation of man's Creation narrative is totally incredible, but that is the point. Regardless of how incredible such conjecture may be, Christians don't know the details of how God created in order to develop a factual creative account. Even if such an anthropological interpretation were to be given a voice in reconciliation, it doesn't dismiss the validity of the Creation narrative. Rather than being dogmatic in perpetuating seventeenth-century ideological views about creation that were developed with only the knowledge of science that existed in that day, this purely speculative account demonstrates that it is possible to interpret the events consistent with anthropological theory without diminishing the literal truth of the Creation narrative. It demonstrates that Creation theory should not be closed to other possible insights of God's handiwork revealed through science. The traditional assumption that the physical and spiritual creations of man were one synonymous event, and all kinds were created independently, is impossible to verify. Notwithstanding the reluctance to look beyond traditional interpretation of the Creation narrative, the body of believers must recognize that God is an innovative omnipotent Creator who provides mechanisms to accomplish his purpose implemented beyond constant oversight. We don't know how creation unfolded. We are left only to agree with the apostle Paul[17] when he said of God, "how unsearchable are his judgments, and his ways past finding out."

Conclusion

The point of this chapter was to examine the Genesis account of Creation from the perspective of its scientific credibility. In contrast to allegations that the Genesis account of Creation was contrary to science, this exposition shows there is congruity between the literal wording of scripture and the scientific evidence associated with the beginning of the universe and life. Are there other interpretations of the details? Of course, and that is understandable given the time period over which these scriptures have been studied, the advancement in scientific knowledge, the orientation of those scholars interpreting the manuscripts, and even the choice of words among the translations of the Hebrew text, but it remains scientifically creditable.

Even given variations in the interpretation of the Genesis account, the relative scientific accuracy of the account written thousands of years before the discoveries of modern science is uncanny to the secularist, but to the Christian, it is an explicit verification of God's word. A beginning, the appearance of first light, the transformation of the atmosphere surrounding the Earth, plants as first life-forms, followed by animals that originated in water and then were brought forth on land, and man as the final life-form to arise, are consistent with the contemporary view of science. The ancient narrative recorded approximately six thousand years ago was written in a form that is credible and current for all time.

Endnotes

1   J. D. Morris, *Creation Basics and Beyond* (215).

2   J. A. Moore, *From Genesis to Genetics* (Berkeley: University of California Press, 2001).

3   T. H. Huxley, "The Cell-Theory," *British and Foreign Medico-Chirurgical Review* 12(1853): 221–43.

4   A. Loeb, "The Dark Ages of the Universe," *Scientific American* 295, 5 (2006):46– 53.

5   Miller, *Finding Darwin's God*, 270.

6   Scofield Reference Bible (New York: Oxford University Press, 1967).

7   J. H. Taylor, *Saint Augustine: The Literal Meaning of Genesis* (New York: Paulist Press, 1982).

8   King James Bible, John 4:24.

9   King James Bible, Genesis 2:7.

10 King James Bible, Genesis 1:26.

11 Mayr, *What Evolution Is*, 236

12 R. J. Guliuzza, *Creation Basics and Beyond* (253).

13 Editors of Encyclopaedia Britannica. 2018. Cro-Magnon Prehistoric Human. https:// www.brtannica.com/editor/the-editors-of- encyclopaedia-britannica/4419.

14 King James Bible, Genesis 1:24.

15 King James Bible, Genesis 1:26.

16 King James Bible, Genesis 2:8.

17 King James Bible, Romans 11:33.

CHAPTER 15
The Essence of Resolution

In the previous chapters, the evidence in support of the two worldviews on the beginning and diversity of life has been presented, perspectives on their reformation given, followed with a rendition of Genesis from the viewpoint of its scientific merit. It is apparent that throughout history, the controversy between the two philosophical models is much deeper than the evolution issue, and it involves the spiritual component of whether the God of the Bible is author of all that exists, or even if there is a God. Anti-theists have attempted to make the controversy between science and religion, but that is only their strategy to subjugate Creation. Scripture says that the basis of the warfare is enmity between man and God,[1] and that describes the situation of the natural state of people who have yet to resolve their unbelief, and it also identifies the origin of the controversy.

This treatise has presented evolutionary theory consistent with the neo-Darwinian frame of reference, well known among scientists but not necessarily understood by the general public. Most have been unaware that the theory is inferential, expanded from demonstrable evidence of adaptive micro-changes within species. That disparity has been disclosed in this discourse. Although the objective of the theory has been to explain the source and transformation of archetypes, that disposition remains hypothetical. The situation is different with Creation. Today's general public tends to view Creation in terms of seventeenth-century theology. While we may understand Christ as the Son of God, his mission, and atoning grace in salvation and healing, that is seeing him only in his messianic form. Christ as the Word in the beginning,[2] existing before time began,[3] the creator of all things,[4] and holding all things together,[5] is a person of God unknown and incomprehensible to our understanding. But that is the personage being presented in this discourse as intelligent cause and thus the source of things revealed by science that are recognized in this analysis as the fingerprints of the Creator. To provide an objective framework of reconciliation of worldviews, it is necessary to integrate both the material and spiritual aspects of the issue.

The Material Context

The primary questions have focused on what caused life's beginning and its diversification thereafter. The material context is about process, whether life came about by the unfolding innovation of divine metaphysical engagement, or by happenstance assembly through the accumulation of errors in the replication of the first cells that resulted in different life-forms, consistent with neo-Darwinism. If by the metaphysical, was the diversity of life accomplished by a progressive creative process, or were the life-forms that appeared, such as before and during the Cambrian explosion, separate concoctions?

The word *evolution* has been applied to embrace adaptation, but that is only relevant in the Darwinist model. The actual biological evidence for adaptive change is a limited level of genetic variation in response to environmental challenges. Such exposure results in a genetic alteration or intraspecific change within the lineage of the organism, and the phenotype that survives best in a given environment because of those slight genetic differences will have a performance advantage in producing more offspring over other individuals in the population. That is also referred to as microevolution, because it involves adaptive alterations of the genome that natural selection will favor. We have seen that this phenomenon of change is not inference but a biological reality confirmed through scientific research and observation. Examples cited were Pacific salmon colonization of diverse habitat, in which incubation temperature determines adult spawn timing, color pattern of the peppered moth with the black spots on the light gray wings providing camouflage against lichen-coated trees to avoid predators, bacteria building resistance to antibacterial drugs, and beak shape of the Galapagos finches corresponding to the source of food. Based on the evidence that microevolutionary change is the process of life-forms adapting to environmental diversity, we can agree that Darwin got that part right. Microevolution is real and is the mechanism that involves variation and natural selection that favors the most accommodating phenotype in environmental challenges.

However, that is not macroevolution. Macroevolution is the interspecific transformation of one kind of plant or animal into another kind. It amounts to the formation of an entirely different archetypical life-form from an existing parental taxon. That is the essence of evolutionary theory. But the evidence used in support of the theory has been largely adaptive radiation, because unequivocal evidence of macroevolutionary change cannot be established by observations in nature or in the laboratory. Real-time proof of accumulating micro-changes would require millions of years to demonstrate that such natural transformation was possible. Fossil evidence is often presented as the primary evidence of evolution, but as Mayr[6] has pointed out, it should be in graded form and continuous, and that is not the case. New species appear suddenly, discontinuities are overwhelming with few intermediates, and those alleged to be transitional forms are contentious inferences. So, when neo-Darwinists talk about the extensive evidence demonstrating evolution, they are referring to observations and research primarily within typological lineages, but that is in the arena of microevolution. Because they believe that such changes accumulate over time leading to macroevolution, they infer change as one continuous process from adaptation on to archetypical transformation. Consequently, archetypical transformation of one kind of life-form into another is inferred by deduction. This amounts to what Hawking and Mlodinow[7] refer to as model-dependent realism,

Ernest L. Brannon

where once a perspective has been established that explains certain events, it is then considered to be absolute truth, and henceforth all such events are interpreted in that light. Macroevolution is model-dependent realism.

Creationists differentiate between the evidence of adaptive change and macroevolution because they see the evidence for adaptation in a dynamic environment, but they don't see any evidence that such changes lead to archetypical transformation. The assumption that micro-changes accumulate beyond type, such as amphibians evolving into reptiles by accumulated changes, has never been substantiated. Darwin speculated about this level of descent, but because he lacked the evidence, it was only hypothetical. That is not to say that the unfolding of processes in design could not have included such macro-changes as a mechanism used by intelligent cause in creating different body plans, but conclusive evidence is simply wanting. The deficiency is demonstrated in the fossil record and by the sudden appearance of diverse animal body plans during the Cambrian explosion, where no common ancestor is apparent, and intermediates linking phyla are absent. Lack of such evidence has implications fitting the contemporary Creation model in chapter 13.

A major disparity in the interpretation of scientific evidence is recognition of what constitutes transitional forms. A criticism is that creationists define the term *transitional form* in a way that is distinctly different from the evolutionists' use of the term. That is true. Evolutionists identify all phenotypic changes above the level of species as macroevolutionary in nature, and transitional forms would be those at the forks of the various branches emanating in the alleged tree of life. But contemporary creationists consider transitional forms to be those involved in changing the body plans from one typological category to another, and there is very limited evidence that such transitions even occurred. The lack of linkages between animal body plans when they first appeared during the Cambrian period[8] indicates that transitions between typological categories or archetypes are missing. Further, later fossils portrayed as transitional forms may only be exotic side branches within the diversity of an archetype. Such a disparity in missing links suggests that archetypes were formed rapidly, either as individual creations or through creative progression, but in relatively rapid succession over geological time.

Practical insight on microevolution within typological lineages is provided by the extent of diversity that occurred when isolated on large ocean landmasses that separated after the breakup of the supercontinent Pangaea. This is effectively demonstrated with the lemurs of Madagascar,[9] which diversified in numerous forms within their archetype during their isolation history. Understandably, evolutionists would classify such significant phenotypic alterations as macroevolution, since the lemurs diversified to the extent of being classified in separate genera and family categories. However, while the diversity of the lemurs was extreme, it has been limited within their typological lineage of the superfamily *Lemuroidea*, and thus their diversity occurred after their own kind. The exploding diversity of lemurs could be viewed as the manifestation of the creative potential embedded by the creative strategy of intelligent cause as the first lemur immigrants spread and involuntarily adapted to the variety of habitats on Madagascar during the sixty million years of isolation in near absence of other primate competitors.

The marsupials,[10] isolated in Australia about the same period during the breakup of Pangaea, are another example of diversity within typological lineages. The marsupials are non-placental and give birth to premature young that are held in a pouch until weaned. They are thought to have originated in the Americas ninety million years ago and had diversified to an unknown degree before their immigration along their migratory pathway from the Americas through Antarctica on to Australia, before those landmasses completely separated. At least five marsupial fossil finds in Antarctica have been identified, so it is uncertain to what level of diversity was represented among the immigrants before being isolated in Australia approximately fifty million years ago. The existence of over two hundred fifty marsupial species makes it very apparent that the diversity within the respective mammalian infraclass has been extensive and includes everything between the red kangaroo to the mouse-size dunnart. Although separated taxonomically, the definite similarities among the various life-forms, such as the wombat and koala, show typological relationships. While both the lemurs and the marsupials are mammals under the Linnaeus classification system, their archetypes are separated in different taxonomic groups and fit well within the concept of each having diversified after their own kind.

The degree of diversity that has occurred within the typological lineages of lemurs and marsupials over the fifty to sixty million years of adaptive radiation is remarkable and demonstrates the latent genetic potential in those lineages and the impending diversity that can arise in all life-forms. The extent of such latent potential has been effectively demonstrated in the variability of the canine species through just a few hundred years[11] in the laboratory of artificial selection that showed myriad diverse forms in size, shape, hair length, color, temperament, and behavior. Thousands of different varieties have been developed, resulting in the most successful artificial selection programs known. A persuasive aspect of the canine evidence is that regardless of major artificial breeding efforts, the changes remained within their canine typological lineage.

But the most impressive example, with the millions of years of adaptive radiation in isolation, is that there has been no evidence of transformation of archetypical kind among the lemurs. There is no evidence of such evolutionary changes that represented transition of the typological lineage or kind in the fifty million years that these life-forms were isolated under circumstances that have provided such opportunity. Although they experienced extreme diversity, the anatomy of those diverse life-forms testifies of their intraspecific ancestry. That also appears to be the case within *Marsupialia*, although just using the marsupium as the defining characteristic isn't sufficient in itself to confirm their common ancestry. There may be more than one typological lineage among the marsupials, especially when convergent evolution cannot be excluded.

Consequently, an important implication forthcoming from the observed persistence of the canine, lemur, and marsupial life-forms is that adaptive radiation of species is bound within limits of their typological lineages. The molecular machinery and its manifestations are established by the origination of the primal intrinsic structural parameters of organismal kind. In those constraints, the diversity within kind results through an involuntary synchronization of the respective phenotype determined by the selective nature of the environmental landscape, but the involuntary options appear to be limited within their intraspecific biological laws of form.

Maximum flexibility within kinds is demonstrated as convergence where very different life-forms show similar functional continuums in structural features when confronted by comparable natural forces. Although the Australian marsupials have been separated from the placental life-forms for at least fifty million years, each has independently diversified in a similar manner when exposed to the same environmental challenges. The various archetypes diversified with similar phenotypes (cat-like, wolf-like, flying squirrel-like, and mouse-like types) and behavior when exposed to and functioning against the same defining forces. The phenotypic patterns reveal how influential ecological dictates are in determining convergent responses when under parallel biological laws of form and place.

Similar examples are present in the plant kingdom. Unrelated cacti and other succulent plants show convergent evolutionary patterns that support the idea that biological laws of form and place are responsible for similarities in phenotype when challenged by concordant environmental conditions. For example, the agave and aloe plants are succulents that form a rosette of many pointed, fleshy green leaves growing from a ground-level base that look very much alike but are unrelated. The agave plant form originated on the Yucatan Peninsula of Mexico, while the aloe plant form originated in the southern part of the Arabian Peninsula and northern Africa. Yet the long thick clusters or rosettes of succulent leaves have assumed a very similar appearance under the same but distant desert-type environmental challenges.

So what can one conclude in resolution of the material context? Neo-Darwinian orthodoxy stipulating the accumulation of small chance mutations culminating in macroevolution that leads to transformation of archetypes and phyletic segregation must remain as a tenuous concept. Evidence in support of that philosophical worldview is weak, and neo-Darwinists have no fallback proposition. The problem for evolutionists is that any deviation from orthodoxy makes purpose an alternative, and that implies intelligent cause. Naturalism's proponents reject that alternative, but their opposition exposes the real underlying issue that the truly omnipotent nature of the functional enterprise that exists in natural phenomena is being dismissed. Evolutionists mistakenly believe that such phenomena go no further than material cause. In contrast, Creation theory recognizes the Creator as the author of natural phenomena in the design of the existential plan of life. That makes propositions embedded in neo-Darwinian orthodoxy, such as the reputed paleontological interpretation of therapsid reptilian evolution leading to early mammalian forms,[12] relevant only if common design were to be dismissed as the source of morphological similarities.

Other related evidence is not as indeterminate. It is apparent from the amassed scientific evidence that the age of the universe and the Earth, and the history of life in the fossil record, cover great lengths of time. The fossil record leaves little question that changes occurred in the morphological characteristics of different lineages of plants and animals, and new forms appeared among those groups by the opportunities made available upon the near extinction of other life-forms. The fossil evidence indicates that major extinction events have occurred at least five times in the past. The largest mass extinction is said to have occurred at the end of the Permian period two hundred fifty million years ago, estimated to have wiped out over 90 percent of all organisms. But life recovered and again diversified. Another was the massive K-T event, when the dinosaurs and an estimated 50 percent of all other life-forms went extinct sixty-five million years ago. Following the removal of the dinosaurs, the mammals were able to grow into dominance and expand into immense diversity within kinds, demonstrating many skeletal features that were similar among archetypes.

An amazing feature in the history of life is the extreme amount of diversity that exists. The enormous number of extant life-forms present throughout the biosphere is incomprehensible, and that is even exceeded by the sheer magnitude of those that have gone extinct over the six hundred million years since multicellular life first appeared in the geological record. The historical amount of plant material represented by massive oil deposits is evidence of the productivity of the past that supported and sustained the very large sizes attained by reptiles and later by some mammals. The indubitable interpretation of the age of the Earth is the radioisotopic data[13] of nuclide half-lives of the elemental isotopes found on Earth and in the universe that indicate billions of years elapsed to prepare for the formation of the Earth, and then billions more to make it inhabitable for life. Life itself was a series of events before culminating in the appearance of man. These particulars are considered scientific evidence that has to be acknowledged and make it apparent that God's creative plan has been recorded in the geological and paleontological history of the planet. The historical information accumulated through processes that conformed to the natural laws he established are evidence of the manner in which the plan was destined to unfold with extreme involuntary diversity of life.

In contrast, if one accepts the neo-Darwinian theory, the conclusion is that life and all of its diversity have been the result of a litany of errors in genetic replication that occurred by chance. This makes all of life represented in the alleged evolutionary tree of life, the population characteristics of all life-forms, and the ecological interrelationships among communities the result of mutations in the genetic code, which amounts to an unrealistic scenario that life's complexity, organization, and structure were the accumulation of random mistakes. Creation theory posits that life was the ultimate creation, and its diversity was in fact a provision in the original design that was to culminate with man.

The Spiritual Context

The focus of the spiritual context is on origin. Science is an instrument through which the origin of process is revealed, and the origin is clearly seen, being understood by the things that are made. That perspective is unanimous among Creation advocates involved in such research today, with the view that the spiritual element is essential in scientific discovery. Although the debate on the literal or allegorical interpretation of the Genesis account of Creation has been ongoing for ages, Darwin's theory of descent amplified the dispute with the early nineteenth-century traditional version of Creation that has reverberated ever since, and in retrospect, it's not entirely justified.

The problem was that instead of considering that God was the origin of what Darwin observed as the basis of descent with modification, anti-theistic scientists encouraged the incongruence of Darwin's theory with the traditional view of Creation. In the scientific arena, that issue drove a wedge between the traditionalist and reformist that has continued to the present, because it has been portrayed as science against religious fundamentalism. The protagonists created an artificial disparity that pitted evolution against Creation, not as an analysis of the evidence, but as a case against divine authorship. In effect, they eliminated God from the scientific perspective on the origin and diversity of life based entirely on their own bias. On the other side of the coin, had the traditionalists given more attention to the scientific views on Creation prior to Darwin, they would have found that earlier scholars such as St. Augustine of Hippo (354–430), St. Thomas Aquinas (1225–1274), Isaac Newton (1643–1727), John Wesley (1703–1791), and Louis Agassiz (1807–1873) gave considerable attention to scientific understanding as they interpreted the account of Creation and were not necessarily committed to regional theological precepts.

The fact of the matter is that the spiritual context of reconciliation is inseparable from material phenomena. Natural laws and matter are the material elements of this world, and in the creationists' perspective, the spirit is the source of material phenomena. Neo-Darwinists have rejected the supernatural from the equation of life, so they are dealing with the only part of reality that they identify with the material world. The prevailing rationale in the secular world is described in scripture[14] when it says, "the natural man receiveth not the things of God: for they are foolishness unto him," and that is the viewpoint of many of those who are imbedded in the neo-Darwinian interpretation of the scientific evidence as model-dependent realism.[15] That is a frank reality of the condition confronting those who have dismissed the God of the Bible and believe it is foolishness. So the disparity between evolution and Creation has its roots in the belief in or rejection of the God of the universe as the interminable element separating the worldviews.

But that is not the entire verse. It goes on to say, "neither can he know them because they are spiritually discerned." The "natural man" views the world intellectually, but in the material perspective, and the spiritual aspect of life is foolishness to him because he is not able to judge spiritual truth. That is simply the result of the state in which we entered this world. We are not automatically the children of God. That is a state requiring a choice that can be defined as a transition of the heart. Spiritual truth requires spiritual discernment, which is lacking as a natural phenomenon when one is born into the world. Consequently, in the materialistic society, the metaphysical aspects of life are viewed as myth and foolishness.

Alleging the lack of spiritual discernment among the advocates of materialism sounds condescending, but the scriptures reveal that there are two birth experiences.[16] The first birth is a physical birth that makes man an object of the world, and that person is referred to as the natural man. The second birth is the spiritual birth that occurs when one invites the Spirit of God to come into one's life. The second birth experience reclaims the lineage with the heavenly father as the child of God and adds entitlement to the promises that God has given to those who accept his provision for all of eternity. They enter that rest proclaimed on the seventh day of Genesis.[17, 18] By definition, the spiritual birth is a choice that adds the spiritual dimension to life and sets the person apart from those who have not taken that step of faith.

Consequently, over much of the last century, scientific inquiry of life's beginning and diversity has largely been unaccompanied by spiritual discernment, because it is not acceptable to stray outside of naturalism's philosophy of limiting inquiry within natural cause. In spite of such limitations of research in the biological arena, most apparent at the molecular level of cell anatomy and function, the fingerprints of intelligent cause become overwhelming. That evidence is everywhere around for us to see, as described in the epistle to the Romans[19] where it says, "the invisible things of him ... are clearly seen, being understood by the things that are made ... so they are without excuse." In retrospect, we are without excuse, especially as scientists, because by our study of the existence and minute detail of the living world, it is apparent that it cannot reasonably be attributed to happenstance mistakes.

Design is the evidence of the spiritual component of Creation. To the scientific mind, that is not simply applying the optimism of faith over secular reason; it is applying the canons of evidence that science has accrued with the perspective of what discernment says is the source. Everything about cell structure and function follow a programmed repertoire, epigenetic expression, and self-organization that shout of creative design. Accepting the explicit evidence around us as testimony of intelligent cause is a difficult chore when intellectually we are satisfied and self-confident in our belief that naturalism provides the answer to life. But the spiritual context opens our eyes to the evidence beyond chance. Resolution employs scientific evidence that purports material cause is, in fact, one of the instruments of the Creator.

The Resolution Platform

As a compendium on the controversy presenting the scientific evidence in support of the origin and diversity of life, the evidence from the material and spiritual elements of the issue have provided the resolution paradigm beyond just the material framework. Darwinism was a process that attempted to explain diversity of life at the level of the organism, and that was a revolutionary concept that swept through the scientific community during most of the twentieth century. The specific details of that concept were covered by Jerry Coyne's[20] description of six components that represented the worldview on the general theory of evolution. But that summary has proven inadequate to account for the diversity of life beyond typological lineages. Over the last half-century, with the advancements in molecular biology and biochemistry that have revealed the complexity of the cell and molecular functions, the deficiency of neo-Darwinian theory has become apparent. The innovative language of the genetic code, its

Ernest L. Brannon

transcription, and its translation into the language of peptide polymers and their biochemical functions have effectively demonstrated the case.

Admittedly, there is much unknown about these processes and the material blueprints imbedded in the cellular form of an incipient embryo. But the evolutionary model illuminated in the six components Coyne described as the general nature of evolution explain change only in the context of adaptive radiation. The origin of archetypes highlighted in the Cambrian explosion as the emergence of entirely new life-forms that are morphologically distinct is a realm entirely overlooked by the neo-Darwinian concept that dwells just on alterations at the genetic level of adaptive change. Concepts that get to the basics involved in the origination of morphologically new body plans and related behavior are not addressed by neo-Darwinism. That conclusion is not confined to supporters of Creation theory but is an increasing view among other scientists[21] apart from any religious affiliation.

The traditional Creation model has also been inadequate to characterize the omnipotent innovation of the Creator. Because they were offended by Darwin's apparent abandonment of God, creationists didn't consider that the evidence Darwin cited for the origin of species was in reality a description of life's provisions generated by the Creator. They missed the potent evidence that demonstrated the supernatural was to be understood by the things that are made: the origin of the Big Bang, the evidence of creative time, and the succession of those events in geological and paleontological history. They gave little attention to the ability of life-forms to adapt to the challenges confronted in dynamic environments as the life insurance endowed in the creatures of the world. That meant they had insufficient understanding of the basic characteristics of life-forms that fell within the definition of kind. The author of Genesis described Creation in a manner current for all time but didn't labor on the pathway of the creative events or on what was meant by the process of "gathering together" or what was involved when the waters and Earth "brought forth" the living creatures, because scientifically, he was given no insight on the processes underpinning those events.

In the pragmatic approach to get past the stalemate in resolution of the controversy, emphasis must be concentrated on the weight of the evidence. The challenge is being able to differentiate between chance and design-discernable functions. The example referenced earlier was the University of Rochester study by Berry Hall,[22] where the gene that produced the galactosidase enzyme that metabolized lactose for food was deleted from *E. coli*. The new biochemical pathway that rapidly developed by another set of genes to replace the loss was attributed to chance. Ironically, the possibility that it was design that ensured such a rapid remedy in face of the highly improbable odds of chance wasn't even considered. Such biochemical reconfigurations are explicit as programed contingencies by design rather than chance, and while it is understandable to acknowledge that material cause is the product of natural laws, it is necessary to recognize that those laws were standards that were endowed by the Maker in the created universe.

Resolution must include reconciliation with revised concepts of the models based on the evidence. Reconciliation here takes the form of a "resolution platform," and it includes what science has revealed over the last half-century, integrated with the substance of the Genesis account. Science has given us great insight about the composition and complexity of Creation but nothing that we can apply with confidence about how the origin of the blueprint of life arose, apart from the substance from which life was made. Scientists of both camps have given their perspectives, but that amounts to a level of faith, because nothing has been revealed about the manner in which life originated or the archetypical mechanisms employed by the Creator in his creative labor. The evidence is in the things that were made, those material things that can be observed. In other words, the truth about the origin of the universe, the world, and life itself can be understood by the things that science has disclosed, including God's eternal power.[23] Therefore, the resolution platform is an assembly of the evidence of what science has revealed as a broader assimilation of the spiritual and material elements associated with the beginning and diversity of life, guided by the truth of what the scriptures reveal.

The resolution platform is composed of seven assertions that reconcile the controversy between Creation and evolution:

1. There was a beginning when the universe, the Earth, and life originated by the power of an extraneous force.

> Science and Creation agree that there was a beginning, when all physical matter originated and provided the conditions for life to occur. The manner in which it occurred is unknown but is recognized as a force outside of the created universe. The force is beyond our comprehension, to an extent that we can only recognize its existence by the evidence of what has been made through the instruments of discovery.

2. Natural laws are the foundation of natural phenomena and are the basis of material cause.

> Science and Creation agree that natural laws function throughout time in a predetermined manner and are carried out involuntarily in a mode that sustains all material functions in the universe. The material phenomena forthcoming from natural laws are instruments involved in the origin and diversity of life, established directly or indirectly by the extraneous force.

3. Formation of the universe, Earth, and life were time-intensive phenomena.

Science and Creation agree that time has progressed from the preparation of the universe, to the creation of matter, the formation of celestial bodies, and making Earth ready for life. Time was involved in the creation of the different life-forms, and in the scientific perspective, there was much time involved in the Creation saga that is consistent with six descriptive phases of the Genesis account.

4. Life is the result of dynamic processes, with standards of elaboration and diversity programmed in the blueprint of the life-form.

Science and Creation agree that the astounding aspect of the system is the dynamic nature of life that has taken form in nearly unlimited manifestations of endoskeletal and exoskeletal constructs. The blueprint is the standard in the elaboration and replication of the genetic and epigenetic aspects of development and function throughout all forms of life. The digital code, RNA polymerase, mRNA transcription, tRNA translation, and the many organelles and their inherent functions, with ATP as the universal organismal energy supply, all disclose that life is a programmed entity. Programming is elaborated by cell differentiation in structure and function, and consummated in the assembly of molecular structure of innumerable life-forms.

5. The source of all life-forms originated from the elements of Earth's matter and was fashioned in sequence over the creative period, forthcoming as different kinds.

Science and Creation agree that the processes involved in the transformation of inert matter into the first living cell are unknown, but the scriptures and the geological/paleontological record indicate that the assembly of life occurred in sequence starting first as plants, followed with animals in the seas that were to diversify into beasts, cattle, and creeping things as descendants of those that moved onto land, and finally man. The different forms of life originated either separately, in which the digital genetic code was endowed repeatedly through different archetypical kinds, or as a progressive series of archetypes emanated via an original ancestral prototype, from which all subsequent kinds were fashioned in succession. While the process remains abstract, the consummation was the complete array of all archetypical kinds of life, such as manifest in the separate animal body plans of the Cambrian explosion.

6. Variation and natural selection are the basic microevolutionary instruments of diversification within lineages of different life-forms after their own kind.

Science and Creation agree that variation of archetypical kinds through adaptive radiation within the typological lineages has resulted in the diversity of the fossil evidence and extant life-forms. Microevolution is a security system in which the hierarchal structure of the genotype enables the acquisition of the adaptive needs of the organism. Such genetic potential is an ingenious mechanism that gives organisms the flexibility necessary to sustain their typological lines consistent with the environmental challenges and opportunities as far as adaptability of the genome of kind will allow.

7. The foremost point of the evidence is that the extraneous force central in all of creation made a universe with properties inevitable for the existence of intelligent life, referred to as the anthropic principle. That principle is manifest within precise measures and fine-tuning to provide, sustain, and adapt life to the nature of the dynamic world that culminated with man.

Science has identified the Big Bang, formation of the galaxies, creation of Earth, and the sequence of life-forms down to the machines and function of the cell as ordered events in precise disposition. Science identifies those things as having been made but has avoided the identity of the maker.

Creation posits that the existence of such order is indisputable evidence of intelligent design. It is evident in the polymer language of the genetic code directing the development and functioning of the cell. It is evident in cell division, cell differentiation, and all of cell machinery. It is evident in the processes that fashioned the molecular biochemical innovations of life destined to unfold in an involuntary manner within structural parameters of nearly unlimited diversity. It is evident among phenotypes that result from designed molecular processes in the form of alterations of the genetic code and epigenetic properties in response to the multiplicity of environmental challenges. It is evident in how irreducible complexity is realized as fated constructs, either at conception, in the same manner as cell differentiation is fated during embryogenesis, or by induction due to encoded contingencies in the Creator's plan. Creationists assert that discovery of those processes has been possible because intelligent cause, the author of natural laws, used mechanisms that can be ascertained through science. Intelligent design, misinterpreted as chance, is the overshadowing paradigm of specific measures accomplished in the multidimensional creative plan.

The seven points of the resolution platform present the symmetry of science with Creation that has been revealed through both discovery and the Holy Scriptures. The complexity of the organism, indeed the complexity of the machinery of the cell, confirms that chance is inadequate to result in the fabrication of life. Resolution recognizes the evidence of an ingenious plan that perpetuated the origin, diversification, and sustenance of life. This is clearly seen by the things that were made, amounting to the sum total of all aspects of the universe, down to the molecular structures and functions of the cell. That manifestation, presented as design, testifies of the existence of the designer, the architect of Creation's plan.

To the Christian, the evidence corroborates the claim that all of creation occurred by the will of God as he declared in the Holy Bible, and there has been no evidence that would dispute his testimony as true. The creative order revealed in the Holy Scriptures is shown correct and credible. Those who give no account to Creation should carefully consider the evidence with an open mind in their search of truth. One cannot look upon the grandeur of life and its assimilation of diversity and beauty as a collection of random mistakes, or see the molecular mechanisms and innovations in the magnificence of the cell, and not recognize the existence of a much superior force than the human mind.

It has been falsely assumed that science has disposed of God, as demonstrated in the November 13, 2006, *Time* magazine article[24] on "God vs. Science," covered earlier involving the debate between Frances Collins and Richard Dawkins. The title was revealing. The article was a straw man, as though there is a dispute that pits science against the concept of God, or that science somehow has disproven God. Collins thwarted such conjecture. He made it clear in the article that science provides the physical revelation of God's handiwork. It matters little how God exercised that handiwork. What matters is making a fair judgment from the evidence, and that evidence reveals the industry of the Creator. Dawkins makes a pertinent final point in the article where he says, "If there is a God it is going to be a lot bigger and more incomprehensible than anything that any theologian of any religion has ever proposed." That is true. We cannot comprehend the full nature and extent of God, and the design he afforded in his Creation is evidence of that truth. But there is a more personal piece of evidence beyond science, and that is the transformation of the heart when accepting the grace of God. Those who have experienced that transformation can attest to its truth, with the hope that others will find their rest in the same. The physical birth into the world gives us a comprehension of material things; the spiritual birth gives us a comprehension of the reality that exists.

Endnotes

1   King James Bible, Romans 8:7.

2   King James Bible, John 1:1.

3   King James Bible, John 17:5.

4   King James Bible, Colossians 1:16.

5   King James Bible, Colossians 1:17.

6   Mayr, *What Evolution Is*, 189.

7   Steven Hawking and Leonard Mlodinow, *The Grand Design* (New York: Bantam Books, 2010).

8   Mayr, *What Evolution Is*, 209.

9   S. M. Goodman and J. P. Benstead, eds., *The Natural History of Madagascar* (Chicago: University of Chicago Press, 2003).

10 M. A. Nilsson and others, "Marsupial Relationships and a Timeline for Marsupial Radiation in South Gondwana," *Gene* 340 (2004):2.

11 B. Bower, "Earliest Known New World Dogs ID'd," *Science News* 193 (2018):8.

12 Mayr, *What Evolution Is*, 15.

13 Miller, *Finding Darwin's God*, 70–71.

14 King James Bible, 1 Corinthians 2:14.

15 Hawking and Mlodinow, *The Grand Design*.

16 King James Bible, John 3:5–6.

17 King James Bible, Genesis 2:2–3.

18 King James Bible, Hebrews 4:1–11.

19 King James Bible, Romans 1:20.

20 Coyne, *Why Evolution Is True*, 3–14.

21 Alan Brush, Eric Davidson, Douglas Erwin, Dean Kenton, Roger Penrose, Richard Prum, Charles Thaxton, Barbara Stahl, among others.

22 Hall, "Evolution on a Petri Dish," 15.

23 King James Bible, Romans 1:20.

24 D. van Biema, "God vs. Science," *Time* magazine 168, 20 (2006).